Our Priceless Heritage

A Study of Christian Doctrine, In Contrast with Romanism

◆

PREPARED ESPECIALLY FOR CHRISTIAN
SCHOOLS AND COLLEGES

By

HENRY M. WOODS, D.D., LL.D.

THE EVANGELICAL PRESS
HARRISBURG, PENNA., U. S. A.

Second Edition
1941

Copyright, 1941

BY

HENRY M. WOODS

PRINTED BY THE EVANGELICAL PRESS,
IN HARRISBURG, PENNA., U. S. A.

DEDICATION

of the First Edition

TO PROTESTANT STUDENTS EVERYWHERE,

THE FUTURE LEADERS

OF

THE CHURCH OF GOD.

"The Glorious Gospel of the Blessed God."
—I TIM. 1:11.

'The Word of Truth, the Gospel of Your Salvation.—EPH. 1:13.

"If ye continue in My Word, then are ye My disciples indeed; And ye shall know the Truth, and the Truth shall make you free." "If the SON therefore shall make you free, ye shall be free indeed."—JOHN 8:31, 32, 36.

"Sanctify the LORD GOD in your hearts; and be ready to give an answer to every man that asketh you a reason of the hope that is in you, with meekness and fear."—I PETER 3:15.

Foreword

THERE are many urgent reasons why the great doctrines of the Christian faith, as set forth in Holy Scripture and re-affirmed at the Reformation, in contrast to the errors of Romanism, should be proclaimed, and their truthfulness and reasonableness be made plain.

It is most regrettable to see the woeful ignorance which prevails, even among intelligent Protestants, regarding the grounds of our faith and the grave errors of Romanism. Romanists are drilled from childhood in the rudiments of their creed, and can give some reasons for their belief. Both belief and reasons may be far from valid—but can the average Protestant do as much for the Truth?

The Church of Rome carries on an incessant propaganda to draw Protestants away from the true faith. Five recent cases came to the writer's mind, in which the usual appeal for "Mother Church," the showy ritual, and attractive music were much in evidence. Rome shrewdly calculates that if Protestants are not actually won as converts, favorable impressions may be made which will blind them to the irreconcilable antagonism between papal error and Scripture truth, and thus at least active opposition may be disarmed. The writer recalls the conversion of two wealthy Protestant sisters to Romanism, who gave a large sum of money to found a Romanist institution in Washington, D. C., but were soon disillusioned by discovering the painful discrepancy between profession and practice which they found in the Roman Communion. They returned to their Protestant faith, though their *wealth did not return with them!* "Surely in vain the net is spread in the sight of any bird!"

At the present time Protestants need to be specially alert, because the three most powerful agencies which mould public opinion are largely under Romanist influence, viz.: the secular press, motion pictures, and radio broadcast. The pope is allowed to broadcast Romanist propaganda to the world, even attempting to justify the gross medieval superstition of *Indulgences.* But no Protestant leader would be allowed equal opportunity to state the truth in reply, for that would be called "controversial," and "intolerant!"

This book is written in no unkind spirit, for the author has had warm friends among Roman Catholics. It is written with the sole desire to *tell the truth,* and to *warn Protestants of a real danger,* a danger to *true religion,* and a danger to *free government;* for genuine allegiance to a foreign prince, as the pope claims to be, is inconsistent with wholehearted allegiance to one's government. Young people especially need to be put on their guard, and no mistaken notion of charity should lead one to remain silent, when the welfare of the Christian Church and free Government are at stake.

Christians should be more active in spreading the truth, and in circulating *attractive Protestant literature.* Fox's Book of Martyrs, and the glorious history of heroic Protestants who died for the faith, like the Huguenots and Covenanters, should be in every home and Sunday School Library; and prizes should be offered to encourage children to read such books and to write short accounts of what they have read. *Never* for economy's sake, or for any other reason, *send children to Romanist schools. Mixed marriages* should be earnestly *opposed,* for in most cases they will destroy the happiness of the home. Truly "perpetual vigilance is the price of Liberty!"

"WATCH YE, STAND FAST IN THE FAITH, QUIT YOU LIKE MEN, BE STRONG!
AWAKE, THOU THAT SLEEPEST!"

Ventnor, New Jersey,
May, 1934

Foreword

TO THE SECOND EDITION

I T IS truly remarked that the great enemies of the Christian Faith are *not outside*, but *inside* the camp, viz.: Indifference and Lack of Vigilance. On all sides there is much discussion of Fascism, Naziism and Communism, while the most subtle enemy of all, dangerous to the soul's salvation, and dangerous to civil and religious liberty, is entirely overlooked. Why the most dangerous? Because the Papal Church is well-organized, well-advertised, and is such an adroit *counterfeit* of Christianity, that the casual observer fails to detect it! What is said of bank notes is true of religion, *the more skillful the counterfeit, the more dangerous it is!*

It is a matter for deep regret that during the past year overtures looking toward diplomatic relations with the Vatican have been made—said to be personal only—though the membership of the Papal Church is only about one-fifth of the population of the United States, or less, if the Church's mode of counting members be taken into account.

Inasmuch as this proposal, while well-meant, is not in accord with the wisdom of our forefathers, who rightly discouraged special favors or privileges to any religious organization, and thus may not be promotive of harmony and the welfare of the Republic, it is earnestly hoped that, in accordance with the sentiments of the large majority of American citizens, further overtures may be discontinued; especially is this important, as the Roman See has openly expressed sympathy with Totalitarian influences in Europe.

Therefore the warning of our First Edition may well be repeated:

AWAKE, THOU THAT SLEEPEST!

WATCH YE, STAND FAST IN THE FAITH, QUIT YOU LIKE MEN, BE STRONG!

Ventnor, New Jersey,
  May, 1941

Contents

Bibliography

The Author gratefully acknowledges his indebtedness to many authorities:—

Gibbon's "DECLINE AND FALL OF THE ROMAN EMPIRE."

Green's "HISTORY OF THE ENGLISH PEOPLE," and other STANDARD HISTORIES OF ENGLAND and other countries.

Guizot's "HISTORY OF FRANCE."

Guizot's "HISTORY OF CIVILIZATION."

D'Aubigné's "HISTORY OF THE REFORMATION."

Ranke's "HISTORY OF THE POPES."

Froude's "HISTORY OF THE COUNCIL OF TRENT."

JOHN HUSS, *by Benito Mussolini.*

"HOW PETER BECAME POPE," *by William Dallmann.*

"CATHOLICISM AND PROTESTANTISM," *by T. Demetrius.*

"THE TEACHINGS OF THE ROMAN CATHOLIC CHURCH."

Motley's DUTCH REPUBLIC.

"SANTA TERESA," *by Dr. Alexander Whyte.*

ESSAYS *by Thomas Carlyle.*

Froude's "SHORT STUDIES," "CALVINISM," and "THE CONDITION AND PROSPECTS OF PROTESTANTISM," etc.

THE WORKS OF TIMOTHY DWIGHT, D.D., *former President of Yale University.*

"THE COUNTER-REFORMATION," *by B. J. Kidd, D.D.*

CHAPTER I

THE CHURCH OF GOD

What is the true Church of God?

The true Church of God is that divinely established society among men, which worships the Holy Trinity alone; which trusts the atoning death and righteousness of the Lord Jesus Christ for salvation; the Holy Spirit as Guide, Sanctifier, and Comforter; the Sacred Scriptures of the Old and New Testaments as its sole rule of faith; and which proclaims the Gospel of God's free grace to all mankind.

THE CHURCH VISIBLE AND INVISIBLE

The Church is often referred to as Visible and Invisible. What is meant by these terms?

The Visible Church is the organized society on earth of those who profess the true Gospel, together with their children. It is also called the Kingdom of Christ, the Kingdom of God, the Kingdom of Heaven, and the family of God on earth. Eph. 5:5, Eph. 3:15, II Peter 1:11, Acts 2:39, 3:25, Westminster Confession of Faith XXV, 2. The Invisible Church consists of the whole body of the saved in every land and of every age, including the redeemed in heaven and all true believers on earth. Col. 1:13, Eph. 3:15, Confession of Faith XXV, 2.

Why is it necessary to distinguish between the Visible and the Invisible Church?

Because the Word of God, though not using these terms, distinguishes between them; and because the Visible Church also contains many who profess faith in Christ who are not truly His; they show by their lives that they have never been "born again," and therefore are not saved. Matt. 7:21-23, 25:12, 44-46, John 3:3, 5, Heb. 10:25-29.

(1)

Does the Church of Rome distinguish between the Visible and Invisible Church?

The Church of Rome does not make this necessary distinction, because it holds a mistaken, mechanical theory of salvation; as if all who submit to the pope, receive the sacraments, and conform to the outward rites of the Church are thereby saved. They fail to grasp the all-important teaching of God's Word, that mere outward conformity to any Church cannot save, but that only through faith in the living Christ, and the power of the Holy Spirit, man must become "a new creature," bringing forth the fruits of righteousness. These fruits the Scriptures declare are necessary for salvation, *not* as the ground, but as *the evidence of it.* See Bellarmine on *the Sacraments:* Luke 6:46, 13:9-25, James 1:22, Eph. 2:10.

Why should all true Christians love, honor and unite with the Church of God?

Because the Church, unlike all other societies in the world, was established by God, not by man. He purchased it with His own precious blood. By uniting with the Church, believers confess Him before men; and because the Church is God's agency for the spread of His saving truth, for the conversion of perishing sinners, and for the instruction, sanctification and comforting of believers. Matt. 10:32, Acts 20:28, II Thess. 2:16, 17, I Tim. 2:15.

Can the Church save men?

No, the Church, its ordinances, sacraments and ministry, though highly important, cannot save men. *Only the Lord Jesus Christ can save.* Sinners must come in faith, and repentance to *Him alone,* to receive forgiveness, "the new heart," and eternal life. John 14:6, Acts 4:12, Ezek. 36:26, John 3:16, 36.

THE MARKS OF THE CHURCH; NOT INFALLIBLE; NOT PERFECTLY HOLY

Is the Church of God on earth Infallible?

No. The Church is not infallible, nor is it perfectly holy; because its members, while sincere, are yet sinful, erring men. *Only Christ* its Lord and Saviour is *infallible and holy;* but at last the Church will be perfectly holy, for Christ will present it before the Father's throne "a glorious Church, not having spot or wrinkle or any such thing." Eph. 5:27.

What grave error does the Church of Rome teach concerning infallability?

It teaches that the Church is infallible; by Church generally meaning the pope. Bellarmine *de Eccles.* 3, 14, *De Rom. Pontif.* 4:4.

Having no sure Scriptural anchorage, the Roman Church has drifted about in perplexity, now affirming that infallibility resides in one place, now in another. The Jesuit writer Schrader speaks of the disputed question whether "the pope in his own person is infallible in matters of faith, or whether he can claim infallibility only at the head of a Council." (Krueger 237.) For nearly two hundred years the Roman Catholic bishops, clergy and laity of England and Ireland *denied* that *the infallibility of the pope* and *his claim to temporal power* over civil governments *were doctrines of the Church.*[1] Keenan's *Cathechism* went so far as to call this dogma "a Protestant invention," insisting, "It is no article of Catholic faith!" Trusting to this assurance of Roman Church leaders, the British Government granted political rights to Romanists.

The Church of God Indestructible

Will the Church of God ever perish?

The true Church can *never perish,* but at last will *surely triumph over all obstacles and foes,* because it is founded on Christ, the Rock of Ages, who has "all power in heaven and in earth," and has declared that "the gates of hell shall not prevail against it." Matt. 16:18, 28:18, Dan. 2:44.

---

[1] Commenting on the solemn assurance, repeatedly given by Roman Catholic bishops and laity, that the temporal power and infallibility of the pope were *not doctrines of the Roman Church,* that eminent authority, the Honorable William E. Gladstone wrote: "Either the See and Court of Rome had abandoned the dream of enforcing infallibility on the Church, or else by wilful silence they were guilty of practising on the British Crown one of the blackest frauds ever recorded in history."

THE CHURCH APOSTOLIC

Is the true Church of God apostolic?

It is; because the doctrines of the Reformed or Protestant Church are the same as those taught by *Christ and His apostles,* all of which were given by God in the *Holy Scriptures.*

THE CHURCH OF GOD UNIVERSAL

Is not the true Church also universal or catholic?

It is; because all mankind being lost sinners, the Gospel of salvation[1] is provided for the whole human race. Our Lord's command was universal, "Go into all the world and preach the Gospel *to every creature";* "make disciples of *all nations."* Obeying this command of our crucified and risen Lord, His faithful followers are publishing the glad tidings of redemption and establishing His Church in every land. Matt. 28:18-20, Mark 16:15, Luke 24:46-48.

To whom does the name "Catholic" rightly belong?

The name Catholic[2] rightly belongs to that body which obeys God's Word and has carefully kept the apostolic faith; The Church which does this is the Reformed or Protestant Church. The Roman Church desires to appropriate this name, but because it *dishonors the Word of God in many important respects,* and has *departed far*

---

[1] Only the Gospel of Christ can save men. There is no other way. Heathen religions and human philosophy, while they may contain some good, *cannot save men.* Teaching as they do the worship of false gods, men and devils, and providing no redemption from sin, they lead men away from God and righteousness, and deceive with false hopes. Acts 4:12, I Cor. 1:21, 23, 24, 10:20.

[2] Concerning Catholicity as a mark of the true Church, St. Chrysostom says: "That may not be considered Catholic which appears to be *contrary to the statements of Scripture." Hom. de Adam et Eva.* St. Augustine declares, "Faith in Scripture is the *most catholic mark of all." Sermon XIV, De verb. Apost.*

The Jesuit Véron, in his Rule of Catholic Faith, Paris 1645, lays down as a test of Catholicity, that is, to make any doctrine Catholic or binding on the consciences of Christians, it must be: 1. revealed in the Word of God. 2. proposed to the faithful by the whole church. Note that *not one of the papal doctrines,* like the worship of Mary, saints and angels, the Mass, Transubstantiation, Purgatory, papal Indulgences, human merit, holy water, forgiveness of sins by a priest, etc., etc., *can stand this test!*

from the *doctrines delivered by the Saviour, it has forfeited all right to be called Catholic and Apostolic.*

THE SEAT OF AUTHORITY

Is the seat of authority, as the Church of Rome teaches, in the Church? That is, should believers accept as final and binding what a Church, or its human leader, declares to be the truth?

Not at all. The seat of authority which binds the consciences of men, is not in any Church or man, but only in *the Sacred Scriptures, the Word of God,*[1] under the guidance of the Holy Spirit. The Scriptures being "the Very Word of God," infallibly reveal God's will to men, and they alone are binding on the conscience.[1]

If the Church is not the seat of authority in religion, what is the meaning of the Scripture, "The Church of the living God, the pillar and ground of the truth?"

This Scripture means that it is the duty and privilege of the Church of God faithfully to *proclaim, preserve, defend* and *transmit, God's Holy Word* and the *saving Gospel it reveals.* It does *not* mean that the truth derives its authority from the Church, nor that the Bible and its saving doctrines are true *because a pope or Church Council declares them to be true;* they are true because they are *revealed by the God of truth,* and partaking of His nature, they will *stand forever.* Psalm 19:7-9, 119:89, 142, 160, John 5:39, 17:17.

THE ROMAN CHURCH INCONSISTENT

Are not our Romanist friends when discussing authority guilty of reasoning in "a vicious circle?"

---

[1] At the opposite extreme from the blind submission to human authority of the Papacy, lies the equally dangerous error of *rationalism* or *Modernism,* which makes reason and experience the supreme arbiter and guide in religion. But reason and experience by themselves are untrustworthy guides, for they spring from our sinful nature and cannot escape the warping effect of ignorance, desire and prejudice. Though opposite extremes, Romanism and rationalism *meet on common ground;* Romanism bowing to *a pope* as supreme authority; rationalism making *Self* the supreme authority. Thus both are forms of Humanism, *exalting man instead of God.* Between these extremes lies the truth; the Protestant faith of Holy Scripture, allowing a proper use of reason and of all human faculties, but *controlled and guided by the Holy Spirit through the Word of God.*

They are guilty of this error. Like a squirrel revolving in his cage, they try to prove the Church by the Bible, and the Bible by the Church!

THE PROTESTANT DOCTRINE TRUE AND CONSISTENT

Is not the Protestant doctrine concerning the seat of authority true and consistent?

The Protestant doctrine concerning the seat of authority is undoubtedly true and consistent. It declares that the Holy Scriptures are *not* dependent for their authority on the *witness and sanction of a Church,* but are *self evidencing* to the reason and conscience of men. Their infallible truth and divine authority are directly impressed upon the heart of the believer by their Author, *the Spirit of truth,* who bears witness *by and with* the *Word.* John 16:13, 14, I Cor. 2:10, 11, Confession of Faith I, 1, 4-8.

Does not history show that the Church of Rome at different times has wavered and shifted her position concerning the seat of authority?

Papal writers show that the Roman Church has shifted its position regarding the seat of authority. At one time it held that authority resided in the Church Councils. Three Councils that of Pisa in 1409, of Constance, 1415, and that of Basle, 1432, decreed that *"even the pope is bound to obey the Councils."* At another time the Church held that authority resided in the Councils together with the pope. At still another time that it resided in the pope alone.[1] This opinion was finally decided upon in 1870, when, as a last hope of bolstering the tottering chair of the papacy, the Vatican Council declared Pius IX infallible, against the strong opposition and greatly to the

---

[1] It would be difficult to find a dogma less accordant with Holy Scripture and reason than papal infallibility. Does calling a mendicant a millionaire make him a millionaire? Neither does declaring an erring and fallible man infallible make him infallible. And how is he made infallible? By being chosen *by* and *from among,* a body of fallible men! The Emperor Ferdinand I discussing this point once said with perfect truth—"As the cardinals are *not good,* how can they choose a *good pope?"* Ranke, *History of the Popes,* Vol. I, page 203. The testimony of pope Adrian VI ought to settle the fiction of infallibility. After confessing that the root of all evils in the Roman Church was found in the priesthood and in the pope, he declared, "it is certain that *the pope can err,* even in *matters of faith,* asserting heresies in his decrees; for *many* of the *Roman pontiffs* were *heretics." Dictates on the 4th Book of Sentences.*

distress of many of his ablest followers. It may well be asked, which pronouncement is "infallible?"

Bishop Strossmayer in the Vatican Council of 1870 strongly opposed the dogma of infallibility, pointing out the many contradictions by popes of their own deliverances and those of other popes. He said, "I should never finish my speech, venerable brethren, if I were to put before your eyes the contradictions of popes in their teachings. If you decree the infallibility of the present bishop of Rome, you must also decree the infallibility of all preceding popes."

The Creed of Pius IV that the Roman Church is the "Mother and Mistress of all Churches" is clearly *untrue*. The New Testament declares that the Church at Jerusalem was the first Christian Church organized on earth. (Acts 1:4, II 41-47.) The second Church was founded at Samaria (Acts VIII 14) and the first Gentile Church was established at Antioch (Acts XI 20). It was from Jerusalem and Antioch that the Gospel first came to Rome, a good while later. In the early Church the highest officials of the Eastern branch were called Patriarchs, the three chief Patriarchates being those of Alexandria, Antioch and Constantinople, which later numbered *80* million Christians. The Eastern or Greek Church, the official title of which is the Catholic Orthodox Eastern Church, has *always repudiated the claims of Rome*. It later became the established Church of the Russian Empire.

The True Church of God is One

Did the Lord Jesus Christ teach the unity of all believers—that His true Church is one?

Attempting to bolster the pope's usurpation of the position which belongs only to the Lord Jesus Christ, it has been alleged that there is need of "an infallible living voice" to interpret Scripture, and decide what is the truth. But there is *no need* of an infallible human voice, because all true believers have *Christ's promise of the Holy Spirit to "guide them into all truth."* John 16:13. That there is no need of "an infallible living voice" is proved from the *history of the Jewish Church,* to whom God gave a revelation 1500 years before Christ, yet they had no "infallible living voice" to keep them from error in interpreting the Old Testament. As they did not have Christ's teaching and example, nor the fullness of the Spirit in the Jewish Church, they needed such an infallible guide *much more than Christians do now."* *Littledela,* page 162.

Our Lord clearly taught the unity of all true believers. In His last intercessory prayer before His crucifixion the Saviour prayed, "That they all may be one." John 17:21, 23.

Was this unity for which our Saviour prayed an external unity, a oneness of ecclesiastical organization?

Not at all. Just here is where the Roman Church errs. The unity for which our Lord prayed was a *spiritual* unity, a oneness of *heart, of faith, love and obedience to Him.*

What Scripture proves that this unity was spiritual, and not of ecclesiastical organization?

The same intercessory prayer proves it; "that they all may be one, *as Thou Father art in Me,* and *I in Thee."* The oneness of Christ and the Father was not an external, visible oneness, but an *invisible, spiritual oneness.*

Did the apostles, through the inspiration of the Holy Spirit, teach the same invisible, spiritual unity?

They did. St. Paul exhorted believers to "keep *the unity of the Spirit."* This spiritual union of believers is based on their *spiritual union with Christ.* "Christ dwelling in your hearts by faith." "Rooted and built up in Him." "One body and one Spirit; one Lord, one faith, one baptism (of the Holy Spirit)." There is no hint of *external, ecclesiastical unity,* but only of unity of the Spirit, the *unity of the Father and the Son,* the unity of *the believer with His Lord,* the unity of *all true believers in Christ, indwelt and guided by one Holy Spirit.* Eph. 4:3-6, Col. 2:7.

Does the papal conception of an external, visible oneness of Church organization, submitting to absolute authority of a pope, agree with the true Scripture doctrine of spiritual unity in Christ?

No. The Church of Rome's dogma of unity, that is, of visible oneness in one Church organization is *wholly different from that of Scripture;* for there may be oneness of external organization, without real spiritual unity; and there may be, and actually is, *real spiritual unity without* oneness of organization.

Not perceiving this important fact, does not the Papal body often wrongly accuse the Protestant Church of schism, of dividing the body of Christ?

Yes; but this accusation is wholly groundless. For in spite of different external organizations, there is a *real and growing unity of spirit among Protestant bodies,* both in the Homeland and on Foreign Mission fields.

The Protestant Church in Essentials One

Do the differences of belief or practice among Protestant bodies concern essential or non-essential doctrines?

The differences in belief or practice of Protestant denominations concern *non-essentials only.* Regarding the great vital doctrines of Christian faith, like the doctrines of the Holy Trinity, the deity and atonement of our Lord Jesus Christ, His substitutionary death on the cross, His resurrection, and coming again in glory; the work of the Holy Spirit; salvation not by works in any degree, but only by the righteousness of Christ; the Bible doctrine of heaven and hell, with no intermediate Purgatory, and no delusive masses for the dead; in these and other doctrines, the *Reformed or Protestant Church is One.* Denominational distinctions are like the differences in the various branches of service in an army; infantry, cavalry, artillery, air service, each has its own organization, its uniform, badge, and equipment, yet all are *truly one.*

Examples of True Unity

What examples of true spiritual unity may be seen in the Protestant Church?

The various declarations of Christian faith, like the Westminster Confession of Faith, the Thirty-nine articles of the Church of England, and those of the Methodist and Baptist denominations, are all essentially the same. In practice, there is an increasing cordiality and sympathy between pastors and congregations of different denominations; the transfer of members from one denomination to another; a brotherly exchange of pulpits; union evangelistic services;

joint Communion of the Lord's Supper; and hearty cooperation in the work of Bible, Tract, and Temperance societies, and in charitable welfare service.

What examples of the true spiritual unity of the Protestant Church are found in the Foreign Missionary fields?

Protestant missionaries in China, Africa, South America, and other lands are closely drawn together not only in preaching services, but also in famine-relief and medical work, and all forms of cooperative endeavor. Protestants thus form a striking contrast to Roman Catholic Missions in China. In earlier times there unfortunately existed such a *spirit of jealousy and strife among the various ecclesiastical Orders of the Church of Rome,* as the Jesuits, Dominicans, Franciscans, etc., that the pope was *compelled to separate them, assigning a different province to each Order! No such lack of concord has ever existed among Protestant bodies.* Though belonging to different societies, Protestant missionaries have uniformly shown an admirably fraternal spirit toward fellow workers of other denominations, because they feel that all are truly *one in Christ.* Gal. 3:28.

UNITY IN DIVERSITY

Is not the unity in diversity, which is taught in Holy Scripture, clearly seen in the Reformed or Protestant Church?

Protestant unity is clearly taught in Holy Scripture, and is a part of that precious "liberty wherewith Christ hath made His people free." Gal. 5:1. This liberty consists of *oneness in essentials* and a reasonable latitude in non-essentials. St. Paul illustrates this by the human body, which has many members each differing from the other, and each having its own special function, as the eye, the ear, the hand, the foot; yet all sympathizing and cooperating, and together constituting *one living organism.* Variety of members so far from hindering the action of the body, really helps it, and makes it more useful. So, says the apostle, with the Church of God and its members. God in His wisdom has bestowed on different groups of men various gifts of thought, character, education, etc. These various gifts He allows to have play within reasonable limits, so that *each denomination contributes something* which *the others do not possess,* and the sum total brings to all variety and enrichment of Christian faith and service. Variety in the branches of the Church no more militates against true spiritual unity than variety in the members of the human body militates against the oneness and efficiency of that body. While it is acknowledged that the principle of unity in diversity has been abused by the forming of needless subdivisions of the great branches of the Church, *the rightness or value of the principle* is *not* thereby *disproved;* for what good gift of God has poor, erring humanity not abused? Rom. 12: 4-8, I Cor. 12: 4-21.

How else may the true unity of Holy Scripture, as contrasted with the Church of Rome's mistaken conception of oneness of ecclesiastical organization, be illustrated?

According to Scripture, the unity of the Protestant Church is that of a *living organism,* Christ being its Head and Life. Col. 3:4. The unity of ecclesiastical organization, as found in the Roman Catholic body, is *mechanical and forced,* because it depends upon the autocratic will of one who controls as he sees fit. The Church of Rome's unity is that of a *barrel,* whose separate staves are held together by *an iron hoop.* Remove the hoop, the staves fall apart, and the barrel no longer exists. There is no life in any of its parts, no natural connection between them, all depends on the *compelling force of the iron band.*[1] How different is the conception of Holy Scripture! The Church is a *living organism* whose Head is Christ; all its parts are *living members,* joined in *one living body to the living Head.*[1] "Grow up into Him in all things, who is the Head, even Christ; from whom the whole body fitly joined together,—maketh increase of the body,—till we all come in the unity of the faith unto a perfect man, unto the measure of the stature of the fulness of Christ." Eph. 4:13, 15, 16.

This is the unity of the Protestant Church; the *true spiritual unity* of Holy Scripture, a *unity in diversity.*

[1] Dr. J. J. Döllinger of the "Old Catholic" movement, wrote: "The papal idea of the Church is a universal empire, spiritually and where possible, physically, *ruled by a single monarch;* an empire of *force and oppression,* where the spiritual authority is aided by the secular arm *in summarily suppressing every movement it dislikes.*" Janus, Preface XV.

CHAPTER II

THE CHURCH'S RULE OF FAITH

What is the Church's Rule of Faith?

The Word of God, the Sacred Scriptures of the Old and New Testaments, is the *only rule of faith and obedience* for all true believers. The Scriptures alone are the standard and test by which we may know whether a church is a part of the true Church of God, or not. Any church whose *doctrine and practice conform to the teachings of Holy Scripture* is a *part of the true Church of God;* and any church which does *not* conform to Holy Scripture in doctrine and practice is *not* a part of the true Church, but is *apostate.*

What Scriptures prove this statement?

Many Scriptures prove it, as 1. Deut. 28:58, 32:46, 47. Joshua 1:7, 8. What is said of the *Law* applies to *the whole Scripture,* for *all of it is the Word of God.*

2. Isaiah 8:20, "To the law and to the testimony; if they speak not according to this word, there is no light in them."

3. Isaiah 34:16, where the Scriptures are called "the Book of the Lord," because through them God speaks to men, and *in this book alone* is *found God's saving truth.*

4. Our Lord's command, "Search the Scriptures"; for He declares they are *a sure witness to Himself as the Saviour,* and to *eternal life in Him.*[1] John 5:39.

5. Our Lord's warning in Luke 16:29-31, "They have Moses and the Prophets; let them hear them. If they hear not Moses and the

---

[1] Later translations rightly follow the King James' Version, making our Lord's words *a command,* rather than *a statement.* Christ was reproving the Jews for not believing in Him as the Saviour. The reason was, that *God's Word was not abiding in them.* If they *really knew* the *Scriptures,* they would *believe* (ver. 38). So He commands them, *search diligently* the Scriptures, and you will *believe that I am the Saviour.* Perhaps some stress the word "think" unduly, as if it indicated doubt,—"in them ye think, ye have eternal life." The real meaning seems to be, "ye *(rightly) think* ye have eternal life."

Prophets, neither will they be persuaded though one rose from the dead."

6. The practice of the apostolic church, which *tested even the preaching of the apostles* by the Scriptures. Acts 17:11.

THE HOLY SCRIPTURES INFALLIBLE

The Holy Scriptures are infallible because they were given by the *God of truth,* "who cannot lie." Titus 1:2.

They are God's voice speaking through inspired men to the heart and conscience of mankind. "All Scripture is given by inspiration of God." II Tim. 3:16. The Scriptures are "a sure word of prophecy," for holy men of old spoke as they were *moved by the Holy Ghost.*" II Peter 1:21. Our Lord clearly proclaimed their infallibility; "The Scripture *cannot be broken.*" John 10:35.

The Scriptures are declared to be "the Word of God that *liveth and abideth forever,*" also, "The Word of the Lord which *endureth forever,*" bringing the Gospel of salvation. I Peter 1:23, 25; II Peter 1:16-19.

The infallibility of Scripture is also shown by all of those passages which our Lord used *as final* to *settle questions* under discussion.

"Did ye *never read in the Scriptures?*" Matt. 21:42. Matt. 27:54, 56.

"But the Scripture *must be fulfilled.*" Mark 14:49.

The finality of Scripture is also shown by His use of the phrase *"It is written."* Matt. 4:4, 7, 10.

Is there not a close connection between the Lord Jesus Christ and the Holy Scriptures, showing their vital importance as the instrument of salvation?

There is a very close connection between Christ and the Scriptures. *Both* are called the *Word of God:* both are the *living Word:* Christ is the living Word *Incarnate,* the Holy Scriptures are the *living Word written.* He who rejects the Holy Scriptures *rejects the Christ who gave them,* and shall *be judged by them at the last Great Day.* John 1:1, 14; 12:47, 48; I Thess. 2:13; Heb. 4:12; Rom. 2:16.

St. Peter's inspired declaration, "The Word of God which liveth and abideth forever," is confirmed by *20 centuries of time.* Genesis and Revelation, New Testament

THE SCRIPTURES SUPREMELY IMPORTANT

What texts show the supreme importance of the Scriptures?

Psalm 19:7, 8. "The law of the Lord is *perfect,* the testimony of the Lord is *sure;* the statutes of the Lord are *right;* the Commandment of the Lord is *pure.*" Here are set forth the purity, certainty, correctness, and completeness of Holy Scripture. They convert the soul, make wise the foolish, give joy to the believing heart, and light to the spiritual eyes. *The whole of the 119th Psalm shows the supreme importance of Scripture.* Also the text, "Blessed are they that hear the Word of God and Keep it." Luke 11:28, Also Joshua 1:7, 8, 23:6, Deut. 6:6-9, Luke 24:27.

What other texts show the supreme importance of the Scriptures as the instrument of salvation?

The Scriptures are "the Word of life." Phil. 2:6. They are "the *Word of truth,* the *Gospel of your salvation.*" Eph. 1:13. They are *"the Sword of the Spirit."* Eph. 6:17.

Through them sinners are *awakened, convicted, converted, sanctified,* and *comforted.* I Peter 1:23, Eph. 5:26, II Thess. 2:13, John 17:17, Rom. 15:4. By believing them, men are *forever saved:* by rejecting them, men are *forever lost.* Rom. 10:8, 9, Mark 16:15. While the vain philosophies of men and destructive criticism will surely pass away, the Scriptures will *stand forever;* "Heaven and earth shall pass away, but My Words shall not pass away." Matt. 5:18, 24:35; Isa. 40:6-8; I Peter 1:24, 25.

Are the Holy Scriptures a perfect, all-sufficient guide?

Through the enlightenment of the Holy Spirit, the Scriptures are a *perfect guide in all things.* The Spirit opens up the Scriptures to make them plain, and *opens up our minds* to receive the truth. Luke 24:32, 45; Acts 16:14. The Scriptures have full divine authority and are *all sufficient for every human need.* By them the believer

---

and Old Testament—the same Author; every part illustrated by the whole, and the whole shedding light on every part. It is organically united. He by whom the first three chapters of Genesis were inspired, saw also in His mind the *last three chapters of the Book of Revelation!*" Saphir, *The Divine Unity of Scripture,* pages 191-193.

is not only made "wise unto salvation," but also is *"thoroughly furnished unto all good works."* II Tim. 3:15, 16.

An admirable statement of the all-sufficiency of Holy Scriptures as the Christian Church's Rule of Faith is found in the Westminster Confession of Faith, chapter I, and in the Larger Catechism, Question 4—"How doth it appear that the Scriptures are the Word of God?" Answer. The Scriptures manifest themselves to be the Word of God by their majesty and purity; by the consent of all the parts, and the scope of the whole, which is to give all glory to God; by their light and power to convince and convert sinners, and to comfort and build up believers unto salvation. But the Spirit of God, bearing witness by and with the Scriptures in the heart of man is alone able fully to persuade it that they are the *very Word of God."* John 16:13, 14; I Cor. 2:6-9.

Did the early Fathers of the Church hold the Protestant opinion concerning the supreme authority of the Scripture as Divine and all-sufficient?

They did. The Protestant opinion concerning the Scriptures was the opinion held *by believers from the very beginning of the Christian Church.* Tertullian (about 150-230), writing against Hermogenes, said: "Let the school of Hermogenes tell us where (in Scripture) such a statement is written. If it be *not written,* then let that school fear the woe which awaits those who *"take from, or add to, Holy "Scripture."* Adv. Hermogenem, XXII. St. Basil the Great declared: "It is useful and necessary that every one should *thoroughly learn out of the divinely inspired Scriptures,* both for the fulfilment of *piety,* and also in order not to become *habituated to human traditions."* From the Short Rules, 95. St. Augustine wrote "Let us hear no more of 'you say,' or 'I say'; but let us hear a *'Thus saith the Lord,'"* Epist. cont. Donat., III, 5.

ROME'S GRAVE ERROR REGARDING HOLY SCRIPTURE

What grave error regarding Holy Scripture does the Church of Rome teach?

The Church of Rome *shamefully disparages God's Holy Word.* It declares that—

"Holy Scripture is *not sufficient*";

"That it does *not contain all that is necessary for salvation*";

"That Scripture is *dark and obscure*";

"That it is *not for the people to read*"; and

"That Scripture is *not the judge of controversy*, nor *an entire rule of faith.*"

Where are these grossly erroneous statements found?

In *standard papal works,* which no Romanist will dare to dispute; as Cardinal Bellarmine,[1] one of the most prominent authorities on papal dogma, whom Pius XI commended. Also they are found in substance in the decrees of the Council of Trent; and in the popes' catalogue of forbidden books. Bellarmine, *De verbo Dei,* 2:15, 3:1,3; 4:3. *Index libr. prohibit, Regula* 4.

POPES HAVE UNIFORMLY OPPOSED THE READING OF HOLY SCRIPTURE BY THE LAITY

It naturally follows from Bellarmine's view of Holy Scripture, which has permeated the priesthood, and is accepted generally in the Church, that the reading of Holy Scripture is *looked upon with disfavor* by the authorities of the Roman Church. They try, of course, to deny this fact when conversing with Protestants. The 4th Rule of the Congregation of the Index of Prohibited Books, approved by pope Pius IV, declares: "Since it is manifest by experience that if the Bible in the vulgar tongue be suffered to be read everywhere without distinction, *more evil than good arises,* let the judgment of the bishop or the Inquisitor be abided by, so that after consulting the parish priest or the confessor they may grant permission to read translations of the Scriptures, made by Catholic writers, to those whom they consider are able to receive no harm; but permission must be given *in writing.* But whosoever shall presume to read the Bible, or have it in possession, *without such written*

---

[1] Roberto Bellarmino; born in Tuscany in 1542, died at Rome 1621. A Jesuit controversialist, professor at Louvain, and in the papal College at Rome; was the author of standard theological works; was appointed Archbishop of Capua and Cardinal. He has been called "the greatest controversialist of the R. Catholic Church." Ranke, *vol.* I, p. 298.

permission, shall *not* receive absolution of their sins, unless they have *first given up their Bibles.* Booksellers who shall sell or furnish Bibles in the vulgar tongue to anyone who has no written license, shall *forfeit the price of the books,* and shall be *otherwise punished* at the pleasure of the bishop. Pope Clement VIII added to the Rule, that "the Holy Inquisition had *taken away from bishops and superiors the power to grant such licenses."* Pope Leo XII in an encyclical of May 3, 1824, exhorted bishops to *turn away your flock from "these poisonous pastures,"* that is, the Word of God in the vernacular tongue! He declared that if the sacred Scriptures be indiscriminately published, *"more evil than good would result!"* Who could fail to see how these leaders have *hedged round the Bible with so many restrictions* that the people are *prevented from reading it?* The bishop and parish priest must first *approve a license to read God's Word,* the translation must be *by a Catholic writer,* the license must be *in writing,* and licenses *cannot be granted even by bishops and superiors!* To read the Scriptures without a license means to be *cut off from absolution for their sins,* unless they have *first surrendered their Bibles!* All of these restrictions make reading of God's Holy Word practically *impossible,* and *directly contradict the Saviour's command,* "SEARCH THE SCRIPTURES!" Think of the popes, who profess to honor God, *daring to forbid the laity* to read *God's own Book of life!* Does not the Church of Rome by such action *condemn herself as apostate?*

THE SUPREME IMPORTANCE OF DAILY READING AND STUDY OF HOLY SCRIPTURES

In painful contrast to the deplorable opposition to the Scriptures of the high authorities of the Roman Church, see how the Word of God constantly urges God's people to *exalt and honor it,* and *make it the rule of their daily life,* and *zealously teach their children.* See how often Moses exhorted the children of Israel concerning the Law of God. "These words which I command thee, this day, shall be in thine heart, and thou shalt teach them diligently unto thy children and shall talk of them when thou sittest in thine house, and when thou walkest by the way, and when thou liest down, and when thou risest up." Again, he exhorts, "Gather the people together, men, women and children and the stranger within thy gates, that they may *hear,* and that *they may learn,* and *fear the Lord your God,* and observe *to do all the words of this law:* and that *their children* may hear, and learn to fear the Lord your God, as long as ye live." So also the prophets stressed the importance of learning the Scriptures. Isaiah exhorts, To the Law and to the Testimony; if they speak not according to this word, it is because *there is no light in them."* Is. 8:20. Of the Levites it is said that King Jehoshaphat sent them throughout the Kingdom to *teach the laity; "having* the *book of the Law of the Lord with them,* they went throughout all the cities of Judah and *taught the people."* II Chron. 17:8, 9. Again, "Ezra the scribe brought the book of the law of Moses and read to the congregation, *both men and women,* from *morning till midday,* and all the people were attentive to the Book of the Law. So they read in the book of the law distinctly, and *gave the sense* and *caused them to understand the reading."* Nehem. 8:1-3, 7, 8.

Again, our Lord reproved the Jews for their *disbelief of the Resurrection."* And Jesus said, "Do ye not err, because ye *know not the Scriptures,* neither the power of God?" Mark 12:24. St. Paul wrote his epistles, for all Christians: "I charge you by the Lord that *this epistle be read to all the holy brethren."* I Thess. 5:27, also Col. 4:16, Phil. 1:1, II Tim. 3:14-17, Rom. 15:4. It has been aptly remarked: "There is nothing about *'poisonous pastures'* in all this!"

Did the Fathers of the early Church share the view of later popes that "the Scriptures are not for the people to read?"

They did *not;* but urged the laity to *obey Christ's command, "Search the Scriptures!"* "We were enjoined by Christ Himself to *put no faith in human doctrines,* but in *those proclaimed by the blessed prophets and taught by Himself."* Justin Martyr, *Dial. with Trypho,* 48.

"It is a manifest falling away from the Faith, either to *annul anything in Scripture,* or to *introduce anything not in Scripture,"* etc. Basil the Great, *De Fide.* So also Tertullian, *Adv. Hermogenem,* 22 and Augustine, *Ep. cont. Donat.* 3:5.

Chrysostom pointed out the great error of the Roman Church: *"This is the cause of all evil, not to know the Scriptures!" Hom.* 9 on *Coloss.* 3.

Again, "The reading of the Scriptures is a *powerful safeguard against sin*, and *ignorance* of the Scriptures is *a dangerous abyss.*" "To know nothing of Scripture is *to risk one's salvation.*" *Hom.* III *on Lazarus.*

"As the Apostle wrote, so did the Lord,—that is, He *spoke through His Gospels, not* so that a few might understand, but *all men.*" Jerome, *Comm. in Psalm 86.*

"What is Holy Writ, but a sort of *letter from Almighty God to His creatures? Study* therefore, and *daily ponder, your Creator's words,* and *learn God's heart in God's words.*" Gregory the Great, *Epist.* 4; *Indict.* 12:31.

How does the Church of Rome try to evade responsibility for this grave sin of opposing their people's reading the Word of God?

The Church of Rome alleges that *Regula 4* of the Index which forbids the reading of Holy Scripture has been *rescinded.* But this cannot be done *without denying the dogma of papal infallibility.* Monsignor Dupanloup in his "Observations," rightly says, "if we declare Pius IX *infallible,* we must declare that *all his predecessors were infallible.*" This is perfectly true, and if the Church's pronouncement against reading the Bible is *rescinded,* then *the pope who made this pronouncement was in error,* and the *dogma of infallibility is thus destroyed.* Into such quagmires of contradiction has the absurd dogma of infallibility led the Roman Church! The truth is, the Church of Rome thus *directly disobeys* the *Lord Jesus Christ's command*—"Search the Scriptures."

Butler's Roman Catholic Cathechism states: "There is *no general obligation incumbent on the laity* to *read the Scriptures,* it being sufficient that they *listen to it from their pastors.*" But this is a weak evasion, a lame attempt to make it appear that the Roman priests give their people what they *really do not give,* i.e., *the whole Word of God.* Cardinal Wiseman trying to gloss over this *grave disobedience of Christ's command by the Roman Church,* said: "Though the Scripture may be *permitted,* we do not *urge them upon the people,* we do not *encourage* them to read them. *Certainly not.*" It may reasonably be asked, *Why not?* The real reason is, the Church of Rome *fears the Bible,* because it *shows plainly how far Romanism* has *departed from the true faith of Scripture!*

3

HOLY SCRIPTURE MUST NEITHER BE ADDED TO, NOR TAKEN FROM

How does God command all men to receive the Holy Scriptures?

God commands all men to receive the Holy Scriptures *in their entirety*, just as He has given them. Nothing whatever is *to be added to* them, or *taken from* them. "Ye shall not add unto the Word which I command you, neither shall ye diminish ought from it, that ye may keep the commandments of the Lord your God." Deut. 4:2.

"What thing soever I command you, observe to do it." Thou shalt *not add* thereto, *nor diminish from* it." Deut. 5:32, 12:32, 18:19-20; Jer. 26:2; Matt. 5:18, 19.

The Word of God presents two solemn warnings of the great sin of tampering with Scripture; one in the Old Testament, given to King Jehoiakim; who when he had received God's message through the prophet Jeremiah, deliberately cut up the parchment on which it was written and burnt it in the fire! For this insult to the Almighty, he was warned that he should be *carried captive to Babylon* and when he died, his body should be *thrown out unburied.* "He shall be buried with the burial of an ass, drawn and cast forth beyond the gates." All of which was fulfilled to the letter. Jer. 36:2-7, 23, 22:18, 19; II Chron. 36:5, 6.

The second warning closes the whole Canon of Scripture. It *foretells the awful curse* which will *surely fall* on those who *add to,* or *take from,* God's Holy Word. "If any man shall add unto these things, God shall add unto him the plagues that are written in this book; and if any man shall take away from the words of the book of this prophecy, God shall take away his part out of the Book of life, and out of the holy city, and from the things that are written in this book." Rev. 22:18, 19.

Do not be deceived! This solemn warning was *not placed by chance* at the *end of the whole canon of Scripture,* for it applies not merely to *Revelation,* but equally to *all the Holy Scriptures,* for all are God's Word! The man who rejects, or doubts, any part of them, does so at *the peril of his eternal condemnation!*

THE APOCRYPHA EXCLUDED FROM SCRIPTURE

Do not the solemn warnings of God concerning His Holy Word (the Old and New Testaments) that nothing should be added to it or taken from it, entirely exclude the Apocrypha from the Canon of Sacred Scripture?

They *wholly exclude the Apocrypha from the Sacred Canon.* The reason is: The 14 books of the Apocrypha are confessedly *the work of men;* the Bible alone is what it claims to be, the *work of God the Holy Spirit.* Having no divine authority the Apocrypha may *not* be used to *establish Christian doctrine,* as Jerome declared in the fifth century.

Note that the Lord Jesus Christ *never recognized them, nor quoted from them.* The apostles and Church Fathers *did not accept them* as a part of Holy Scripture.

They are *never mentioned in the New Testament.*

They were *not included in the Hebrew Scriptures.*

They were *never referred to in the Talmud.*

It was not until the Council of Trent, about the middle of *the 16th century* (1545-1563) that the Roman Church declared the Apocrypha to be *a part of the Sacred Scriptures.* The Protestant Church has *never recognized these books.*

TRADITION NOT A PART OF THE RULE OF FAITH

What should be the attitude of the true Christian Church toward Tradition?

Tradition, even as part of the rule of faith, should be *wholly rejected:* 1. because the Holy Scriptures are the Church's *perfect, God-given guide;* 2. because tradition is *man-made and imperfect;* and 3. because the Lord Jesus Christ *mentioned tradition only to condemn it and warn against it.*

What Scriptures prove that this is true?

Those in which our Lord *rebuked the Pharisees for doing just what the Church of Rome does,* viz.: professing to believe the Scriptures, but *really rejecting* them *to follow the traditions of men.*

1. "Why do ye transgress the commandment of God by your tradition?" Matt. 15:3.

2. "Ye have made the Commandment of God of none effect by your tradition." Matt. 15:6.

3, 4. "In vain do they worship Me, teaching for doctrines the commandments of men." Matt. 15:9, Mark 7:7.

5. "Laying aside the Commandment of God, ye hold the tradition of men." Mark 7:8.

6. "Full well ye reject the Commandment of God that ye may keep your own tradition." Mark 7:9.

7. "Making the Word of God of none effect through your tradition." Mark 7:13.

Thus in seven declarations our Lord showed *the antagonism* between tradition and the Word of God, and warned men that if they hold tradition, *their worship of God is in vain!*

THE APOSTLES TESTIFIED PLAINLY AGAINST TRADITION

Did St. Paul warn believers against tradition?

He did. "Beware lest any man spoil (rob) you—*after the tradition of men, and not* after *Christ.*" Col. 2:8. Paul declared that *before* his conversion he was *zealous for the traditions of his fathers;* but that *after* his conversion he *"counted all such things as loss for Christ."* Gal. 1:14-16, Phil. 3:7.

What was St. Peter's testimony concerning tradition?

St. Peter *testified against tradition,* addressing both Jews and Gentiles in his general epistles. He warned against "the vain conversation *received by tradition* from your fathers"; that since Christ had redeemed them by His precious blood, they must follow *Him,* and *not* follow the manner of life *which tradition had formerly led them to follow.* I Peter 1:18, 19.

THE CHURCH OF ROME'S GRAVE ERROR CONCERNING TRADITION

What does the Church of Rome teach concerning Tradition?

The Church of Rome teaches: "That we ought to serve God *according to the tradition of the ancients.*" And, "That we ought to receive with the obedience of faith many things which are *not in the Scriptures.*" Bellarmine, *De verbo Dei.* 4:4; Cotton 2:34, 35.

Some papal writers, in order to justify their disobedience, and make wrong appear right, have dared *falsely to call* tradition "the *unwritten Word of God!"* Dr. S. J. Hunter, an English Jesuit, exalts Tradition above the Divine Word, saying, "The Church *could dispense with Holy Scripture,* but *cannot* dispense with *tradition";*— "Tradition is *of wider scope*—and *more necessary."* Do not these declarations plainly show that Jesuitism is *apostate?* A Romanist book, published in Brazil, with full ecclesiastical sanction, says: "Today we live *one-tenth on the Bible,* and *nine-tenths* on *tradition.* The Bible perhaps does *not* contain *all essential truths.* Tradition is *greater than the word of the Bible!" Outlines of Dogmatic Theology,* Vol. I, pages 153-155, *O Biblismo, Du Bois,* Para, 1921, page 96.

Is not this teaching of the Roman Church directly contrary to Christ's command and the Holy Scriptures, and therefore, a mark of apostasy?

It is the *great sin of apostasy.* It places the teaching of sinful men on the *same level as the Word of Almighty God;* and it directly *disobeys the divine command* that nothing shall be *added to* what God has enjoined—"Ye shall *not add* unto the *Word which I command you."* Deut. 4:2.

Two Scriptures texts have been quoted by Romanists as seeming to countenance tradition, viz.: II Thess. 2:15, 3:6. Do these justify tradition in the sense in which the Church of Rome uses it?

No, they do *not.* St. Paul uses the word in its original sense, as simply indicating "that which *was delivered"* or *"handed down";* and *not* in the sense in which the Church of Rome uses it, for he is speaking of *doctrines which he himself had delivered;* he says, "Hold the traditions ye have been taught whether by word or our epistles"; and "Withdraw from every brother that walketh not after the tradition *which ye received of* us." It is thus clear that these texts give no support to the Roman doctrine of tradition.

It should be carefully noted that practically the whole Roman system of doctrine and worship is based on Tradition, and *not on the Word of God.* Leading papal authorities have acknowledged this fact. When the Council of Trent was discussing the Church's Rule of Faith, and some present wished to declare the Holy Scriptures to be the Rule, Cardinal Reginald Pole of England insisted that *the Scriptures alone* should *not be declared the Rule of Faith;* for said he, "Our beliefs and our worship in *their entirety depend upon Tradition.*" And his opinion *prevailed in the Council.*

If our Lord and His apostles thus clearly opposed tradition, why does the Church of Rome insist on teaching it?

Because the Roman Church uses tradition *to try to justify dogmas and practices* which are *plainly contrary to the Word of God.*

We see then that the Holy Scriptures alone are the Rule of Faith for the true Church of God. They were the *sole rule of the Apostolic Church,* and of *the Church for centuries later.* As we have already seen, Justin Martyr, Tertullian and Basil the Great testify to the Holy Scriptures as the *Church's sole divine guide.* So also *Chrysostom* (died 407) in his sermons *Hom. IX on Colossians* 3, and *Hom. II.*

St. Augustine said: "You aske me where the Church is; "I answer, *'Search the Scriptures.'*" Christ did not say "Search *tradition,*" but the Scriptures *alone,* for they are the Church's *all-sufficient guide, the Very Word of God.* I Thess. 2:13.

The valiant John Huss[1] also loyally held the Word of God as the *true Rule of Faith.* He said: "Let us make matters clear. What I call apostolic orders are the teachings of Christ's apostles. When the orders of the pope are in harmony with these teachings, I am ready to listen to them; when they are contrary to them, *I refuse them obedience, even if I were to see kindled before my eyes the fire which was to burn my body.*" Mussolini's *John Huss, the Man of Truth,* p. 53.

---

[1] John Huss, the great reformer, was born in Bohemia in 1369. After graduating in the University of Prague, he began to lecture on the writings of Wycliffe, and became Rector of the University and pastor of Bethlehem chapel. Opposing the abuses of the Church of Rome, he incurred the bitter hatred of the hierarchy, and was summoned to appear for trial before the Council of Constance. Though guaranteed a safe conduct by the Emperor Sigismund, the Council declared that "faith need not be kept with heretics," and *burned him at the stake* July 6, 1415. The martyr exhibited *a noble faith and courage to the end,* and foretold *the triumph of the Gospel* for which he laid down his life. Said he, *"the image of Christ shall never be effaced from men's hearts,* but *shall be written there by much better preachers than myself. The nation that loves Christ shall rejoice and I,* as one awaking from the dead, will *leap with exceeding joy!"* Pope Adrian at the Diet of Nuremberg recalling Huss' words declared, *"The heretics Huss and Jerome are now alive again in the person of Martin Luther!"* D'Aubigné's *History of the Reformation.*

In the matter of God's Holy Word and Tradition has not the Church of Rome often violated God's express commands and therefore comes under His condemnation?

The Church of Rome has introduced *many sinful inventions* which *God's Word does not permit,* and *disregards many things* which He has *commanded.* God's Word commands that the Holy Trinity alone is to be worshipped; the papal Church disobeying the Divine Command sinfully worships *saints, angels* and *Mary.* God warns in His Holy Word that *no image, picture or representation of any kind* is to *be used* in *worship,* for they are an *abomination* in His holy sight; yet Rome *fills her Churches* with these *abhorred images,* even bowing down to the image of *Peter* in the Vatican and *kissing his toe!* The Church of Rome has *sinfully taken away from the Lord's Supper, depriving the laity of the wine* and has *added the invention of the Mass, falsely exalting* a sinful priest as able to *change a wafer into the Son of God!* Rome has taken away Confession of sins *from the Creator,* and has *added it* to a *sinful priest who falsely claims to forgive sins.* The Roman Church has *added* many *false mediators* and thus dishonors the *one Divine Mediator.* I Tim. 2:5. It has invented a place called *purgatory* and *makes gain by falsely professing to save men from it.* It has taken away *the true Repentance of Scripture* and has *added penances and false Indulgences:* It has taken away the Word of God from perishing men, and has substituted *false human tradition.* For these and other grave transgressions the Church of Rome must *face Condemnation at the Judgment bar of God.*

Chapter III

THE CHURCH'S HEAD AND FOUNDATION

Who is the Head of the true Church of God?

The Lord Jesus Christ is the only Head of the true Church of God.

Who is the Foundation of the true Church?

The Lord Jesus Christ is the only Foundation of the true Church of God.

Why is the Lord Jesus Christ the only Head and Foundation of the true Church?

Because He is God and therefore LORD of all. And only God has all the perfect attributes which are needed to fill these great offices. "God manifest in the flesh," and "In Him dwelleth all the fulness of the Godhead bodily." I Tim. 3:16, Col. 2:9—the fulness of Divine wisdom, power, love, righteousness, and holiness. Also, He founded the Church; He redeemed it with His precious blood; He promised to be with His people to the end of the world (or age); and because at last He will bring His Church safe to heaven, to reign with Him in glory for evermore. Matt. 16:18, 28:20, Acts 20:28, I Cor. 1:30, Rev. 3:21, 21:9, 10, 11:15.

What fatal error does the Church of Rome teach concerning the Head and Foundation of the Church?

The Roman Church teaches that *the Pope of Rome is the Head and Foundation of the Church of God.* "The Pope is the Chief Priest, *the Head,* the Husband, *and the Foundation of the Church.*" "That St. Peter had not only a primacy of order, but also a primacy of *dominion and jurisdiction.*" Bellarmine, *De Rom. Pontiff,* 2:31, 1:10,11.

An authorized Roman Catholic catechism asserts that "St. Peter is *the supreme Head of the Church.*" By the Rt. Rev. J. H. Oechtering, *imprimatur* of Archbishop Glennon of St. Louis, Mo., 1907, page vii.

Are not these assertions blasphemous, *making a sinful human being usurp the high place of the living God?*

They are *blasphemous,* and a mark of *apostasy,* for no sinful human being may usurp the place which Christ alone fills. *Only God* can be the *Head and Foundation of the true Church.* It is "the Church of the living God." I Tim. 3:15.

Is not the sin of the Roman Church, in declaring the pope to be the Head and Foundation of the Church of God, essentially that of the fallen angels *who rebelled against Almighty God, strove to usurp the sovereignty of the universe, and are kept in everlasting chains in darkness to await the great Judgment Day?*

It is essentially *the same great sin.* There is the same rash *pride, self will, unholy ambition,* and *rebellion against the Lord of hosts,* under *the appearance of piety;* and there will be the *same awful condemnation.* Jude 6, II Peter 2:1-4, II Thess. 2:3, 4, Ezek. 28:2, 8.

CHRIST THE ONLY HEAD AND FOUNDATION OF THE CHURCH

What Scriptures prove that the Lord Jesus Christ is the only Head *of the true Church of God?*

1. God the Father "gave Him to be *the Head over all things to the Church,* which is His body." Eph. 1:22, 23.

2. "Grow up into Him in all things who is *the Head, even Christ.*" Eph. 4:15.

3. The husband is the head of the wife, even as Christ is the Head of the Church. Eph. 5:23.

4. "He is the Head of the body, the Church." Col. 1:18.

5. As there is only "one body," so there can be *only one Head.* Eph. 4:4, 5.

What Scripture proves that Christ alone is the Foundation of the true Church?

"Other foundation can no man lay than that *is laid,* which is *Jesus Christ.*" I Cor. 3:11.

Does Ephesians 2:20 afford any ground for calling a pope the foundation of the Church of God?

None at all. This text teaches that the prophets and apostles were inspired of God specially to write the Holy Scriptures without error, and were sent by Him to proclaim His Gospel and establish the Church. But the Lord Jesus Christ, because He is God, and has provided a perfect atonement for sin, and because of His resurrection from the dead, and His intercession in glory, is the *only foundation of salvation,* from whom all grace, power and holiness proceed.

How are we sure that the papal explanation of this text is wrong?

Because it directly contradicts the declaration of I Corinthians 3:11, that *Christ is the only Foundation;* and because it would prove that there should be not one pope merely, but *about thirty popes at the same time,* for prophets as well as apostles are included.

The assumption of the Roman Church that a human head of the Church was needed is *false,* and based on ignorance or unbelief; for our Saviour declares plainly that He Himself would be *constantly present with His followers* to *do all that the Church needed to have done for it.* He said: "Lo! I am with you always, even unto the end of the world (or age)!" Matt. 28:20. And after Christ's ascension to heaven we read in Mark: "And they (the Apostles) went forth and preached everywhere *the Lord working with them* and *confirming the Word with signs following.*" Mark 16:20. Christ was present through His Holy Spirit to teach, "to guide into all truth," to save men, and to sanctify and comfort His people. All through the Book of Acts we read that the Christians in simple faith appealed to Him and *always had His presence and help given them.* John 14:16, 17, 26, 15:26, 27, 16:7-13; Acts 1:24, 2:42, 4:24-31, etc.

HOLY SCRIPTURE PROVES THAT ST. PETER WAS NOT THE FOUNDATION OF THE CHURCH OF GOD

The Church of Rome tries to use Matthew 16:18, 19 to prove the papacy, alleging that Peter was the rock *on which Christ built the Church; but does it correctly interpret this passage?*

No. The Church of Rome *wholly misinterprets it.* When our Lord said, "Thou art Peter, and on this rock I will build My Church," if he had meant that *Peter was* to be the foundation, the natural form of the statement would have been, *"Thou* art Peter, and *on thee* I will build My Church"; but He *does not say this,* because it never was His purpose that *a sinful man should be the rock on which the Church was built.* Note carefully that in the expression "on this rock," our Lord purposely used a different Greek word πέτρα, *pétra* from that used for Peter Πέτρος *Pétros.* He did this to show that *not Peter,* but *the great truth which had just been revealed to him,* viz.: that *our Lord was "the Christ, the Son of the living God,"* was to be the *Church's foundation.* Built on this divine foundation, the Christ, the ever-living Saviour, the gates of hell should never prevail against the Church. But built on *the well-meaning but sinful Peter, or on any other man,* the gates of hell *would surely prevail;* for a little later our Lord had to *severely rebuke Peter,* calling him *"Satan!"* "Get thee behind Me, Satan," thou art *an offense unto Me;* for thou savorest not the things that be *of God,* but *those that be of men."* Verse 23.

Is this the interpretation of Protestant commentators only?

No. It is the interpretation which has *uniformly prevailed in the Church of God from the days of the apostles.*

The fathers of the early Church, Ambrose, Basil, Chrysostom, Hilary and Jerome all make "the rock" on which the Church was founded to be *not Peter,* but the *great truths confessed by him.*

St. Augustine, in his treatise on the first epistle of John, asks, What do these words mean, "on this rock I will build My Church?" He replies, "On this faith that thou art *the Christ, the Son of the living God."* On this rock which thou hast confessed, I will build My Church; for *Christ was the rock."* Again in his 13th sermon, Augustine practically repeats the same words, adding, "I will build My Church upon *Myself,* who am *the Son of the living God;* upon *Me, not* upon *thee."* This is also the interpretation of a majority of learned Roman Catholic commentators. Of 61 Roman expositors *only 17* explained 'the rock' as referring to *Peter; 44 of them* held the Protestant interpretation that *Christ, not* Peter, was the rock on which the Church was built. It is *only since the Council of Trent,* in the 16th century, that the mistaken view which makes Peter, not Christ, 'the Rock' on which the Church was built, has prevailed.

THE POWER OF THE KEYS BELONG TO ALL TRUE MINISTERS OF CHRIST

"The Power of the Keys," the "binding and loosing," the "opening and shutting" of the Kingdom of heaven, belongs not only to the apostles, but *also to all true ministers of the Lord Jesus Christ.* Tertullian in the 2nd Century rightly said, "Everyone who confesses Christ as Peter did, also *carries the Keys of heaven as he did.*" *Scorpiace,* Shotwell, page 295. This power is *declarative,* for the actual exercise of the power, "the opening and shutting," "the admitting to, or excluding from," the Kingdom of heaven, belongs to CHRIST ALONE; for HE ALONE *knows the hearts of men,* and *He alone can forgive sins.* This divine power he holds as *Lord of the Resurrection,* Rev. 1:18, and *He claims* the *exclusive right to exercise it.* Rev. 3:7. Any other interpretation makes Scripture contradict Scripture.

What acts of Peter show that he was weak and erring, and could not be the foundation of God's Church?

His sinful sleeping in Gethsemane, during Christ's agony, when he should have been *watching and praying, as his Lord commanded.* Matt. 26:40. His rash act in cutting off the high priest's servant's ear, for which Christ *rebuked him.* Matt. 26:51, 52. After boasting that he was willing to die for Christ, he *shamefully denied his Lord three times,* even with *oaths and curses!* Matt. 26:74. Even after Pentecost Peter *gravely sinned.* At a crisis in the Church when dealing with the Gentile Christians, Peter was *guilty of deceitful conduct,* and drew upon himself *in public* a *stern reproof from St. Paul.* Gal. 2:11-13.

Does Scripture show any real primacy of Peter among the apostles?

It does *not,* except perhaps in a readiness to be spokesman for the disciples. The apostles, while differing in ability, all seem to have been of *equal rank.* St. James was the *leader* of the Church in Jerusalem; he pronounced the decision arrived at in the General Council, and *probably presided over it.* Acts 15:13-19.

While all the apostles had equal authority, James seems to have had *a kind of leadership;* he is several times mentioned first. "Go, show these things unto *James,* and to the brethren." Acts 12:17. "Paul went in *unto James.*" Acts 21:18. "And when James, Cephas and John, who seemed to be pillars," James is here put *before Peter.* Gal. 2:9.

Also, St. Paul wrote *much more of the Scriptures* than St. Peter,[1] and seems to have established *many more churches.*

But the best proof is a man's own testimony. *What does St. Peter say* of himself? *Does he claim to have been a pope, or to have primacy above the other apostles?*

No. Surely if Peter had been a pope, or "the supreme head of the Church," or of rank superior to the other apostles, *he would have declared it in his general epistles,* for that was the place of all others to *assert his authority,* and popes have never been slow to make claims, for themselves. But Peter does *not* make *any claim whatever* to superiority. He does *not* call himself *Pontifex Maximus,* or any such title. He simply speaks of himself as *a presbyter, an ordinary minister of Christ.*[2] It is from this apostolic office that the Presbyterian Church takes its name,—the *"Church of the Presbyters."* That this was the original, apostolic form of Church Government set forth in Holy Scripture, eminent scholars of different Communions testify; among others, Anglican leaders, like Bishop Lightfoot, Dean Stanley, etc.

What were Peter's exact words in declaring that his office in the Church was simply that of presbyter (elder)?

Peter said: "The presbyters (elders) who are among you I exhort, *who am a fellow-presbyter.*" I Peter 5:1. The Greek word is συμπρεσβύτερος *sumpresbúteros,* meaning *'joint' or 'fellow'-pres-*

---

[1] If Hebrews is included among the Pauline epistles, there were *14 epistles* written by St. Paul, and only *2 short ones* written by St. Peter.

[2] It is noteworthy that one of the greatest apostles, he who leaned on Christ's bosom, who wrote the most spiritual of the Gospels, three epistles, and received a special revelation of things to come, viz.: St. John, *does not speak of himself at all as an apostle,* but *only as a presbyter.* "The Presbyter unto the elect lady"; "The presbyter unto the well-beloved Gaius." II John, 1. III John, 1. This was *not accidental,* nor merely *from humility.* It seems to have been done in order to show that the office of the apostle was *only temporary,* and that the office of presbyter was to be the *permanent, important one* in the Christian ministry.

byter. St. Peter thus puts himself where he rightly belongs, on the *same level as other presbyters or ministers;* for the Scriptures clearly teach *the parity of all Christian ministers.* The humility and self-forgetfulness of Peter shown toward the end of his life in his epistles, is in marked contrast to the impulsive, self-assertive spirit seen in his earlier years. Toward the end, as he grew in grace, he had much to say of *meekness* and *humility,* "Yea, all of you be clothed with humility; for God resisteth the proud, and giveth grace to the humble. Humble yourselves therefore under the mighty hand of God," he constantly *exalted Christ, not* self, "and when the chief Shepherd shall appear, ye shall receive a crown of glory that fadeth not away." How entirely different was that humble presbyter from the popes of Rome!

The Testimony of the Fathers Proves Clearly There Was No Pope in the Early Church

It cannot be repeated too often that there was *no hint of a pope in the early centuries of the Church.* Christ was still faithfully acknowledged as the *only Head and Foundation. Nor* did the Christians of those early times believe that Peter had a primacy, or was *exalted in any way above the other apostles.* That great error was reserved for the Dark Ages of ignorance and superstition, which soon descended upon the Church. This is proved by the fact that there is *no mention of a pope,* or of *any primacy of Peter* in the *three oldest creeds of Christendom,* the Apostles', the Nicene, and the Athanasian: and, as already stated, it is *only since the Council of Trent* (1545-1563) that Peter was *held to be the rock on which Christ built the Church.* How different it is now! For now the papacy is declared to be *a fundamental dogma of Romanism, necessary to salvation!* Boniface VIII radically changed the faith of the Church, when he wrote in the bull. *Unam Sanctam,* "We declare that *every human creature is subject to the Roman pontiff;* and we pronounce this to be *altogether necessary to salvation."* (Nov. 18, 1302.) *Wholly different* was the *belief of St. Jerome,* when writing against Jovinian in 393, "Thou sayest the Church is founded on Peter, albeit the same is true *of all the apostles,* and they *all received the Keys of the Kingdom of heaven."* And he might have added as Tertullian declared, "and *true of all Christian ministers as well!*" St. Augustine distinctly wrote "We who are Christians, in name and deed, do *not believe in Peter,* but IN HIM *on whom Peter himself believed.*" "*He, the Christ, is Peter's Master* in the teaching which leads to life everlasting, and He is *our Master too.*" *De civit. Dei.,* xviii, 54. Bishop Bossuet protested *against the false claims of the popes,* saying, "*That very late invention,* that bishops receive their jurisdiction *from the pope,* and are as it were, *his Vicars,* ought to be banished from Christian schools *as unheard of for twelve centuries!*" Bossuet, *Defens, Declar, Clari Galli,* viii, 14.

Church history thus plainly shows that the belief of the early Christian church concerning its Head and Foundation were *essentially those held by the Protestant Church of the Reformation;* that the papacy was an *invention of later centuries* which was gradually built up by a series of *encroachments on the rights and liberties of the clergy and laymen,* and by means of *documents* which *were acknowledged by Roman Church leaders to be fraudulent.* St. Peter *never claimed to be a pope,* or *the Head of the Church;* he was *not* "the rock" on which Christ built the Church. The Lord Jesus Christ is the *only Head of the Church,* and *He alone,* is its *everlasting Foundation.* It was centuries later, when the Church had *forgotten the Scriptures,* had lost its *original simplicity and spiritual power,* and had been *submerged by a flood of worldliness* and unholy ambition, that *popes began to appear.*

"According to the Sacred Record, *Peter never celebrated 'Mass,'* nor did he *hear Confessions.* He *never directed a soul to pray to Mary or to the Saints,* nor to *use beads.* He never *advocated the use of 'holy water,' scapulars,* and *relics.* He never ordered the people to *abstain from meat on Fridays,* and *during Lent.* He *never* declared that *priests and nuns should not marry.* He *never presented his foot to be kissed.* He *never lived in a palace,* with soldiers to guard him, and multitudes of servants to wait on him. *Why* did Peter *not do these things?* Because he *never was pope.*" MacFaul's, "*Is there salvation within the Roman Catholic Church?*"

Chapter IV

THE CHURCH'S OBJECT OF WORSHIP

Who is the Object of Worship in the true Church of God?

Holy Scripture teaches that the sole Object of Worship is the one true and living God, Father, Son and Holy Spirit. He alone, as our Creator, our Providential Ruler, our Lord and Saviour, our Divine Guide, Sanctifier, and Comforter, the glorious Trinity, is worthy of all adoration and praise; being infinite, eternal, unchangeable, perfect in wisdom, power, holiness, justice, truth and love; and He alone as the Hearer of prayer and Giver of all good, is to be invoked and supplicated. "For of Him, and through Him, and to Him are all things; to whom be glory forever. Amen." Rom. 11:36, Psalm 65:2, Ex. 15:11, Ps. 90:2, Ex. 34:6, 7, Is. 49:26, John 15:26, 16:13, II Thess. 2:13, Rev. 4:8.

God the Holy Trinity Alone to be Worshipped

May saints, angels, and Mary, the mother of our Lord, be invoked, prayed to, or receive any form of religious worship?

They may *not*. Though we may greatly respect and love them, The Word of God clearly teaches that *no religious worship* of *any kind* or *degree* may be paid to any person *except the Holy Trinity*. To bow down to, invoke, pray to, or worship anything else than the *one true God* is *the great sin expressly forbidden by the First* and *Second Commandments*. This is not only the teaching of Holy Scripture, but also was the practice of the apostolic and early Christian Church.

St. Clement of Alexandria, A.D. 200, wrote: "Since there is only one good God, both we ourselves and the angels supplicate *from Him alone*." St. Athanasius, A.D. 370, wrote concerning the Arians who denied Christ's deity: "But if they say these things are spoken of the Son, let them confess that the saints did *not think of calling on a created being* to be their helper and their refuge." Ironside's *Letters*, page 29.

(34)

Whom did our Lord Jesus Christ teach all men to worship?

Christ clearly taught that *God alone should be worshipped.* "Thou shalt worship the Lord thy God and *Him only* shalt thou serve." Matt. 4:10, 19:17.

What did the Apostles teach concerning the Object of Worship?

The Apostles taught that *all forms of religious worship* should be rendered to *God alone.* When the Roman centurion prostrated himself before Peter, Peter *forbade him* saying: "Stand up, I myself also am a man." That is, "Do not bow down to me; I am a *sinful man like yourself.*" Acts 10:26.

How different was the apostle Peter from the popes, who expect visitors to kneel down before them, and kiss their hand, foot, or ring! The apostle John wrote that when he fell down to worship the angel who showed him wonderful things to come, *the angel reproved him,* saying: "See thou do it *not,* for I am thy fellow servant; *worship God!*" This solemn admonition to worship *God alone* was given on two other occasions. Rev. 19:10, 22:9.

THE CHURCH OF ROME'S GREAT TRANSGRESSION

Has not the Church of Rome departed far from the true faith in worshipping, and praying to, human beings?

The papal Church has *departed far from the true faith* in committing the great sin which God calls *"rebellion" against Him.* To take the worship, reverence or appellation of the Almighty Lord of heaven and earth, and give any part of them to sinful human beings is *a fearful impiety,* which will *surely bring condemnation* at the Judgment Day. Jer. 28:16, Num. 14:9.

Has not the Church of Rome been guilty of this great sin in paying to the pope the reverence or worship due to God alone?

It *has been guilty of this great sin.* In a gloss of the Roman Canon Law the words "our Lord God the pope" appear. It declares that "to believe that our Lord God the pope has not power to decree as he has decreed, is heretical." *Extravagantes of pope John XXII, Cum Inter, Tit.* XIV, *cap.* IV, *Ad Callem Sexti Decretalium,* Paris, 1685.

4

Writers on the Canon Law have said: "The pope and God are *the same;* so he has all power in heaven and on earth." Barclay, *Cap.* XXVII, page 218.

Pope Nicholas I (died 867) declared, "the appellation of God was *confirmed by Constantine on the pope,* who, being God, *cannot be judged by man." Labb. Dist.* 96, *Can.* 7.

The Doge of Venice asserted that he would honor Clement VII *"as a deity on earth."* Pastor, *History of the Popes, vol.* IX, *page* 246.

The Pope on August 22, 1929, referring to the political troubles in Malta, which had been caused by *the unjustifiable demands of the Roman Church authorities* there, declared to Maltese citizens, that "to be *with the Bishops and the Pope* meant to be *with Jesus Christ,* of whom they must think when they *looked at a Bishop,* and that *whoever is not under the protection of the Pope* shall be *overcome!"*

Pope Leo XIII blasphemously said: "I occupy the place *of Almighty God on earth!"*

The statement of Dr. Timothy Dwight, former President of Yale University, died 1817, is absolutely accurate. He wrote, "The bishops of Rome have arrogated to themselves the peculiar titles of Jehovah, *Dominus, Deus noster, Papa,* and have accordingly granted absolution from sin and passports to heaven. They have *abrogated the commands of God; substituted for them contrary precepts; ascended the throne of the Redeemer; assumed the absolute government of His Church; claimed the world as their property; and declared all mankind to be their vassals. Beyond all this* they have *given openly and publicly indulgences,* or *permissions to sin. Thus has 'this Man of sin, this Son of perdition, exalted himself above all that is called God, or that is worshipped.' Thus has he, as God, sat in the temple of God, showing himself to be God."* II Thess. 2:3, 4, *Theology Explained and Defended, vol.* 4, *page* 10.

This blasphemy is repeated when Romanists *call a parish priest God!* Archbishop F. V. Kendrick, quoting Alphonso Liguori concerning the seal of the Confessional, says: "A priest is brought as a witness (in Court) only as a man; and therefore without injury to conscience he can swear that he does *not know things which he knows only as God."* Here is not only blasphemy against the Holy Trinity in *calling*

Has not the Church of Rome also departed far from the true faith in worshipping or praying to saints and angels?

It has. It *commits grievous sin* by worshipping, or praying to saints, angels, etc. Rome teaches, "That we ought to worship angels, and give religious service to saints." And, "that we ought to pray to saints." Bellarmine, *De Cult. Sanct.* 1:11-14, *De Sanct. beat* 1:19. Council of Trent, *Sess.* 25.

The Bible teaches that it is a grave sin to worship, or pray to saints and angels for they are *not God-appointed mediators* or *intercessors.* The Lord Jesus Christ is the *only God-appointed Mediator.* All worship and prayer are to be offered in *His name alone.* To pray to, and seek help from saints and angels, is not only *useless,* but it *dishonors Christ, to whom all praise and honor belong.* I Tim. 2:5, I John 2:1, Heb. 12:24, Col. 2:18, Judges 13:16, Rom. 11:36, Rev. 1:5, 6.

EARLY CHURCH FATHERS OPPOSED THE WORSHIP AND INVOCATION OF SAINTS AND ANGELS

Note that there are *only 4 examples* in the New Testament of acts of reverence offered *to saints and angels* and *in all these cases* they were *promptly rejected and forbidden,* as showing disloyalty to the true and living God. Acts 10:25, 26, Acts 14:13-15, Rev. 19:10, Rev. 22:8, 9.

The early Fathers of the Church rightly opposed such worship and invocation. Irenaeus, A.D. 180 said: "The Church *does nothing*

---

a man God, but it also *justifies lying and perjury;* it teaches that a priest *can break his solemn oath to God* with *a clear conscience, swearing* that he *does not know* facts which *he knows perfectly well!* Jesuit theology in other places teaches the same thing. Peter Dens asks the question, "What answer ought a Confessor to give, when questioned about a truth which he *knows from sacramental confession only?"* He replies: "He ought to answer that he *does not know,* and if necessary, *confirm it by an oath!"* This shameful violation of God's moral law, *justifying falsehood and perjury even in the professed service of the God of truth,* explains the severe condemnation of papal teachings by Lord Acton, a Roman Catholic, who said: *"I do not know of a religious and educated Catholic who really believes* that *the See of Rome is a safe guide to salvation.* It (Ultramontanism) not only promotes, it *inculcates, distinct mendacity and deceitfulness.* In certain cases it is made *a duty to lie."* *Introductory Memoir to Lord Acton's Letters,* by Herbert Paul, *page* IV. *(Italics are by the author of "Our Priceless Heritage.")*

by invocation of angels, but by directing her prayers *to God in the name of the Lord Jesus Christ.*" So also St. Clement.

Origen, A.D. 230. "Every prayer and supplication, intercession and thanksgiving is to be *sent up to God.* It is *not right to invoke angels.* If they knew, they would not suffer us to *pray to any other but God.*"

Athanasius, A.D. 370. "Let the followers of Arius confess that the saints did not think of calling on *a created being* to be their *helper and refuge.*" *Orat. cont. Arianos,* i: 62.

St. Augustine said: "Let not our religion be a *cultus of dead men.* They (the saints) are to be honored by way of imitation, *not worshipped by way of religion.*"

Council of Laodicea, A.D. 360. "Christians *ought not to invoke angels.* To do so is to *forsake Christ and be guilty of idolatry.* Let such a one be *anathema.*"

DOES NOT THE CHURCH OF ROME COMMIT GREAT SIN IN THE WORSHIP AND INVOCATION OF THE VIRGIN MARY?

The Church of Rome *commits grievous sin against God* in the worship and invocation of the Virgin Mary. Such worship *directly disobeys God's commandment,* that *He alone* is to be worshipped and invoked, and gives to the creature the worship and reverence which *belong only to the Creator.* Rom. 1:25. The Church of Rome makes Mary usurp the place of her Lord and Redeemer. It calls Mary the "Queen of heaven," the "Door of Paradise," the "Salvation of the Living and the Dead," the "Mother of God,"[1] and other idolatrous titles. These titles are *false* and are *directly contrary to the Word of God.* Heaven has no "Queen." This highly improper title is borrowed from *heathenism.* Jer. 7:18, 44:17-25. Chinese sailors worship an idol they call the Queen of heaven. The titles "Door of Paradise," "Salvation of the Living and the Dead," *usurp the place of Christ and rob Him of His glory.* Our Lord declared plainly, *"I am the Door; by Me if any man enter in, he shall be saved."* John 10:9. *"I am the Way, the Truth and the Life: no man*

---

[1] Church history shows that the Nestorians were bitterly persecuted because they protested against this *false and unscriptural title.*

cometh unto the Father, *but by Me.*" John 14:6. If these words of
Christ are true,—and they *certainly are*—then the worship of Mary,
saints, etc., is *a gross sin.* In asserting that Mary is "the Salvation
of the living and dead," the Church of Rome *directly contradicts
St. Peter,* who said of Christ alone, "Neither is there salvation *in
any other;* for there is *none other name under heaven given among
men whereby we must be saved!*" Acts 4:12. The title "Mother of
God" is *blasphemous! God has no Mother.* He is "the King, eternal,
immortal, invisible." Mary was the *mother of Christ's human body
only;* Christ was *Mary's Creator, existing from all eternity.* John
1:1, 3, Heb. 1:2. Christians should never forget that Christ's human
relationships were *not those of ordinary human beings.* He was
Almighty God. While he lovingly performed the duty of a filial son
when on earth, even in His agony on the cross providing for His
mother in the flesh (Luke 2:51, John 19:26, 27), yet more than
once He *reproved the mistaken tendency to exalt the earthly relationship* at the *expense of the divine,* the physical bond at the expense
of the *spiritual,*[1] which is the *very mistake that the Church of Rome*
makes. Luke 2:48, 49, John 2:4, Matt. 12:48-50, Luke 11:27, 28.

THE CHURCH OF ROME EXALTING MARY, DISPARAGES CHRIST THE LORD

Have not prominent Roman leaders disparaged Christ *while exalting Mary, imputing to her a loving sympathy and patience greater
than that of our blessed Lord?*

Prominent leaders like Alphonso Liguori (died 1787), in their
desire to exalt Mary, have made assertions which *disparage our
blessed Saviour and detract from His perfectly holy character.* In
his "Glories of Mary," Liguori declares, "Mary is our *only refuge and
help.*" "Often our prayers shall be heard *more quickly* by applying
to Mary *than to the Saviour.*" "At the command of the Virgin, *all
things obey,* EVEN GOD!" Liguori quotes Anselm as saying, "*It is*

[1] That the spiritual bond which makes believers in Christ members of God's family
is *more important than the physical bond of flesh and blood,* is clearly taught by an
incident recorded in three of the Gospels. Dear and tender as were the ties which bind
us to parents and brethren, yet those which *bound Him to true believers were more
tender and sacred.* Earthly ties are *transient,* but the tie which bind believers to
their Lord are *eternal* and *make them truly members of God's family.* Rom. 8:14,
16, 17, Matt. 12:46-50, Mark 3:31-35, Luke 8:19-21.

safer and better to call on the blessed Virgin than on Christ." Liguori also speaks of Christ as *"irritated by our sins,"* and that when this is so, Mary intercedes and secures for the suppliant *blessings which otherwise might not be obtained.* What *awful blasphemy* and *gross dishonor to our Lord and Saviour* such statements are! Could anything be farther from the truth! Our blessed Saviour has *infinitely greater love and mercy than all human beings combined!* He assures us, "I have *loved thee with an everlasting love!"* Jer. 31:3. He is not only able, but willing, "to *do exceeding abundantly above all that we ask or think,"* for His is *"the love that passeth knowledge."* Heb. 2:17, 18, 4:14-16, Eph. 3:19-21.

Was not the worship of and prayer to Mary a corruption and perversion of later times which the Fathers of the early Church strongly opposed?

This worship of and prayer to Mary was a *false worship,* which the early Church leaders *strongly opposed.* They worshipped, and prayed to God the Holy Trinity, *alone. They declared that Mary sinned in wavering faith,* and at the Judgment Day will be judged *like other Christians.*

St. Hilary of Poictiers, A.D. 350, said: "If the Virgin, who conceived God, is *to come into the severity of Judgment,* who will dare to be judged by God?" Comment on Psalm 118.

St. Basil the Great, Ambrose, Chrysostom, and Gregory of Nyssa, A.D. 390, *all explain the sword of Simeon's prophecy* as *Mary's wavering faith* at the time of Christ's Passion. Luke 2:34.

St. Epiphanius, died 403, declared, Mary's body was holy indeed, but she was *not deity.* She was honored, but was *not given to us to worship.* Wherefore the Gospel warns us, *"Woman, what have I to do to thee? Mine hour is not yet come."* John 2:4. He (Christ) says this that people may understand that the holy Virgin *was not more than human.* Let Mary be honored, but let Father, Son and Holy Ghost be *worshipped. Let no one worship Mary."* Adv. *Haer* lxxix.

St. Jerome, A.D. 418, agrees with Origen, and those above, in charging Mary with *temporary unbelief* which pierced her as a sword. *Comment in Lucan,* Luke 2:35.

St. Cyril of Alexandria, A.D. 440, declares Mary *not only failed at the Cross from grief and feminine weakness*, but was committed to St. John's care that he, as a theologian, *might teach her truths which she did not know."*

From these quotations it is clear that the worship and invocation of Mary was condemned and rejected by the early Church. Mariolatry grew and became common, only as the *Word of God was neglected*, and *apostasy spread through the Church.*

From the number of Churches dedicated to the Virgin Mary in Rome, she would seem to be *honored more than God or the Saviour.* Out of more than 400 churches, and chapels in the city, *only 5 are* dedicated to the *Holy Trinity, 15 to Christ, 2 to the Holy Spirit* and *121 to the Virgin Mary!* Moreover the *Raccolta* shows that language used in prayer to Mary is *identical with that used to God;* so that the assertion of apologists that she is *merely asked to pray for us*, is clearly *contrary to fact.* Littledale's *Plain Reasons*, page 55.

What should be the attitude of true believers regarding Mary?

All Christians should hold the mother of our Lord *in high respect and affection*, as a noble woman, rich in faith and Christian character, who was greatly blessed of God. But like all other human beings, *she was a sinner,* and *needed salvation. She herself felt this*, for in her song of praise she said, "My Spirit hath rejoiced *in God my Saviour."* Luke 1:47. Christians should *never worship her, nor pray to her, nor bow to her image or picture;* for to do this is the *great sin of idolatry. Only God the Holy Trinity is to be worshipped and invoked:* "for of Him, and through Him and to Him are all things, to whom be glory forever, Amen." Rom. 11:33-36, Rev. 1:5, 6, 5:12, 13, 7:12, 19:1, 6.

The worship of angels is also clearly forbidden in Holy Scripture not only in the *Ten Commandments*, and because they are *created beings*, but also in Col. 2:18 and Judges 13:16.

ALL IMAGES AND REPRESENTATIONS OF ANY SORT ARE FORBIDDEN IN WORSHIP

In worshipping the Holy Trinity is it proper to use images, symbols, or pictures of any kind?

No. The Word of God *strictly forbids the use of any likeness or representation whatever in religious worship.* Not only images and pictures, *but any symbol or representation of God or of man are excluded.* The use of such things is a *very heinous sin, a flagrant violation of God's Commandment.* Note the Second Commandment of the Decalogue (Ex. 20:4) where the prohibition is explicit *and repeated*—"*any image* or *any likeness of anything* that is in heaven above or in the earth beneath or that is in the water under the earth: thou shalt not bow down to them nor serve them." "Take ye good heed to yourselves lest ye corrupt yourselves, and make you a graven image, the *similitude of any figure,* the likeness of male or female." *God thus forbids the use of all shapes, resemblances, and symbols whatever.* Deut. 4:15, 16, 5:8, 12:30-32; Acts 17:29, 30.

Note that the Church of Rome in attempting to evade the guilt of gross disobedience to God in using images, *often prints the Second Commandment in small type and appends it to the first Commandment;* then to retain the proper number of the Commandments she divides the Tenth Commandment into two parts, thus making *two commandments treat of the same subject, covetousness!* But that the II Commandment as found in the Protestant Bible, forbidding images, was the *original form as given by God to Moses,* is proved by the *Jewish Scriptures,* which *held the same form as the Protestant Bible,* long before the Christian Church was established. It was also *so held by the Eastern Church,* and by *Origen and St. Jerome.*

The Lord also *denounced an awful curse on anyone who should break the Second Commandment.* Deut. 27:15. After commanding that the images of the heathen whom Israel conquered should be *destroyed by fire,* God commanded that *even the silver and gold of them should not be kept,* for "it is an *abomination to the Lord thy God.*" They should *not allow anything associated with an image or idolatry* to come into their homes; "*neither* shalt thou *bring an abomination into thy house,* lest *thou be a cursed thing like it;* but thou shalt *utterly detest it,* and thou shalt *utterly abhor it,* for it is *a cursed thing.*" Deut. 7:25, 26. Our Saviour also clearly forbade the use of any visible object or symbol when He stressed *the spirituality of true worship;* "God is a spirit and they who worship Him must worship him *in Spirit and in truth.*" John 4:23, 24.

THE CHURCH OF ROME DELIBERATELY BREAKS
THE SECOND COMMANDMENT

What does the Papal Church teach regarding the use of images, pictures, etc., in religious worship?

The Papal Church teaches that it is right to use images, pictures, etc., in religious worship. Directly contrary to God's command, the Church of Rome declares that *"we ought to worship images,"* and that *"God may be represented in an embossed, graven or flat picture."* Bellarmine *De imag. Sanct.* 2:7-10, 12. The 25th session of the Council of Trent decreed that the images of Christ, the Virgin Mary and of other saints are *specially to be had and retained* in the Churches, and *that honor and veneration are to be paid to them.* The creed of Pope Pius IV declares: "I most firmly assert that the *image of Christ,* of the *Mother of God, ever Virgin,* and also of the *other saints* ought to be had and retained and that *due honor and veneration are to be given to them."* The catechism of the Council of Trent asserts: "It is lawful to have images in the Church, and to give honor and worship unto them." Note that the second Council of Nice, A.D. 787, which the Church of Rome *acknowledges to be orthodox,* declared "that Christians should not only serve and honor images, but *adore and worship them";* that is, *honor them as if they were God Himself!* The Church of Rome has been guilty of gross profanation in *dressing up an image of God as a pope, with papal robes, mitre and triple crown!*

Is not the Papal Church guilty of idolatry in having an image of St. Peter in the Vatican, where thousands of Romanist Pilgrims bow down to it and kiss its foot?

The Papal Church is thus *guilty of a great sin against God,* and must be considered *apostate.* Millions of deceived worshippers have *literally worn away the metal foot by their kisses, imagining* that they *were performing a pious act,* when *really they were breaking God's holy commandment,* and *heaping up condemnation* to themselves, against the awful day of Judgment.

How do Romanists try to evade guilt for their great sin?

The Papal Church has *invented several terms* to express, as it supposes, various degrees of worship, as *latreia, douleia, hyperdouleia,* etc. But this is mere self-deception and *juggling with words*, because God's command is *clear and absolute*, and *prohibits every form and degree of religious worship. God has made no exception to His law* and *no man may dare to make one*, without being guilty of *great impiety.* Note that the excuses which the Church of Rome makes to evade her guilt of the sin of idolatry are *the very same that the heathen offer for their worship of idols.* God's prohibition applies *to every form of idolatry*, whether to the idol worship of Hinduism *or that of Rome:* the images of *St. Peter or of Mary is just as truly an idol as any idol of Buddhism*, and at the Judgment Day God will *hold the leaders of the Roman Church responsible for deceiving the people* and *leading them into apostasy.*

Do not the Holy Scriptures repeatedly use the strongest language to warn against the great sin of image worship, and the worship of any other being than the Holy Trinity?

The Scriptures do often *use the strongest language to warn against these grave sins.* All such worship is called an *"abomination,"* a *"detestable thing."* The word "abomination" occurs over 50 times in the Bible, generally referring to *images and false worship.* I Kings 11:5, 7, Matt. 24:15, Mark 13:4.

All representations used in religious worship are included in what *St. Peter calls "abominable idolatries."* I Peter 4:3. Whoever uses or tolerates them is a *"teacher of lies."* Hab. 2:18.

The worship of anyone or anything beside the one true God is called *"fornication," "Adultery,"* as being among *the most loathsome of sins.* To worship images or human beings is to *forsake our Creator,* just as *an unfaithful wife,* following a stranger, *forsakes her husband.* The whole of the prophecy of Hosea is pervaded by the thought of *this dreadful sin.* Hosea 2:2, 7, 8, 13; Ezek. 16:15-32; Eph. 5:23-31.

DID NOT THE EARLY CHURCH STRONGLY OPPOSE THE WORSHIP OF IMAGES?

Yes. As long as the Church *remained true to the Bible,* it *strongly opposed the worship of images,* and *the use of representations of every kind.* Lactantius, A.D. 300, said: "It is indisputable that *wherever there is an image, there is no religion." Div. Inst.,* 11, 19.

St. Irenaeus (120-190) mentions the use of images of Christ and the honor done them as a *peculiarity of the Carpocratian heretics,* distinguishing them from orthodox Christians. *Adv. Haer.* i, 25.

Origen, 230, said, "Those are the *most untaught, who address lifeless objects* and imagine that the hands of mechanics can fashion *likenesses of Divinity.* What sensible man can help smiling when he sees a learned man *turning to images and offering his prayers to them?* Origen, *Cont. Cels.,* vii, 44; viii, 17.

St. Augustine quotes the Word of God—"Confounded be all they that serve graven images, that boast themselves of idols." "Thus it is plain," Littledale affirms, "that *down to St. Augustine's death, A.D. 430,* there *was no devotional use of pictures and images among Christians, and even very little merely for decorative use.*" Gregory, called "Great," died 604, wrote: *"In every possible way avoid worshipping images,* and let the people humbly prostrate themselves *in honor of the Almighty and Holy Trinity alone."*

But the Church gradually became corrupted, and departed from the doctrines of God's Word. Thomas Aquinas, died 1274, taught that "the *same reverence should be shown toward the image of Christ as toward Christ Himself! and seeing that Christ is adored with the adoration of latreia (supreme worship) so His image should be adored with adoration of latreia."* *Sum. Theol.,* xxv, 3. Thomas thus incurs the condemnation of the spiritual blind mentioned by the Psalmist in Ps. 115:8.

The plain teaching of Scriptures is, *God alone is entitled to the worship and adoration of our hearts:* He must *have our whole worship,* or *none at all, for* the worship of a "divided heart" is hypocrisy. "I am Jehovah; that is My name, and my glory will I not give to another, neither My *praise to graven images."* Isa. 42:8. God's Word clearly shows that the Latin Church in giving *part of its worship to Mary, saints and angels, breaks God's First Commandment;* in *using images, the crucifix, etc., in worship, it breaks His Second Commandment.*

In worshipping God, what does Scripture teach regarding multiplicity of ceremonies, ritual, vestments, genuflections, sign of the cross, turning toward the East, etc.?

All of these things, *having no warrant whatever in Scripture,* are *wrong;* for *no* ceremony or religious rite may be *added to what God has commanded in His Word.* They were *entirely absent from the Apostolic Church;* there is no hint of them in the Book of Acts, or the Epistles. They are *all contrary to the "simplicity and sincerity" which the Gospel enjoins.* II Cor. 1:12, 11:3; and are *a part of that formalism and will-worship against which the inspired Word warns all Christians.* Col. 2:18-23. For as genuine devotion of the heart declines, men strive to make up for its loss by multiplying external rites, which in the sight of God are *not only of no value,* but *are a mockery.* Isa. 1:11-14, Matt. 23:5, 23.

Cardinal Newman acknowledged that the paraphernalia of the papal Church, as incense, candles, holy water, processions, tonsure, vestments, images, etc., are all of pagan origin. *Essay on Development of Christian Doctrine,* 1846, page 359.

He might have added that the *office and name of the pope* were suggested by that of the *Pontifex Maximus, the head of heathen religion in Rome.* The alb, cope and maniple were copied from the vestments of pagan priests: so also the practice of facing eastward in services. The perpetual burning of lamps in churches was borrowed from the Vestal Virgins, who day and night kept burning lamps before the shrines of ancient idols. Gregory I, as bishop of Rome, *had advised the use of heathen rites* in *order to attract them to the Church!*

Both Gregory and Newman thus showed *how little they knew of the holiness of God, and of the true spirit of the Gospel.* Their method was *compromise with evil, to win popularity; letting down the Gospel standard to the level of the heathen, instead of raising up the heathen to the Christian standard, as St. Paul did.* How *different* was the *apostolic way! "In simplicity and godly sincerity," not* as *pleasing men, but God, who trieth our hearts." "Be ye separate,* and touch not the unclean thing!" *Anything connected with false gods, or with pagan worship, was to be abhorred as "fellowship with devils," or as a foul garment infected with leprosy or pestilence.* "Hating even the garment spotted by the flesh." I Cor. 10:20, 21, II Cor. 6:14-17, Jude 23.

CHAPTER V

APOSTOLIC SUCCESSION

What is the meaning of apostle in Scripture?

The Greek word ἀπόστολος, *apóstolos*, means "one sent forth," that is, one sent forth by Christ to preach the everlasting Gospel of the grace of God. The apostles were special ministers ordained by Christ to proclaim the Gospel and to plant the Christian Church. They had special qualifications to do this. They had seen the Lord, and been able from personal knowledge to bear witness to His death and resurrection. They had the gift of inspiration of the Holy Spirit; and were endued with special power to work miracles.

What Scriptures prove these statements?

Those which record Christ's Great Commission. Matt. 28:18-20, Luke 24:48, John 20:22, 23, Mark 16:15. His command to preach the Gospel. "Preach the Word." Matt. 10:7, II Tim. 4:2. "Preach the Gospel to every creature." Mark 16:15. "Ordain presbyters in every city." Titus 1:5. "They ordained presbyters in every city." Acts 14:23. St. Paul's words: "Am I not an apostle? Have I not seen the Lord?" I Cor. 9:1. St. Peter's words, when Matthias was chosen to take the place of Judas, "Wherefore of these men that have companied with us all the time that the Lord Jesus went in and out among us, must one be ordained to be a *witness with us of His resurrection.*" Acts 1:21, 22. "And with great power gave the apostles *witness of the resurrection* of the Lord Jesus." Acts 4:31, 33.

What Scriptures show that the apostles were specially inspired by God the Holy Spirit to write the Epistles?

"For this cause also thank we God without ceasing because when ye received the Word of God which ye heard of us, ye received it not as the word of men, but as it is in truth the Word of God, which effectually worketh also in you that believe." I Thess. 2:13. "All Scripture is given by inspiration of God, and is profitable for doctrine

(47)

for reproof, for correction, for instruction in righteousness, that the man of God may be perfect, thoroughly furnished unto all good works." II Tim. 3:16, 17. "We have also a more sure word of prophecy,—for the prophecy came not in old time by the will of man; but holy men of God spake as they were moved by the Holy Ghost." I Peter 1:19, 21.

Many Scriptures also show that the apostles had special power to work miracles; as, Matt. 10:18, Luke 10:17-19, Acts 3:6, 9:40, 41, 20:9, 10, etc.

Did St. Paul know Christ personally when He was on earth?

No. He was qualified to be an apostle by a special revelation of the Lord. He did *not* derive his authority from the other apostles. Gal. 1:1, 16, 2:6.

Does not the Church of Rome now claim that its ministers; pope, bishops and priests—are essentially the same as the apostles, and have the same power and authority?

This claim is made, but it entirely lacks the support of Holy Scripture.

Has any Church leader since the days of the apostles had power to work miracles, as raising the dead to life?

While God has been graciously pleased to give His people many wonderful answers to prayer, yet there is no trustworthy evidence that anyone in the Christian Church since the days of the apostles has had the power of working miracles! Some in the Papal Church have claimed to possess this power, but their claims are not supported by adequate evidence.

It is reported that on one occasion as the pope was showing visitors the treasures of the Vatican, he remarked, "Certainly St. Peter's successors cannot now say as he once said, 'Silver and gold have I none.'" Acts 3:6. *"No,"* was the ready response, *"nor* can they now *say as he said, 'Rise up and walk!'* "

What are some of the miracles the Church of Rome claims to have wrought?

Madonnas winking their eyes; images moving without human aid. The Virgin Mary's cottage in Nazareth flying (or carried by angels) from Palestine to Loretto, Italy, on December 10, 1294. Fire brought down from heaven in Jerusalem at Easter, visible to bystanders, etc., etc.

Do not Romanists also claim that miraculous cures are wrought at certain shrines, as Loretto, Lourdes, and at Malden, Mass.?

Yes, but those who report these cures were mostly ignorant people who labored under great excitement; and their claims are similar to those of hypnotists, of psychiatrists, of Christian Scientists so-called, and of devotees of idolatrous cults in the Orient.

What proof is there from Romanist sources that most of what are claimed to be miracles, never took place?

The testimony of many intelligent members of the Church of Rome who declare that the reputed miracles were *never wrought,* but were 'pious frauds'; also the bitter protests of Romanists in Palestine, who insist that Mary's cottage has *never been moved,* but is *still in Nazareth!*

About the year 1932 newspapers reported wild excitement at Malden, Mass., where marvelous miracles of healing were alleged to have taken place at the grave of a priest. Vast crowds gathered at the cemetery; large gifts of money were made by those who sought healing; and a shocking lack of reverence and decorum were manifested, so that Church authorities deemed an investigation necessary. An official report was later published under the authority of Cardinal O'Connell, that there was *no evidence of any miracle,* but that what was considered miraculous could all be *explained on natural grounds.*

A dispatch in the public press of September 30, 1939 reported in substance that pope Pius XII regretted the destruction of images in Poland, by which, he alleged, "many miracles had been performed." It is sad to see a religious leader allowing himself thus to be misled by vague rumors of miracles, as if there were no commandment in the Decalogue *strictly forbidding the use of images* by believers. The pope evidently differs from St. Paul who warned against "dumb idols," saying, "we know that an idol is nothing in the world." I Cor. 8:4. He also differs from the Psalmist, who spoke of images as blocks of wood or metal, that "neither see nor hear nor speak nor move." "They that make them *are like unto them:* so is *everyone that trusteth in them."* Psalm 115:5-8.

Have not such alleged miracles done great harm to Christianity?

They have done immense harm, by leading intelligent people, who perceived the imposture, to mock at religion, and to reject the genuine miracles of our Lord and His Apostles.

THE APOSTLES HAD NO REAL SUCCESSORS

Did Christ's apostles have any real successors? That is, did Christ's ministers who succeeded the apostles and carried on the work of the Christian Church, have the gifts and power that the apostles had, viz.: the gifts of inspiration and of working miracles?

No. After the death of the apostles, the apostolic office ceased. The special gifts of the apostles were bestowed to do a special work. When that work had been accomplished, the Church well established, and the Holy Scriptures of the New Testament completed, the *special gifts ceased.* Inasmuch as one of the great functions of the apostolic office was to bear personal witness to our Lord's death and resurrection, it was impossible for those who succeeded the apostles to bear such witness, having never personally known our Lord. And after St. John completed the Book of Revelation, the Canon of Scripture was *closed,* and the special *gift of Inspiration ceased.* But though the special gifts of the apostleship ceased, the greatest gift of all, still remained in the Church, viz.: *the Holy Spirit, with His life-giving power.* John 14:16, 15:26, 16:7-13.

After the Apostleship ceased, what permanent offices still remained in the Church?

After the Apostleship ceased, the permanent offices of presbyter, viz.: the minister of the Word; the ruling elder, and the deacon, remained. The minister, who was both teaching and ruling presbyter, served as pastor, evangelist and teacher; proclaimed the Gospel, established congregations, and administered the sacraments. I Cor. 12:28, Eph. 4:11, 12.

Beside the pastor or minister, there was in each congregation a bench of ruling presbyters. Titus 1:5, I Tim. 5:17. These were spiritual officers. In addition, there were deacons, whose business it was to administer the charitable and business affairs of the Church; though they also took part in spiritual duties, as preaching the Word, etc. Acts 6:1-4, 8:5, 12.

No Priest but Christ in the True Church of God

Does the Word of God anywhere teach that the Christian minister is a priest?

The New Testament *nowhere teaches* that *the Christian minister is a priest*. In the Old Testament dispensation under Moses there were priests, who offered animal sacrifices in the Tabernacle and in the Temple; but Scripture teaches that they were only temporary and symbolic: "for it is not possible that the blood of bulls and of goats should take away sins." Heb. 10:4. The ancient sacrifices *pointed to Christ,* the *one great Divine Priest to come,* who on Calvary should offer the *one atoning Sacrifice* for sin, viz.: *Himself.* After Christ had come, the priesthood and sacrifices of the Old Dispensation, being but types and shadows which were fulfilled in Him, *forever passed away.* Search the New Testament from beginning to end, and we find but *one Priest, the Son of God,* and but *one Sacrifice,* Christ's precious body, which He offered for the sins of the world *"once for all."*

Is there clear proof of this in Holy Scripture?

There is abundant proof; for nearly the whole Epistle to the Hebrews was written to make this plain. It is stated beyond the shadow of a doubt, that all human priests and all animal sacrifices have passed away; that Christ the one Divine priest alone remains, and His one atoning sacrifice of Himself on Calvary, offered once for all. Heb. 7:11, 12, 18-24, 8:5-8, 13, 9:8, 9, 11-28, Col. 2:17-23.

A careful examination of these and other passages in the Epistle to the Hebrews indicate a contrast between the many priests of the Old Dispensation and the *one great Divine priest* of the New Dispensation. The former are spoken of in the plural, the latter *always in the singular.* The Levitical priests had sin, and must offer sacrifice

5

for their own sins; but the one Divine priest of the New Dispensation
had no sin, and therefore offered no sacrifice for Himself. The
Levitical priests were temporary, and soon passed away, but the
one Divine priest was eternal: "Thou (Christ) art a priest *forever*";
"Made after the power of *an endless life*." So also of the sacrifices.
Those offered by the Levitical priests were imperfect, and must be
repeated; they were animals, "the blood of goats and of calves";
were *symbolical* and must *soon pass away;* "they could not take away
sins" (Heb. 10:4). But the sacrifice of the one Divine priest of the
New Dispensation was His own precious body and blood, a perfect
and eternal sacrifice made on Calvary once for all, and *atones for
the sins of the whole world*.

THE CHURCH OF ROME'S DEADLY ERROR

*Does the Church of Rome teach that its ministers are priests, and
that they offer a real atoning sacrifice for sins?*

Yes, sad to say, the Church of Rome teaches this *deadly error,*
which *strikes at the very heart of the Gospel*. For if the Roman
clergy are real priests, and offer a genuine atoning sacrifice for sin,
then the Word of God is not true, and Christ's atoning death is *not
the only way of salvation*, as the Bible says it is. Acts 4:12, John 14:6.

Liguori, in his book entitled, "The Dignity and Duty of a Priest,"
declares that in giving or refusing absolution, *God Himself is obliged
to abide by the judgment of His priests!* In other words, the
sovereign, holy Lord of heaven and earth must *bow to the decisions
of a weak, sinful human being!* Is not this *horrible blesphemy?*

An authorized Roman Catholic booklet, "The Priest," by Curé d'Ars, pages 22,
23, asks, "What is a Priest?" Answer. "A man who *holds the place of God,* a man
clothed with *all the power of God*. When the priest forgives our sins, he does not
say, *"God* forgives you," he says *"I absolve thee."* Again it says, "Without the priest,
the death of our Lord would be *of no avail*." "If you had no priest here, you would
say, "What is the use of coming to the Church? Our Lord is no longer here. Where
there is no priest, there is no sacrifice, and where there is no sacrifice, *there is no
religion*." How foolish and false this is! and *how blasphemous the boast* made on
page 26; "See the power of the priest! *By one word he changes a piece of bread into
a God!"* How different is the statement of Holy Scripture! "For by one offering He
(the Son of God) hath *perfected forever them* that are sanctified." Heb. 10:14. No
less than 10 times in Hebrews does the apostle emphasize the one perfect atoning
sacrifice which Christ offered for us on Calvary, a Divine sacrifice which is *eternally
efficacious*, and can *never be repeated*.

The Pope Is Blasphemously Called Christ

The plain statement is made by L. Lucantonio in his book *La Supernazionalità del Papato* that *"the Pope here on earth is Christ"* (*Il papa qui in terra è Cristo.*) This is "a very recent work, dedicated to Cardinal Gasparri, the Papal Secretary of State" under Pius XI.

But does not the Word of God speak of a "royal priesthood?"

Yes, but note carefully that this is said *not* of ministers *only*, but of *all believers*. I Peter 2:5-9. St. Peter was addressing *all Christians*. Note also that he used the words "priesthood" and "sacrifice" *figuratively*. The sacrifice they offer is declared to be a *spiritual* sacrifice; not a slain animal, but *praise* and *thanksgiving*. Exhorting believers generally, the apostle says, "by Him (Christ) therefore let us offer the *sacrifice of praise* to God continually, that is, the fruit of our lips, *giving thanks to His name*." Heb. 13:15. Addressing *all Christians*, he also says: "Ye are a *spiritual* house, a *holy priesthood*, to offer up *spiritual* sacrifices, acceptable to God by Jesus Christ." I Peter 2:5. The "royal priesthood," also called "a holy nation, a peculiar people," was the *whole body of believers*, whose privilege it was to show forth the praises of Him "who hath called you out of darkness into His marvelous light." Thus all who are called out of darkness into Christ's marvelous light, and who praise Him for salvation, are *New Testament priests*, and there *are no others*.

Bishop and Presbyter Are One

What is the meaning of "bishop" in Holy Scripture?

The Scriptures teach that the office of bishop and presbyter are one and the same. The Greek word for bishop ἐπίσκοπος *episcopos*, means "overseer" or "supervisor." It indicates the function of the presbyter or minister, viz.: supervising or overseeing the congregation. The bishop did not belong to a higher order than the presbyter, for in the Apostolic Church there was *only one order* of ministers.

What clear proof does Scripture give that in the Apostolic Church presbyter and bishop were one and the same office?

St. Paul, addressing the Ephesian presbyters (elders), *reminds them that they are bishops,* appointed by the Holy Ghost, to oversee the congregation. Acts 20:28. Also after directing that "presbyters be ordained in every city," he goes on to state in the same connection what *the bishop ought to be,* showing that he used presbyter and bishop *as convertible terms.* I Tim. 3:1, 2, Titus 1:5.

What was the teaching of the Fathers of the early Church concerning the ministry of the apostolic age?

The Fathers of the early Church, following Holy Scripture, taught that Christian ministers were presbyters, and that bishop and presbyter were only different names for *the same office.* Thus Polycarp, Irenaeus, Clement of Rome, and Tertullian testified. So also Firmilian, leader at Caesarea, who declared: "In Presbyters is vested the power of baptizing and imposition of hands, i.e., ordination. Hilary, bishop of Poictiers, died 368, says: "Presbyters were at first called bishops." Jerome, of the 5th century, states: "Among the ancients presbyters and bishops were *the same.*" Again, "A presbyter is the same as a bishop, and originally the Churches were governed by the *joint Council of presbyters.*" (i.e., *the Presbytery.*)

What was the doctrine of the Churches at the time of, and following, the Reformation?

The same doctrine concerning the identity of presbyter and bishop, and of government by presbytery, was taught not only by leaders of the Church of England, as Archbishop Cranmer, Bishops Jewell, Willet, and Stillingfleet, but also by all the Reformed Churches of Switzerland, Savoy, France, Germany, Hungary, Poland, and the Netherlands.

In "The Institution of a Christian Man," a work approved by the above Archbishop and Bishops, as well as by King and Parliament of England, it is declared; "In the New Testament there is *no mention of any other degrees,* but of Deacons or Ministers and of Presbyters or Bishops."

What was the teaching of the University of Oxford on this subject?

The teaching at Oxford was identical with that already mentioned. Dr. Raynolds, Professor of Divinity in Oxford, declared that "for 500 years before his time the University taught that *all pastors, whether called bishops or priests,* have *equal power and authority* by the Word of God." Dr. Holland, King's professor of Divinity at Oxford, says, that "to affirm the office of bishop to be different from that of presbyter and superior to it, is most false, contrary to Scripture, to the Fathers, to the doctrine of the Church of England, yea, to the *very Schoolmen themselves.*" Bishop Burnet, of the 18th century, declares, "I acknowledge bishop and presbyter to be one and the same office." Dr. Whitby, died 1726, who was zealous for Episcopacy, states concerning the allegation of some that Timothy and Titus were *diocesan bishops,* says: "I can find nothing in any writer of the first 3 centuries concerning *an episcopate of Timothy and Titus,* nor any intimation that they *bore that name."* President Timothy Dwight of Yale wrote: "It is certain that Timothy was an evangelist, and therefore, *not* a *diocesan bishop;* because Paul directs him in II Timothy 4:5 to 'do the work of *an evangelist.'* An evangelist was an itinerant minister, and could *not* be a diocesan bishop whose business it is to rule and abide in his own diocese."

These facts show that diocesan bishops are not of Scriptural, but of human origin. *Theology, Explained and Defended,* by Rev. Timothy Dwight, vol. IV, pages 241, 242, 1828.

Is this apostolic doctrine that bishop and presbyter are the same office still held by the Church?

This apostolic doctrine is still held by the Presbyterian and other branches of the Reformed Church. We have already seen that eminent scholars of all Communions, like Dean Stanley, Bishop Lightfoot, Professor Schaff, and others, agree that in Scripture and apostolic practice *bishop and presbyter are the same office.*

APOSTOLIC SUCCESSION

What is meant by Apostolic Succession?

In common language it means that the power and grace which Christ bestowed on the apostles to fit them for the ministry, when

He breathed on them and said, "Receive ye the Holy Ghost" (John 20:22, 23), they transmitted by the touch of their hands to the ministers whom they ordained. These ministers in turn, by the laying on of hands, passed on divine power and grace to those whom they ordained; and so on down the centuries, it is held that what the bishop confers in ordination by the touch of his hands is essentially the same divine power and grace as that originally bestowed by Christ on His apostles. In other words, the power and grace which Christ and His apostles communicated to the ministers who succeeded them, has been *passed on by an unbroken line of bishops, through the touch of their hands, down to the present time, and may be obtained in no other way.*

Is this doctrine taught in the Holy Scriptures?

No, there is nothing like it taught in the Word of God, but just the *opposite.* This exclusive and magical conception of divine grace, mechanically transmitted through the touch of human hands, is entirely *without support in Holy Scripture,* and is opposed to the whole tenor of divine teaching. The Word of God teaches that all power and grace are bestowed *directly by the Holy Spirit,* and are *not dependent* on *the touch of human hands.* Moreover God's gracious gifts are not dependent on, or confined to, any *special line or succession of men for transmission.* He is sovereign Lord, and bestows His gifts *whenever and wherever He wills;* and while He is often graciously pleased to use human instruments, yet they are *not necessary to impart His gifts.* I Cor. 12:11, Acts 11:17, Acts 15:8, 9. The mistake which Peter and the early Jewish Christians made regarding admitting Gentiles to the Church, and insisting that Gentiles must submit to circumcision, is the mistake the Church of Rome now makes in claiming exclusive power and privileges for her priests as the sole depositories of God's saving grace.

An eminent historian wrote: "The corruptions of the Church had all grown out of one root, viz.: the notion that the Christian minister was a *priest,* who possessed *mystical power conferred through episcopal ordination.* But religion, as Luther conceived it, and (as the Word of God teaches), did *not* consist in certain things done to and for a man by a so-called priest. Religion was the devotion of each individual soul to the service of God. *Masses* were *nothing, absolution* was *nothing.* A clergyman differed from a layman only in being set apart for the *special duties of teaching*

What is meant in Scripture by the imposition, or laying on, of hands?

According to Scripture, the laying on of hands for ordination had a two-fold reference, one to God, the other to the Church. On the one hand, it signified that the Church trusted God, in answer to prayer, to fulfil His promise, and grant to the candidate *all divine power and grace needful* for the *ministry.* On the other hand, the Church thereby officially *recognized* the candidate as *suitable for the office,* and conferred on him the Church's *authority to serve as a minister.*

What do the Scriptures indicate as all-important in ordination?

What the Scriptures stress as all-important in ordination is not the *human element,* but the *divine;* not the laying on of hands, but BELIEVING PRAYER. *God, not* man, bestows the grace and power. He bestows it *directly* in *answer to prayer,* and the blessing, like all other divine blessings, *is received by faith alone.* The Apostolic Church *realized its absolute dependence upon God;* it looked to Him *in faith* to *bestow all needed grace;* and believing prayer is never made in vain. Acts 1:24, 8:15, 13:3, 4, etc.

APOSTOLIC ORDINATION WAS ADMINISTERED BY THE PRESBYTERY

According to Scripture, how was apostolic ordination usually administered?

Scripture indicates that apostolic ordination was administered by the Presbytery,[1] that is, by several ministers *acting conjointly.* St. Paul reminded Timothy that he was set apart for his work "by the laying on of the hands of the Presbytery." I Tim. 4:14. The apostles acted together in ordaining deacons. Acts 6:6. No apostle seems to have been present in sending forth Barnabas and Paul.[2] Acts 13:3.

---

and *preaching.* In getting rid of episcopal ordination, the Reformers dried up the fountain from which the *mechanical and idolatrous conceptions of religion had sprung." Times of Erasmus and Luther.* J. A. Fronde.

[1] Jerome wrote that in the early Church, bishops were consecrated by the *body of Presbyters* from which they were taken, that is, by the Presbytery. Jerome died in the 2nd decade of the 5th century.

[2] Only ordinary ministers, as Simeon called Niger, Lucius and Manaen, spoken of as "prophets and teachers." Acts 13:1.

"They laid their hands upon them." So, too, the Samaritan Christians thus received the Holy Ghost. Acts 8:17.

But does not St. Paul also speak of the "laying on of my hands?" II Tim. 1:6.

Yes, but there need be *no contradiction in this,* for St. Paul took part *as a member of the Presbytery.* Compare St. Peter's speaking of himself as *your "fellow-presbyter."* I Peter 5:1.

Does the Word of God anywhere give ground for the belief that Roman bishops or any minister, have power to bestow the Holy Spirit or His gifts by the touch of their hands?

No. No Roman bishop, nor any man, has this power. The dogma was a medieval invention to exalt the pope and the Roman hierarchy. The Holy Spirit now as of old, *Himself bestows* all grace and power in answer to *the prayer of faith;* His gifts have *never* been *mechanically conveyed by human hands.*

There Is No Unbroken Line of Papal Succession

As a matter of historic fact, has there ever been, from the days of the apostles down to the present time, as Rome alleges, an unbroken line of popes and bishops?

History shows that there has been *no continuous, unbroken line of popes and bishops.* The supposed line has been *often broken,* and that for *long periods.* The gaps between popes create vast gulfs which cannot be bridged, and *destroy all possibility* of anything like a *continuous succession.*

Is this merely the opinion of writers unfriendly to the papacy, or is there clear historic evidence that there has been no unbroken line, no real continuity?

There is abundant evidence from eminent Roman Catholic historians that there has been no continuous line of popes, and therefore *no real succession.* Cardinal Baronius, an outstanding papal historian, wrote that IN A LIST OF 50 POPES, THERE WAS NOT ONE PIOUS OR VIRTUOUS MAN AMONG THEM; THAT FOR LONG PERIODS OF YEARS THERE WAS NO POPE AT ALL, AND AT OTHER TIMES TWO OR THREE POPES

AT ONCE; ALSO THAT THERE WERE MORE THAN 20 SCHISMS, ONE OF WHICH CONTINUED FOR 50 YEARS, THE POPES OF ROME AND THOSE OF AVIGNON EXCOMMUNICATING EACH OTHER, AND YET CONFERRING ORDERS ON THEIR SEVERAL CLERGY! ANN. ECCLES. AN. *912*.

Do not these facts, and the undoubted history of the papacy for centuries, conclusively prove that there is no such thing as Apostolic Succession?

They do prove that Apostolic Succession, as held by the Church of Rome and its imitators, has had *no real existence in fact;* it is only the child of a fertile imagination. Both Scripture and history show that it is *neither apostolic* nor *a succession;* it is not a succession, because there is *no unbroken line;* it is not apostolic, because, as Baronius declared, there *have been many popes,* who were *"neither pious nor virtuous."* John Wesley was right, when in 1784 he wrote to his brother Charles: "I firmly believe that I am a Scriptural *episcopos,* as much as any man in England, or Europe. For the uninterrupted 'succession' I know to be *a fable* which no man ever did, or can, prove."

The Impossibility of Any Real Apostolic Succession[1]

A careful student of Church History writes: "The condition of the Church of Rome about the 10th century destroys the last shred of possibility that the Roman Church of today inherits the line of succession of the apostles. *No pope for nearly a thousand years* has had *canonical election to the Roman See,* and the claim of Apostolicity and infallibility is thus *completely voided.* A second gap of 34 years from 1012 to 1046 is caused by unworthy and simoniacal popes. Again a complete break occurs in the 70 years' 'captivity' at Avignon. Next, at the Council of Constance in 1414 there were 3 rival popes, Gregory XII, John XXIII and Benedict XIII, all of

---

[1] The testimony of the High Churchman, Archbishop Laud, is significant. He said: "I do not find one of the ancient Fathers that makes continued succession a necessary mark of the true Church. The succession is not tied to place or person, but to the *verity of doctrine.* This was the uniform opinion of High Churchmen at the time of, and after, the Reformation. They did not hold the doctrine of succession imposed by the Council of Trent, but fully *recognized the valid orders* of *other Reformed Churches.*

whom were set aside by the Council as illegitimate, and thereby invalidated all quasi-papal acts, including the creation of cardinals which was done between 1378 and 1414. There has been no possibility of a legitimate election and succession since 1492, when the electoral body was *vitiated at its very source." Littledale, pages* 219, 223.

So corrupt had the Roman See become that a period of this century was called the *"Rule of the Harlots or Prostitutes,"* for licentious women, Theodora, and her two daughters, practically controlled the selection of popes. This name was given to the period not by enemies of the papacy, but by *Roman Catholic historians themselves. How Peter Became Pope,* by Dallman, page 44.

The Council of Pisa in 1409 deposed the rival popes, Gregory XII and Benedict XIII, declaring that "there was no soundness in the Church from the sole of the foot to the crown of the head." These popes refusing to yield, they were again deposed, together with pope John XXIII, by the Council of Constance in 1415. All three were condemned for a long list of crimes. Concerning John XXIII, John Huss said: "You preachers who affirm that the pope is a god on earth, that he could not sin nor commit simony, that he is the sun of the holy Church, answer me. Behold, this terrestrial god has been declared guilty of so many sins, that he has *fled!* Ah, if Christ had said to the Council, 'let him among you who feels himself free from the sin of simony, condemn the pope,' all of you would, I believe, have fled away! Why then did they kneel down before him and kiss his feet and call him 'most holy father,' knowing that he was *a heretic and a murderer,* as *has since been proved?"* Mussolini's *John Huss,* page 89.

If the dogma of Apostolic Succession has no real basis in Scripture or history, how did it come to be accepted in the Church?

Because it is a plausible theory which appeals to the imagination; it invests the papacy with an *air of antiquity and dignity.* It appeals to *pride* and *love of power;* it became rooted in an age of ignorance and superstition; it spread *through the incessant propaganda of those who profited by it,* that is, the whole hierarchy; and finally, because the *entire mechanical system* of *the Roman Church depended on it.*

How does the dogma of Apostolic Succession enhance the power and prestige of pope and hierarchy?

The dogma practically gives absolute power to the Roman hierarchy by making it a close corporation which supposedly holds a *monopoly of divine grace and salvation.* The laity are made dependent on the parish priest, the priest on the bishop, and the bishop on the pope. Access to God and salvation for the laity can be had, practically, *only through the priest,* on whom they are dependent for sacramental grace, and the bishops and clergy are *dependent absolutely on the pope.* Only those on whom a recognized bishop of the Church has laid his hands can perform the duties of priest; and only those can be bishops on whom the pope, either directly or through his representative, has laid his hands. No one outside of the supposed line of succession, *no matter what his spiritual qualifications may be,* can have any authority or perform the rites of the Church.

Is not this system which makes of the Christian ministry a close corporation, alone controlling and dispensing God's grace and salvation, wholly contrary to the doctrine and spirit of the true Gospel?

This system, which gives practically *autocratic power to pope* and *clergy,* who are supposed to *hold a monopoly of the free grace of God,* and shuts the door of salvation against all who do not bow to their claims, is *wholly alien to the Gospel of Christ.* There is absolutely no warrant for it in Holy Scripture nor in apostolic practice. It was not inspired by the Holy Spirit, but was devised by ambitious, selfish men, who saw the power and wealth of secular rulers, and wished *to secure the same for themselves* in the Church of Christ. How different is the spirit of pride, self-sufficiency and love of wealth and power of the Papacy, as contrasted with the meekness, humility and self-sacrifice of the apostles, who sought no preëminence or glory for themselves, but ascribed all grace, power and glory to the Holy Trinity!

THE LAITY SHARED IN THE MANAGEMENT OF THE APOSTOLIC CHURCH

Did not the Christian laity have a share in the management of the Apostolic Church?

Not only does the Bible show there was no pope in the Apostolic Church, but it shows also that the laity *undoubtedly shared in the management of the* Apostolic Church. The people elected their officers. They voted in the selection of deacons. In Acts 6:1-6 we read, "the whole multitude of believers" chose them. In the General Council at Jerusalem the laity took part through *representatives chosen by the congregation.* Acts 15:6. In verse 22 it is said: "It pleased the apostles and the presbyters with the whole church (i.e., the laity) to send chosen men of their own company," that is, representatives *chosen by and from the people.* Again, the official letter to Antioch was sent not only in the name of the clergy, but also in the name of the laity; "the apostles, presbyters and *brethren" (laity),* verse 23. Thus it is clear that in the Apostolic Church the laymen had a part in the administration of Church affairs, not only temporal, but spiritual; for all the matters cited above relate to spiritual or doctrinal matters. Not only did laymen share in the management of the Church in apostolic times, but they continued to do so *for centuries thereafter.* History shows plainly that clergy and laymen *elected their own bishops* until the 11th century, the time of Hildebrand. In 1059 pope Nicholas II changed the election of pope from clergy and people to a bench of cardinals. Since that time the choice of bishops has *belonged exclusively to the pope.* Dr. Luchaire rightly declares that the papacy *absorbed all the living forces of the religious world,* and *suppressed all the liberties* which the *Church of old had enjoyed!* Note that the pope by increasing the number of bishops was able to control Church Councils. Pope John XXIII appointed 50 bishops in order to control the vote of the council of Constance! Creighton, *History of the Papacy,* vol. I, page 317.

Where there were no dioceses to be filled, there were imaginary or fictitious ones ready to hand, and titular bishops can always be appointed. Lord Acton referred to such, as appearing in the Vatican Council of 1870. Formerly there was no law or probitition preventing any cleric or laymen from being elected pope. But later the choice was narrowed down to the bench of cardinals and since 1378, a cardinal has always been elected pope. The cardinals thus gradually formed an electoral *oligarchy superseding election by clergy and the people.* Note how far from the practice of Holy Scripture the Church of Rome has departed! Popes have gradually *usurped all power and authority* and both clergy and people have been deprived of their *God-given right of Church administration*, just as the people have been deprived of their right to partake of the wine in the Lord's supper!

What is the doctrine and practice of the Reformed Church?

The Reformed or Protestant Church of all denominations, following Scripture, has *restored the apostolic practice*, and gladly accords to all church members the right to participate in the management of Church affairs.

Does the Word of God anywhere teach that salvation or the reception of divine grace is dependent on any human being?

The Word of God nowhere teaches that salvation is dependent on pope, bishop, priest, *or any human being*. Salvation depends on God alone; and all who truly obey His Word, forsake their sins, and trust only in the Lord Jesus Christ as Redeemer, are *saved forever*. Jonah 2:9, Mark 1:15, Acts 4:12, 16, 31.

Judging by the only right Standard, the Holy Scriptures, what Church should be considered the true Church of God?

Judging by the Scriptures, the Church which worships God alone, which trusts Him only for salvation, which loyally obeys the Word of God as its sole rule of faith, and which ascribes all glory to Him, should be considered the true Church; and we believe that the Reformed or Protestant Church is this true Church. For with all the sins and faults of its members, which we *freely confess with deep sorrow*, it most nearly conforms in doctrine and practice to the true Church of Christ in the Scriptures.

Is the Roman Catholic Church a part of the true Church of God?

Judging by Scripture, our only God-given standard, one is bound to hold that the Roman Church is *not a part of the true Church of God;* for on almost every vital doctrine, as we have seen, it has *departed far from the teachings of God's Word,* has put sinful human beings in the place of God, and therefore must be considered apostate.

Does this statement imply that there are no true Christians in the Church of Rome?

Not at all. Thank God there are true Christians in the Church of Rome. But they are good Christians, *not* because *of papal teachings,* but *in spite of those teachings.* Romanism rightly understood is a totally different thing from the true faith of Holy Scripture. It is what St. Paul calls "another Gospel," that is, a *counterfeit Gospel.* Gal. 1:6-9. The papal system is like a thick, iron crust, which has formed over the true Gospel, and shuts the soul off from Christ and salvation. By God's mercy some have been *enabled to break through this iron crust of false dogma* and *reach the living Christ.* But many seem to trust merely to pope and priest and dead rites, and lack that vital faith in Christ and His Truth, which *alone can save.*

To rely on a priest or any minister for absolution or forgiveness, and to trust to the *counterfeit atonement for sin* which is *offered in the Mass,* is indeed a *false* hope which will *utterly fail the sinner in the Day of Judgment.* I Cor. 3:11-13, II Peter 2:1.

CHAPTER VI

THE DEVELOPMENT OF THE PAPAL SYSTEM

What is the meaning of the title, "Pope"?

The word pope is derived from the Greek, Πάπας, πάππας, *papas, pappas,* Latin *papa,* meaning "father." In the early Church of both East and West, the title was applied to all bishops. In the Eastern branch of the Church the same word, with the circumflex accent, πᾶπας, was applied to all priests. The bishop of Rome did not obtain the exclusive use of this title until the time of Hildebrand (Gregory VII), 1073-1085. In other words, before Gregory VII, there was no real pope, as understood later, because *all bishops were called popes.* The student of history must be on his guard not to attach to the title as used in the early Church, the meaning it came to have in later centuries.

It has already been shown that St. Peter and the Apostolic Church had no thought of a pope. St. Paul well expressed the conviction of the apostles, when speaking of Apollos and himself he said, "Who are we, but ministers?" I Cor. 3:5.

The papal office was the product of selfish ambition in much later times. The bishops of Rome ignoring Christ's declaration, "My Kingdom is not of this world," and taking advantage of the political prestige their city had enjoyed for centuries as the Mistress of the World, schemed to secure the power and wealth that the Emperors of the Roman Empire enjoyed, and decade by decade pushed their false claims to secular and religious power until the people of Europe, ignorant of the true teachings of the Bible, and absorbed in their own worldly interests, gradually came to acknowledge them. Moreover it should be remembered that Scripture and secular history afford no evidence that St. Peter was ever in Rome! Had he actually been in Rome, he would surely have spoken of it in his epistles. And St. Paul would almost surely have mentioned it, for he speaks of Luke, Mark and others, who were not so prominent as Peter, being in the capital. II Tim. 4:11, 12, 21, etc. Showing the nebulous

basis for belief that Peter was ever in Rome, the only text which
Cardinal Bellarmine cites to prove this supposition is I Peter 5:13,
where mention is made of *Babylon*. The natural interpretation of
this is, that *Babylon on the Euphrates river* is referred to. This is
the opinion of eminent scholars, among them Erasmus, a Romanist,
who was considered the great scholar of his age; and of Dr. J. J.
Döllinger, considered the great scholar of the Roman Church in the
19th century. Scaliger, who also had a reputation for profound
scholarship, once declared that St. Peter's alleged residence and
episcopate at Rome ought to be *classed with "absurd legends."*

No Pope in the Early Centuries

*Is there trustworthy evidence that there was no pope, not only
in the first century, but at the end of the third century?*

There is clear evidence that there was no pope at the end of the
third century. In A.D. 270 Stephen, bishop of Rome, reinstated in
office certain unworthy ministers who had been forced to resign. A
protest against Stephen's action having been made, Cyprian of
Carthage called a meeting of bishops, *who reversed the decision of
the bishop of Rome.* This could not have been done, had Stephen
really been a pope. That there was no pope in the Church at that
time is also proved by a declaration of Cyprian's to his brother
bishops: "No one of us sets himself up as 'bishop of bishops,' or
forces his colleagues to obedience by tyranny; for every bishop in
the free use of his liberty and power, has *his own right of judgment*,
and can no more be judged by another, than he himself can judge
the other!"[1]

Again, the sixth Canon of the Council of Nice, A.D. 325, declared
that the Patriarchs of Antioch and Alexandria possessed the same
authority over their dioceses that the bishop of Rome had over his.
This pronouncement was reaffirmed by the Council of Chalcedon,

---

[1] In 1563 a statement was widely circulated from the Vatican, purporting to have
come from Cyprian's writings, which acknowledged the bishop of Rome to be
Universal Bishop. This statement, Archbishop Benson of Canterbury declared, came
from a fraudulent document. He remarks, "Papal apologists have steadily maintained
the grossest forgeries in literature. There never was a viler fraud than this, nor one
so easy of detection." *Life of Cyprian*, Benson.

451, which also rejected as forgery a clause that had been inter-
polated into the 6th Canon, alleging "that the Roman Church had
always had a primacy." Roman Catholic authorities, like Bishop
Hefele, agree that this interpolation was *fraudulent*. Thus it is
clear that there was no pope in A.D. 451![1]

Was there any real pope in the 6th Century?

Not yet; for Gregory I, who was bishop of Rome from 590 to 604,
denounced the Patriarch of Constantinople for assuming the title
of Universal Bishop. Gregory declared that this title was "a mark
of Anti-Christ, a name of blasphemy," and anyone who assumed it,
"exalted himself above all other bishops." Later, Gregory stooped
to accept the empty title for himself from the usurper Phocas, who
murdered the Emperor and his whole family, and seized the imperial
throne. Gregory flattered the murderer and praised his horrible
crime, in order to gain Phoças' support against the Patriarch of
Constantinople; and his reward for the base act was the empty title,
and the humbling of his rival, the Patriarch. In 596 Gregory sent
Augustine (Austin) with 40 monks to England to try to bring
Britain into union with Rome.

THE RISE OF MOHAMMEDANISM

*What false religion arose in the 7th century, for which the grave
errors of the Greek and Roman branches of the Church were largely
responsible?*

The Arabian Mohammed (*Hegira*, 622), abhorring as a violation
of true religion the worship of images, saints and the Virgin Mary,
which was practiced by the Greek and Roman Churches, founded
the religion of *Islam* for the worship of the one true God. This cult
spread rapidly, and has ever since been an unrelenting foe of the
Christian religion, and the greatest hindrance to its progress in
Moslem lands. *Life of Mahomet*, Sir William Muir.

*Even in the year 800 was not the Emperor called "Bishop of
Bishops"?*

---

[1] The African Church of the 5th Century was undoubtedly independent of the
bishop of Rome's jurisdiction; for an African Council, of which Augustine of Hippo
was secretary, decreed that "whosoever wills to appeal to those beyond the sea
(that is, beyond the Mediterranean Sea, *to Rome*) shall not be received to the
Communion by any one in Africa."

6

Yes, the Emperor Charlemagne received this title and *wielded the power of Head of the Church*. Though, through ceaseless propaganda, the papal idea was steadily gaining ground, the bishop of Rome had not yet attained the position and power of Universal Bishop. Charlemagne tried Leo III, bishop of Rome, for grave crimes. The Emperor also summoned Church Councils, appointed bishops, and was called "Bishop of bishops," *exercising the power and performing the functions, which later belonged to the popes.* His acceptance of the crown from Leo on Christmas Day, was *not* an acknowledgment that the Bishop of Rome was his superior, but was a shrewd political move to confirm his authority over Italy and Southern Europe; for later, when dying, Charlemagne himself, and *not* the bishop of Rome, crowned his son Louis as his successor to the throne.

The Holy Roman Empire

The foundation for the Holy Roman Empire was laid by Pepin, the father of Charlemagne. Pepin, by usurpation and with the assistance of the pope, became King of the Franks in 751. In payment of his debt to the pope, he gave the pope the Exarchate of Revenna together with the territory of Bologna and Ferrara which formed the nucleus of the *Papal States*.

The Holy Roman Empire began with Charlemagne who succeeded his father as King of the Franks and was crowned Emperor by the bishop of Rome, Christmas Day, 800. As already stated, he accepted the crown from the bishop of Rome, *not* because he acknowledged the bishop as his superior, but because he wished to secure his aid in gaining control over Italy and Southern Europe. The Emperor claimed to represent the Emperors of ancient Rome; the Empire was called "Holy" from its connection with the Church, and comprised the German speaking peoples of Central Europe, with other parts of Europe. Otto I, King of Germany, became Roman Emperor in 962. Later, representatives of the Hapsburg line of Austria, occupied the Imperial Throne. The Empire declined through the 17th and 18th centuries, until Francis of Austria finally abdicated as its last Emperor in 1806.

The Great Schism in the Christian Church and Rise of the Roman Catholic Church

When did the Great Schism between the Eastern and Western branches of the Church take place, and to what was it due?

The Great Schism[1] between the Eastern and Western branches of the Church began in the 9th century and was completed in the 11th century. It was due in large part to the arrogant claims and persistent encroachments of the bishop of Rome, to which the Eastern and senior branch of the Church naturally would not submit. There had long been a bitter rivalry between the two religious leaders of Rome and Constantinople, which finally culminated in their complete separation, the Latin Church being established over the West, and the Orthodox Greek Church, whose Head was the Patriarch of Constantinople, over the East: both claiming to be Catholic or universal, and Apostolic. Thus the Roman Catholic Church, so far from originating in the apostolic age, *really began with the Great Schism* between the Eastern and Western branches of the Church. The date of this final separation was July 16, 1054, during the reign of Henry III of Germany, called the Emperor of the "Holy Roman Empire." At that time Michael Caerularios,

---

[1] Roman Church historians also use the term "The Great Schism," to denote the split in the Roman Church caused by the conflicting claims of rival popes, which extended *for 39 years, from 1378 to 1417.* The contest became so acute and the scandal so widespread, through the unseeming wrangling of claimants and their mutual imprecations, that although such action was contrary to the theory that the Pope alone could convoke a Council, a number of Cardinals met and issued a call for a General Council at Pisa in 1409 to compose the quarrels of the rival popes. This Council met and deposed two claimants to the papacy and elected Alexander V as pope, thus increasing the number of claimants to the papal throne to three. Later the General Council of Constance (1414-1418) was convened, which elected Martin V as the sole pope. This Council enacted the "Five Articles of Constance"; these asserted the Council's authority in all matters of faith and discipline, which all Christians, *even the pope,* were bound to obey, and in case of refusal to obey, all Christians, *even the pope,* were liable to ecclesiastical punishment and to civil sanctions. The legality of Martin V's election, and the existence of the papal office depended on holding that the Council of Constance was a *legal body.* But the "Five Articles" would make the Council supreme over the pope, and thus endanger papal absolute power. So by a mental somersault, more dextrous than honest, the papal candidate recognized the validity of the Council's action in electing him pope, but refused to recognize the Council's action, *making the pope subordinate to a General Council!*

Patriarch of Constantinople, and Leo IX, bishop of Rome, completely severed ecclesiastical relations, and established separate Churches, which ever afterward were maintained as independent organizations.

THE EASTERN BRANCH OF THE CHRISTIAN CHURCH WAS OLDER AND FOR CENTURIES WAS MUCH MORE INFLUENTIAL THAN THE WESTERN BRANCH OF THE CHURCH

In order to get the true perspective of history it cannot be repeated too often that the Roman Catholic Church and her system of dogmas did *not begin in apostolic times,* but *centuries later.* In the early years of the Church the Eastern branch, as regards seniority and influence, *far surpassed the Western or Latin branch,* and maintained this leadership *at least for several centuries.* The great leaders of the early Church were mainly from the East, as Irenaeus, Ignatius, Eusebius, Chrysostom, Origen, Athanasius, and many others, called the Greek Fathers. It was through the work of the Eastern branch that the Coptic Church was founded in Egypt, and the Church established in Armenia, Ethiopia or Abyssinia, and India. Another proof of the early leadership of the Eastern branch is seen in the personnel of *the early Church Councils.* This was *overwhelmingly Greek.* At the Council of Nice, A.D. 325, out of 315 members present, *not more than 8 members represented the Western section of the Church.* So also of the Council of Constantinople in 381; and that of Ephesus in 431, under the leadership of Cyril of Alexandria, the influence of the Greek or Eastern branch was largely predominant.

Showing that there was no real pope then, it should be remembered also that these Councils were convoked, *not* by the bishops of Rome, but *by the Emperor* in Constantinople, who acted practically as the Head of the Church. The Emperor *summoned Councils,* sometimes without informing, and *sometimes against the wishes,* of the bishop of Rome. As has been mentioned, even *as late as the 9th Century,* the Emperor Charlemagne acted as Head of the Church and was called "Bishop of Bishops." Thus the papacy and the bulk of the papal dogmas did *not come into existence till hundreds of years after the age of the apostles.* Many Roman Catholics of repute testify to this. Antonio Pereira of Lisbon declared that the papal doctrines as distinguished from Apostolic Christianity were introduced by *the false decretals* (i.e., *not earlier than the 9th Century*). F. W. Barkovitch wrote that "the decretals were full of principles *hitherto unknown* in the Church of Christ."

What four important events, occurring not far apart, mark the full development of the Papacy?

The four events are, the rise of the ambitious Hildebrand as Gregory VII, claiming supremacy, not only over the Church, but also over all civil governments; the assumption by him of the *exclusive title of pope;* the deprivation of the laity of the *right to share in the government of the Church,* including the election of their superiors; and the final separation of the Church *into the Latin and Greek branches.*

On what did Hildebrand mainly base his exclusive claims to temporal and spiritual power?

Hildebrand based his claims to temporal and spiritual power largely upon documents, later known to be *fraudulent,* viz.: the so-called *"Donation of Constantine"* which appeared *in the 8th* century. It purported to be an edict of Constantine the Great, bestowing on the bishop of Rome *control of Italy and the West,* and conferring on him and the Roman clergy the *same rights and privileges* which the *Emperor and the Roman Senate enjoyed.*

The "Isidorian or Spanish Decretals" appeared in the *9th* century, and professed to be a code of Church laws, compiled by Isidore, bishop of Seville, who died in 636. These *spurious decretals* also magnified the power and privileges of the bishop of Rome and his clergy. They were brought to Rome and presented to the bishop of Rome *by Rothad, bishop of Soissons in 860.* A later compilation of letters, which purported to be ancient, and false decrees, called *Gratian's Decretum,* the work of an Italian canonist, Gratianus, appeared about *1150-51.* This Decretum of Gratian became the great authority on ecclesiastical law throughout the Middle Ages.

THUS BY FORGERY WAS FOISTED ON THE CHRISTIAN CHURCH OF THE WEST THE OFFICE OF POPE, WITH ITS CLAIMS OF TEMPORAL AND SPIRITUAL POWER, AS THE UNIVERSAL BISHOP OF CHRISTENDOM!

THE PAPACY BASED ON COUNTERFEIT DOCUMENTS

Were these documents on which the papacy was founded, really proved to be false?

Competent authorities of the Roman Catholic Church testify that without doubt these documents, which refer to the rights and privileges of the papacy, were forgeries. The Roman Catholic writer Schick quoted Antonio Pereira of Lisbon, declaring that the *Roman dogmas,* as *distinguished from apostolic doctrine,* were introduced by *these false decretals.* Similarly, F. W. Barkovitch wrote, "The decretals are full of principles *hitherto unknown in the Church of Christ."* Archbishop Hincmar of Rheims, called the decretals *"a honeyed poison cup."* The Roman Catholic writer Scherer declared, "He who knowingly lies and forges, as *Pseudo-Isidore,* forfeits all claim to the title of *an honest man."* By Pseudo-Isidore he meant, the forger of the "Isidorian Decretals." Cardinals Baronius, Bellarmine, and Fleury, as well as De Regnon of Paris, *all asserted that these documents were fraudulent.*

Even Pope Pius VI, 1789, rejected them as false. He said, "Let us put aside this collection of decretals *to be burned with fire!"*

Lord John Acton, professor of history in Cambridge University in 1895, whom Cardinal Vaughan declared to be an orthodox Catholic, wrote: "The passage from the Catholicism, or Universal faith of the Fathers, to that of the modern popes was accomplished by *wilful falsehood;* and *the whole structure* of traditions, laws and doctrines, that support the theory of infallibility and the practical despotism of the popes, *stands on a basis of fraud."* Lord Acton was an honest man, an earnest seeker after the truth. Though all his life a member of the Roman Church, at least in name, he clearly saw and boldly asserted that modern papal teachings, like those of the Council of Trent, are *based on fraud,* and *do not represent the doctrines of the early Christian Church. North British Review,* October, 1869, page 130.

NOT ONLY THE OFFICE OF SUPREME PONTIFF, BUT ALSO ITS POWER AND PRIVILEGES WERE FOUNDED ON FRAUDULENT EVIDENCE

That leading scholar of the Roman Church, Dr. J. J. Döllinger, wrote: "The Donation of Constantine and the Pseudo-Isidorian

Decretals were imposed upon the Church about A.D. 750 and A.D. 850. For 700 years they were considered authentic, but about the middle of the 15th century they were abandoned as spurious. The towering fabric of a factitious papal sovereignty, however, raised in part on their authority, remained to crush the spirit of truth, and to harass the natural liberties of man." Janus, pages 94, 95, 105, 106.

The distinguished historian Hallam wrote: "Upon these spurious decretals was built the great fabric of Papal supremacy over the different national Churches,—a fabric which has stood after its foundations crumbled beneath it; for no one for the last two centuries has pretended to deny that *the imposture is too palpable* for any but the most ignorant ages to credit." *Middle Ages,* edition 1869, page 348.

The general conviction held by sincere and profound students of history that the papal system was based on deceit and forgery was expressed by the French theologian Gratry in a letter to Dechamps. "Do you know, Monseigneur, in the history of the human mind any question, theological, philosophical, historical, or otherwise, which has been *so disgraced by falsehood, bad faith, and the whole work of forgers,* as the papal system? I say it again, 'It is a matter *utterly gangrened by fraud!'*" Gratry, *Letter* II.

Did later popes, knowing that their power and privileges were acquired by fraud ever relinquish any part of them?

No one ever heard of their doing so. Though the popes *knew* that the whole fabric of the papal system was *built on forgery,* and therefore they *had no right to it,* they *still held tenaciously to it, and its emoluments.*

Does the Word of God give any warrant for various grades of clergy? In the Apostolic Church do we read of popes, cardinals, archbishops, bishops, canons, monsignors, etc.?

The Word of God gives *no warrant whatever* for any of these grades, but rather *warns against them.* These various grades were copied from the different ranks of officials under secular rulers. Selfish ambition, love of wealth, pomp and display, led leaders in the Church to *disregard our Lord's words,* "My Kingdom is not of this world," and *seek their own worldly advantage*. The Saviour severely reproved the spirit of pride and self-seeking which actuated them, as wholly inconsistent with the humility and self-sacrifice of the Gospel. The standard set up for His followers was that by which He lived; *"Even as the Son of man came, not to be ministered unto, but to minister, and to give his life a ransom for many."* Matt. 18:1-4, 20:20-28, Mark 9:33-35, 10:42-45.

Are not the spirit and style of living of popes, cardinals, bishops, etc., wholly opposed to that of Christ and His apostles?

The spirit and style of living of popes, cardinals, etc., is as far removed from the simplicity and self-scarifice of Christ and the apostles, as their unscriptural dogmas are different from His Gospel. The popes claim a Kingdom of this world; Christ said: "My Kingdom is *not* of this world."

The popes live in a large and expensive palace;
Our Lord "had not where to lay His head." Matt. 8:20.
The popes affect pomp, and ride on men's shoulders.
Cardinals affect "thrones" and call themselves "princes";
Christ said: "I am among you as he that serveth." Luke 22:27.
The popes have men kiss their feet;
The Lord of heaven and earth washed men's feet. John 13:5.
Popes wear a triple crown of gold;
Our blessed Redeemer wore a crown of thorns!
Popes and bishops arrogate to themselves lordly power;
St. Peter exhorted: *"Be not lords over God's heritage."*
Popes and prelates seek much wealth;[1]
St. Peter enjoined: *"Not for filthy lucre."* I Peter 5:2.

---

[1] Quoting von Bezhold, Mussolini wrote: "The Church of Rome had become a slave of profound commercialism, had been bound over to the God Mammon, to the money that undermines all faith. The Curia had become a *gigantic money-making organization;* the saying that in Rome everything was for sale was by no means an exaggeration; for with money one could buy anything, from the smallest prebend to a cardinal's cap, from permission to use butter on fast days, even to absolution for murder and incest." Mussolini's *John Huss, the Man of Truth.*
Catholic Encyclopedia, Vol. V, pp. 118D, 119A.
Catholic Encyclopedia, Vol. VIII, p. 14B.
Bryce, pp. 219, 220.

In style of living there is hardly a feature in which they do not disobey the command, *"Be not conformed to this world."* Rom. 12:3.

Toward the end of the 14th century, in Edward III's reign, the pope's annual revenue from England was *five times greater than the King's income.* In addition, the Church owned *about one-third of England's territory.* Cardinal Wolsey was reported to be one of the richest men in Britain. His banquets and entertainments were *far more lavish than those of King Henry VIII.* The Church owned about *one-fifth of France, one-third of Germany,* a large part of Spain and of Italy, beside parts of Austria, Poland, and other countries. The great wealth of the religious Orders, especially of the Jesuits, and their *constant absorption of lands and money at the expense of the poor people,* was assigned as one of the chief causes of the revolution in Spain, which established the Republic. These well-known facts of history prove the correctness of the statement that the Roman Curia—the Vatican—had become "a gigantic money-making," instead of a "soul-saving," organization.

What were the main causes of the so-called Dark Ages?

Beside the fall of the Roman Empire in 476, and the destruction caused by vast hordes of barbarians who poured like a devastating flood over Europe—the Goths, Vandals, Huns, etc.—the chief causes of the Dark Ages were *moral and spiritual,* due to *the substitution of the papal system for the pure Gospel,* and to false leaders in the Church. These men, attracted by the rich prizes of wealth, power and pleasure, which the high offices of the Church offered, thought of *self* and *not* of Christ. They departed farther and farther from God's Word and the apostolic faith, and turned more and more to "the weak and beggarly elements" of human tradition. They substituted a *pope for Almighty God;* a *sinful human priest* for the *Divine Saviour; mechanical rites* and sacraments for *the Holy Spirit;* a *bartering of papal indulgences* for the *free grace of God;* and *"dead works"* of human merit instead of *vital godliness;* these grave errors, together with the deception of the people by *false miracles,* and *wonder-working shrines* and *relics,* produced their natural result,—*gross darkness* and *widespread moral corruption.*[1] Isa. 60:2, Jer. 2:13, Gal. 6:7.

Papal Control Brought Moral Ruin

Though the Christian Church was not originally papist, did not the popes gain control and hold it for a long time? What was the result?

Yes, just as is seen now in political parties in the State, the popes gained control of the Church, and *held it for centuries,* until they brought the Church to *the verge of ruin.* But all the time that vice and misrule were rampant, Christ still had *His loyal servants who kept the faith,* and handed it down to later generations. That the Church was brought to the brink of destruction, hear the testimony of Cardinal Baronius, among many who might be quoted. *"A few years before the heresies of Luther and Calvin, there was neither justice in the ecclesiastical courts, nor discipline in the morals of the clergy, nor knowledge of sacred things, nor respect for holy things; in short, there was scarcely any religion left!"* Baronius, *Concio, 28.*

Erasmus, a Roman Catholic, wrote: "I have made up my mind to spend the rest of my life in retirement from a world which is *everywhere rotten.* Ecclesiastical hypocrites rule in the courts of princes. The Court of Rome (Papacy) has clearly *lost all sense of shame, for what could be more shameless than these Indulgences?"*

Again, "All sense of shame has vanished from human affairs. The very *height of tyranny* has been reached. The pope and Kings count the people, *not* as men, but as *cattle* in the market." Erasmus' *Letters.*

Savonarola at Florence declared, "The scandal begins at Rome and goes throughout the whole.[1] The bishops are worse than Turks and Moors. The priests sell the sacraments; they traffic in the Mass; in short, *everything is done for money.* At Rome it has become a saying, 'If you will ruin your son, *make him a priest!'* "

---

[1] "All know the condition to which the Catholic Church had sunk at the beginning of the 16th century. An insolent hierarchy with an army of priests behind them, dominated every country in Europe. The Church was like a hard nutshell round a shriveled kernel. The priests, in parting with their sincerity, had lost the control over their own appetites, which only sincerity can give. Religious duty no longer consisted in leading a virtuous life, but *in purchasing immunity for self-indulgence,* by one of the thousand remedies which Church officials were ever ready to dispense *at an adequate price.* The spiritual organization of the Church was *corrupt to its core.* It was impossible to conceal the contrast betwen the doctrines taught in Catholic pulpits and the creed of which they were the *counterfeit."* Prof. J. A. Froude's *Calvinism.*

Chancellor John Gerson, of the University of Paris (died 1429), after declaring that the papacy was *founded on fraud,* and that the ecclesiastical rulers put up the Church *for sale,* said, "The present day Church is *not a*postolic, but *apostate,* from which one must *flee far, far!"*

GOD RAISED UP THE PROTESTANT REFORMATION
TO SAVE TRUE RELIGION

At the time when piety and virtue all seemed *lost,* and the powers of evil *triumphant in the world,* an all-wise and merciful Providence interposed to save true religion. Truly "man's extremity is God's opportunity!" At the beginning of the 16th century, Europe was *sunk in spiritual death* under the iron yoke of the papacy. "That haughty and dissolute power, like the ancient Assyrian King, boasted of his supremacy which none could withstand. (Isa. 10:13, 14.) In the language of the *Encyclopedia Britannica:*[1] "Everything was quiet, every heretic exterminated; and the whole Christian world supinely acquiesced in the enormous absurdities inculcated by the Romish Church." At the Lateran Council which closed in 1517, an orator ascended the platform, and amid the thundering applause of a vast assembly, proclaimed in the presence of the pope: "There is an end of resistance to the papal rule and religion; *opposers exist no more;* the whole body of Christendom is now seen to be subjected to its Head, *to Thee!"* That very year the Almighty's appointed time had come, and as in the handwriting on the wall of Belshazzar's palace, God spoke through an obscure monk; a voice that resounded through Germany, Italy and the whole of Christendom, shaking *the very foundations of the papal power* and arousing nations from the slumber of centuries!"

GOD'S FAITHFUL WITNESSES DOWN THE AGES

Who were some of the sincere believers who kept the true faith alive, and often sealed their witness with their blood?

The Cathari[2] (early "Puritans"), Paulicians, Nestorians, Wyclif-

---

[1] *The seventh edition,* Encyclopedia Britannica, *article, "Reformation."*

[2] The Cathari were falsely charged with Manichaeism, and wild stories were told of secret immorality, which candid Inquisitors admitted had no foundation in fact. They strongly opposed sacredotalism for they knew its emptiness. St. Bernard said

ites, Hussites, Waldenses,[3] etc. Though the faith of some of these may have been incomplete, as they groped their way in ecclesiastical darkness, yet the germ of truth was held. As in Elijah's time, God never left Himself without a witness. In spite of cruel persecutions, there still remained the faithful "7000," who had *not bowed the knee to the Baal of papacy, of sacerdotalism,* and *the worship of Mary, saints and images.* I Kings 19:18, Acts 14:17.

Is the accusation of the Church of Rome, that these Christian bodies in different centuries and the Protestant Church since the Reformation, are all schismatics who have separated from the true Church, founded on fact?

No. Holy Scripture shows plainly that these bodies of Christians, and the Protestant Church, are *in no sense schismatics* because they have *kept the true faith of Scripture,* and what they separated from was *an apostate Church.* The Church of Rome is the *real schismatic,* because it *departed far from the faith;* the Papal Church forced the break with the Eastern Church by its unreasonable demands, and Rome is *now the schismatic,* because *it forced the Protestant Reformation* by *its false doctrines and moral corruption.* Protestants were obeying our Lord's command when they *withdraw from the apostate Church,* for He said: *"Come ye out from among them, and be ye separate!"* II Cor. 6:14-18, Rev. 18:4.

---

of the Cathari: "If you interrogate them, *nothing* could be *more Christian;* as to their conversation, nothing can be *less reprehensible,* and what they speak they *prove by their deeds.* As for the morals of the heretic, he *cheats no one,* he *oppresses no one,* he *strikes no one.* He eats not the bread of idleness, for his hands labor for his livelihood. Their strict morality was never corrupted, and 100 years after St. Bernard, the same testimony is rendered to their virtues. Lea, *History of the Inquisition,* vol. 1, page 102.

[3] In a venerable document called, "The Noble Lesson," written about the year 1170, the Waldenses gave faithful testimony to the truth of the Gospel and against the anti-christian system of Papal dogmas. The document declares: "Antichrist is the falsehood of eternal condemnation, covered with *the appearance of the truth and righteousness of Christ.* Its essence is a *vain ceremonial;* its foundation, *false notions* of *grace and forgiveness;* its tendency, *to lead men away from Christ.* The Papal system *defrauds God* of the worship due to Him, by rendering it to *creatures, saints images, and relics.* It *defrauds Christ* by attributing justification and forgiveness to Antichrist's authority and words, to the intercession of saints, to the *merit of men's works,* and to *the fire of purgatory.* It *defrauds the Holy Spirit* by attributing regeneration and sanctification to the *mechanical operation of the two sacraments, baptism* and *the Eucharist.*"

THE ROMAN CHURCH NOT THE MOTHER CHURCH OF CHRISTENDOM

Protestants are often urged to return to "Mother Church." Is the Roman Catholic Church the true Mother Church?

No. The Roman Catholic Church is *not the Mother Church of Christendom, nor is it the Mother Church of Protestants in any sense.* We have already seen that the Eastern branch of the Church was older than the Latin branch, as is proved by statements of the Book of Acts. If the name Mother Church is properly applied, it should be given to the *Church at Jerusalem,* and after it, *the Church at Antioch.* Acts 11:22-26, 15:2. The Eastern branch of the Church was far more influential than the Church of Rome for centuries, as is clearly proved by the personnel of the early Councils of the Church, which were *overwhelmingly Eastern.* Moreover as we have already seen, the Roman Church cannot be considered the Mother Church because it *departed far from the apostolic faith,* its chief doctrines being *wholly opposed to the teachings of the Bible.* Either in the apostolic age, or soon thereafter; missionaries from Jerusalem and Antioch, planted Christian Churches in various eastern countries, as the Armenian, the Coptic in Egypt, the Ethiopian in Abyssinia, etc. These churches were independent and had *no connection with Rome.* When the Jesuits went to India, they *found primitive Nestorian Churches there,* which recognized the *patriarch of Babylon* at *Mosul* as *their chief,* and as the *pastor of the universal church.* They did *not recognize the pope* of Rome, of whom they *knew nothing.* These primitive churches were later led to enter the pale of the Roman church. Ranke, *History of the Popes,* Vol. II, page 81.

ENGLAND, FRANCE AND GERMANY RECEIVED THE GOSPEL FROM THE EAST, NOT FROM ROME

Was the Church of Rome the first to carry the Gospel to France, Great Britain, and Germany?

No. Tertullian, Eusebius, and other Church historians testify that the Gospel was brought to France and Britain by missionaries *sent directly from the East, long before the papacy was thought of.* The same is true of Germany. Cardinal Baronius records that the Gospel was *carried to Britain in the apostolic age;* so also do the learned

Mosheim, and the Roman writers, Dod and Lingard. It should be carefully noted that Britain's connection with the Church of Rome did not begin *till 500 years later*, when *Gregory I*, bishop of Rome, *sent Augustine (Austin) with about 40 colleagues to try to bring the English Church into union with Rome*. This was in *A.D. 596*. Irenaeus, a *native of Asia Minor*, and a student of the venerable Polycarp of Smyrna, *preached the Gospel in France* and was in charge of the work in Lyons, where he died A.D. 202. Many believe that the Culdee Church in North Scotland and the Orkney Islands, as well as the founders of what later became the Waldensian Church, may be traced back to *apostolic times*, and for centuries the Culdees maintained their independence of Rome. The Waldenses, *though long harried and martyred by papal persecutions, have never submitted to the papacy*. Thus it is clear that Britain, France and Germany did *not owe* their conversion to Christianity to *the Church of Rome*, but as the eminent jurist Blackstone wrote, "*the ancient Church of Britain, by whomsoever planted, was a stranger to the bishop of Rome, and all his pretended authority*."

THE REFORMED OR PROTESTANT CHURCH BEGAN AT PENTECOST, NOT AT THE REFORMATION

Did the Reformed or Protestant Church begin, as some allege, at the Reformation in the 16th century?

It did *not*. Though the name "Protestant" began at that time, to distinguish it from the papal body, Protestant doctrine, which is the true criterion by which to judge any Church, *began at Pentecost;* for Holy Scripture shows plainly that Protestant doctrines were the *original apostolic doctrines*. The Protestant Church of the Reformation did *not originate new teachings;* it was simply *a revival, a continuation of the primitive apostolic church, with the Lord Jesus Christ as its only Mediator and Head, the Holy Spirit as its Teacher and Sanctifier,* and *the Word of God as its divine law and sole rule of faith*. The Reformation merely swept away the grave errors which false leaders had introduced and *reinstated those precious doctrines which Christ had originally given* to save the world. After several centuries, through false leadership and gradual corruption the Christian Church entered the tunnel of the Dark Ages, when the popes gained control; but at the Reformation the Church *emerged again into the sunshine of God's saving grace;* never again, please God, to be eclipsed or obscured. The Reformers rightly called the Church's reappearance LUX EX TENEBRIS, the "Light shining out of Darkness!" And the motto of the Scottish Church, symbolizing the re-publication of God's precious Word and the Church's trial by fire, *applies* also to the noble martyrs of every Reformed Communion, who witnessed for God in the face of persecution and death,—"The Bush that burned, *but was not consumed!*" Ex. 3:2, Rev. 2:10. The English speaking world will *never forget "the noble army of martyrs"*—Ridley, Latimer, Anne Askew, Wishart, Margaret Wilson, and a host of others, *who died for their Protestant faith!* These martyrs met death with such calmness and courage that some of the vast crowd of spectators were by their noble example *won for Christ.* Latimer said to his companion Ridley, just before they were burned at the stake October 15, 1555: "FEAR NOT, BROTHER: WE SHALL THIS DAY LIGHT SUCH A CANDLE IN ENGLAND AS SHALL, BY THE GRACE OF GOD, NEVER BE EXTINGUISHED!" Bishop Hugh Latimer once quaintly said: "The most diligent prelate in all England is *the Devil.* He is never out of his diocese. His office is to *hinder religion,* maintain superstition, and *set up idolatry!* Where the devil is resident, then away with books and *up with candles!* away with Bibles and *up with beads!* away with the light of the Gospel, and up with the light of candles, *yea at noonday!"*

Why was the Reformation Church called Protestant?

Because in 1529 at the Diet of Spires (Speyer), Germany, the name was given to Martin Luther's followers to distinguish them from the followers of the pope. Romanists have stated that this name is purely negative, but this is a *mistake;* standard lexicons show that it means not only to *protest against what is false and wrong,* but also *positively* to *profess and declare that which is true and right.* The Protestant body protested against the Church of Rome's grave errors, and her unchristian attitude toward those who did not submit to her demands; and it also *proclaimed the true Gospel,* and their *right to worship God according to conscience and the Word of God,* under the imperial government of Charles V. Opposed to Rome's false dogmas of a pope and indulgences, Luther and the brave Reformers proclaimed *Christ* as the *only Head and Lord of the Church,* and *salvation not by dead works* of human merit, but *by faith in Christ's redeeming blood,*—"THE JUST SHALL LIVE BY FAITH."* This glorious life-giving truth the Holy Spirit had revealed to the *prophet Habakkuk 600 years before Christ;* Habakkuk passed on this sacred treasure *to St. Paul;* St. Paul *to Augustine;*[1] Augustine to *Bernard*[2] *of Clairvaux,* and Bernard *to Martin Luther.* Here is the *only true apostolic succession,*—not a magical something, supposed to be *mechanically conveyed by men's hands,* but *a spiritual succession of godly men, full of faith and the Holy Ghost,* who *received and handed down* THE ETERNAL TRUTH OF GOD'S FREE GRACE AND SALVATION IN CHRIST THE SON OF GOD ALONE! Heb. 2:4, 10:38, Rom. 5:1.

Concerning the character of Luther, Prof. Froude of Oxford says: "Luther himself was one of the grandest men that ever lived on earth. Never was anyone *more loyal to the light that was in him, braver, truer,* or *wider-minded in the noblest sense of the word.* The share of the work that fell to him, Luther accomplished most perfectly. In an age when the absolutism and intolerance of popery

---

* JUSTIFICATION BY FAITH IN THE RIGHTEOUSNESS OF CHRIST—This was the central truth of Luther's preaching. If we inquire what was the faith which chiefly inspired the Reformers, we shall find that the main article was the doctrine which as preached by Luther had given rise to the whole Protestant movement. Conterini wrote a treatise on it, which Pole speaks of in highest praise: "You have brought to light the jewel which the Church kept half concealed." Pole was of opinion that the Scripture, taken in its profoundest context, preaches nothing but this doctrine. He esteemed his friend, happy that he had been the first to promulgate *"this holy, fruitful and indispensable truth."* We see in the following passage how distinctly he taught this doctrine. "The Gospel is no other than the blessed tidings that the only-begotten Son of God, clad in our flesh, hath made satisfaction for us to the justice of the Eternal Father. He who believes this enters into the Kingdom of God. He enjoys the universal pardon; from a carnal, he becomes a spiritual, creature; from a child of wrath, a child of grace. He lives in a sweet peace of conscience."

[1] The great Augustine of Hippo, Africa, who died A.D. 430.

[2] Bernard wrote: "Thou art as strong to justify as thou art to pardon. Wherefore whosoever smitten with compunction for his sins, hungers and thirsts after righteousness, let him believe on Thee, who justifieth the ungodly; *and being justified by faith alone, he will have peace with God!"*

This truth was also powerfully proclaimed by that shining light of the English Church, Richard Hooker; "Let it be counted as folly, or phrensy, or fury, or whatsoever; it is our wisdom and comfort; and WE CARE FOR NO KNOWLEDGE IN THE WORLD BUT THIS; that MAN HATH SINNED, AND GOD HATH SUFFERED; THAT GOD HATH MADE HIMSELF THE SIN OF MEN, AND THAT MEN ARE MADE THE RIGHTEOUSNESS OF GOD!"

dominated Europe, Luther *stood for liberty of conscience*. He said, "the Papists must bear with us, and we with them. If they will not follow us, we must *not force them*. Wherever they can, they will hang, burn, behead, and strangle us. I shall be persecuted as long as I live, and *most likely killed!* But it must come to this at last,— *everyone must be allowed to believe according to his conscience, and answer for his belief to his Maker*."

WHY A REFORMATION?

Why was the Protestant Church also called Reformed?

Because under the misrule of the popes, the Church had become *so corrupt*, that it must either be *reformed or perish*.

Do papal historians acknowledge that there was great corruption in the Church and urgent need of reformation?

While some Roman Catholic books do not candidly present the facts and keep the laity and youth of the Church in ignorance of true history, yet outstanding papal writers have plainly presented the shameful corruption of the Church and the urgent need of reformation.

Pope Adrian VI (1522, 1523) acknowledged, and instructed his nuncio at the Diet of Nuremberg to acknowledge, that the revolt of Germany against the Church had been *provoked by the immoralities and abominations of bishops and clergy*, and *especially of the* "HOLY SEE" ITSELF.

He said: "For a long time many abominations have existed near the Holy See; everything has been turned to evil. From the head corruption has spread to the members; *from the pope to the prelates;* we have *all gone astray;* there is *none of us that hath done well, no, not one*." Reinaldus, vol. II, page 363.

Cardinal Caraffa, who became pope Paul IV, said: "A reformation is now *so necessary* that it cannot be omitted *without mortal sin*."[1]

---

[1] The moral and spiritual corruption which forced a reformation pervaded all grades of the clergy and religious orders. Outrageous criminals, pleading "the benefit of the clergy" purchased exemption from the punishment which justice and the public welfare demanded. The great abbeys in England in the reign of Henry VII were notoriously corrupt, but probably not worse than those of other reigns and of other countries. A picture of their profligate brutality given by Cardinal Morton cannot for decency's sake be publicly described. The original account of these abbeys, presented in the Cardinal's report, called Morton's Register, is still preserved in the Archbishop of Canterbury's Library at Lambeth, London.

7

Cardinal Baronius, the historian of the Vatican, wrote concerning the deplorable condition of the Church in the 10th century: "How DEFORMED, HOW HIDEOUS WAS THE ASPECT OF THE CHURCH OF ROME WHEN IT WAS GOVERNED SOLELY BY SHAMELESS PROSTITUTES, WHO AT THEIR PLEASURE CHANGED THE POPES, DISPOSED OF BISHOPRICS, AND WHAT IS STILL MORE TERRIBLE, PLACED IN THE HOLY SEAT OF ST. PETER THEIR PARAMOURS AND BASTARDS!" *Ann. Eccles.—ann. 912.*

Baronius called Boniface IV, who was bishop of Rome in 896, and pope, *"a monster of vice."* Confirming Baronius' statements, another papal historian, Du Pin, remarks, "In such terms as these does the Cardinal lament the sad state of the Church during the 10th century"; adding, that "no one may suppose that the Cardinal wrote as an enemy of the Church."

ST. BRIDGET TESTIFIED AGAINST THE POPE

"The Revelations of St. Bridget," who died 1373, declared by pope Benedict XIV authentic, states, *"The pope* is a *murderer of souls;* he destroys and flays Christ's flock, more cruel than Judas, more unjust than Pilate. All the Ten Commandments he has changed into this one, *Money, money!* The pope and his clergy are *forerunners of Antichrist,* rather than servants of Christ."

The Bohemian chronicler A. di Cescky Brod, wrote: "Among the ecclesiastics there was no discipline; among the bishops, public simony; among the monks disorder without end; among laymen, no abuse that the ecclesiastics had *not already practised."* Mussolini, *John Huss, the Man of Truth.*

A ROMAN CATHOLIC ARCHBISHOP TESTIFIES TO THE GROSS IMPIETY OF THE ROMAN SEE

Gilbert Genebrard, Archbishop of Aix-la-chapelle, who died 1587, declared: "During nearly 150 years *about 50 popes have been apostates,—apostatical,* rather than apostolical. That is to say, *about one-fifth of all the popes* who have ever sat in the papal chair are hereby charged with *grievous criminality."* Littledale, *Plain Reasons,* page 209.

Concerning the godlessness and immorality of the papacy, Froude the historian, remarks, "No imagination could invent, no malice could exaggerate, what the papal court really became *under Alexander VI, Julius II and Leo X."*

Leo X scoffed at religion, saying to Cardinal Bembo, "All know how well the *fable of Christ has served us and ours!"* Krueger, page 166; Schick, page 241.

Did the Presbyterian Church begin with John Calvin[1] in Switzerland in 1536, or with John Knox[3] in Scotland in 1560?

No. The Presbyterian Church began in the age *when St. Peter called himself "a fellow-presbyter,"* and St. Paul enjoined, *"Ordain presbyters in every city."* Calvin and Knox *merely republished the Bible doctrines of saving grace,[2]* which had been buried under a

---

[1] John Calvin in one brief sentence expressed a wellnigh perfect summary of the true purpose and aim of all human life,—TO KNOW AND DO THE WILL OF GOD! This purpose and aim was fulfilled in his own noble life and character. Few leaders of men have appeared in history whose life was as pure and devoted to God and humanity, and whose influence for good was as profound and far-reaching as that of Calvin. He may be considered the outstanding theologian and Bible expositor of the Reformation.

[2] "Calvinism has ever borne an inflexible front to illusion and mendacity. It is enough to mention the name of William of Orange, or of Luther,—for on the points of which I am speaking, Luther was one with Calvin,—of your own Knox, and Andrew Melville, of Coligny, of our English Cromwell, of Milton, of John Bunyan. These were men possessed of all the qualities, which give nobility and grandeur to human nature—men whose life was as upright as their intellect was commanding, and their public aims untainted with selfishness; unalterably just where duty required them to be stern, but with the *tenderness of a woman in their hearts;* frank, true, cheerful, humorous, as *unlike sour fanatics as it is possible to imagine any one,* and able in some way to sound the keynote to which every brave and faithful heart in Europe instinctively vibrated!"

"The battle fought in Scotland was in reality the battle *between liberty and despotism;* and where, except in an intense and burning conviction that they were maintaining God's cause against the devil, could the poor Scotch people have found the strength for the unequal struggle which was forced upon them? Enlightenment you cannot have enough of, but it must be *true* enlightenment; and in the passion and resolution of brave and noble men there is often an inarticulate intelligence deeper than what can be expressed in words. It was thus "the Covenanters fought the fight and won the victory." Froude's *Calvinism.*

[3] John Knox, the hero of the Reformation in Scotland, was born at Haddington in 1505. Educated at the University of Glasgow, he was much influenced by George Wishard, who was burned at the stake as a martyr for his Protestant faith in 1546.

mass of Romish sacerdotalism and superstition, viz.: the Divine Sovereignty, the Kingship of *Christ as the only Head of the Church*, His *one atoning sacrifice for sin*, the New Birth and Sanctification by the Holy Spirit and the parity of the Christian ministry. These apostolic doctrines they proclaimed, as well as the *principles of civil and religious liberty*, just as Luther republished the cardinal doctrine of *justification by faith alone*. The *name* was new, but *not* the *doctrines and polity*.

Can one trace in history the gradual departure from apostolic doctrine and the introduction of the grave papal errors, which undermined the Christian Church *and* destroyed the original Christian faith?

Yes. Roman Catholic writers themselves have supplied abundant evidence by which *the downward course of the Church under papal misrule* can be traced, as it abandoned the simplicity and purity of apostolic times, and sank deeper and deeper into the mire of superstition and ungodliness; for as the papal system grew, *vital religion declined.*

In the 8th century (about A.D. 788) the worship of *saints, angels, and the Virgin Mary* came to be a common practice of the Church; and about the same time *images, the crucifix, etc.*, were *introduced.*

So-called "holy water" was borrowed from paganism about the year 1000.

The enforced celibacy of the clergy, monks and nuns, was introduced about 1074-9.

When the French captured the castle of St. Andrews, where Knox had taken refuge, he was condemned to the galleys as a common criminal. Eighteen months later when released, he went to England, preached at Berwick and Newcastle, and in 1554 visited Calvin in Geneva. Returning to Edinburgh in 1559, he bravely contended for the faith with Queen Mary, who was determined to force Romanism on the Scottish people. In 1560 Knox's Confession of Faith was adopted by the Scottish Assembly without change, and later his "History of the Reformation of Religion within the Realm of Scotland" was published in 6 volumes. Knox's great constructive work was the firm establishment of the Presbyterian Church in Scotland. Knox was a man of vigorous intellect, of great faith, courage and firmness of character. Queen Mary once said she "feared the prayers of John Knox more than all the armies of England." Knox died peacefully in Edinburgh in 1572, the year marked by the brutal massacre of the Huguenots in Paris on St. Bartholomew's Day.

Mechanical praying by rote with rosary beads, as in Buddhism, followed in 1090.

The sale of papal indulgences, which caused *unspeakable scandals throughout Europe,* was formally recognized about 1190.

The errors of Transubstantiation and the Mass became fixed dogmas at the Fourth Lateran Council under pope Innocent III in the year *1215.*

Auricular Confession of sin to a *priest, instead of to God,* also in 1215.

The false dogmas of Purgatory and Masses for the dead became fixed about 1438.

Tradition, and the *14 books called the Apocrypha,* were made canonical by the *Council of Trent (1546-1563).*

The invention of Papal Infallibility was adopted by the Vatican Council *in 1870.* Thus, as history plainly shows, radical departures from the apostolic faith, extending from the 8th to the 19th centuries, have *destroyed the precious system of saving truth* delivered by the Lord Jesus Christ to His Church, so that *now only an empty name and dead form is left* in the Roman body. So far was the Roman Catholic body from being the original Christian Church and its doctrines being the same as those taught by the apostles, as Rome alleges, history shows that the papacy and the bulk of papal dogmas did not come into existence *until hundreds of years after the apostolic age.* The list of radical changes given above shows plainly that melancholy process of decay, how the original powerful doctrines of God's saving grace have been *totally changed* or *buried,* under a mass of *sinful superstitions, which have led men far away from Christ and righteousness.*

TAKE WARNING FROM THE APOSTASY OF THE ROMAN CHURCH!

The apostasy of the Church of Rome presents *a solemn warning to the Reformed Church* of the ruin which is *sure to come* when leaders *presume to depart, even a little,* from the Church's God-given guide, the Holy Scriptures. For the command of God is explicit and repeated. "WHAT THING SOEVER I COMMAND YOU, OBSERVE TO DO IT.

THOU SHALT NOT ADD THERETO, NOR DIMINISH FROM IT." To disobey this plain command is *fatal;* it places one in *rebellion against God,* and *cuts him off from salvation.*

No tradition of men or human opinion may be substituted for the Word of the living God. The Church's safety, as well as the salvation of the individual, *depends on whole-hearted obedience to the whole Word of God,* and *in humble constant dependence on the Holy Spirit of God.* In view of the delusions of Modernist unbelief and of destructive criticism[1] of the Bible, which are *leading many to make shipwreck of their faith,* God is "solemnly warning us of the Protestant Church",

"This book of the Law shall not depart out of thy mouth—turn not from it to the right hand or to the left!" Deut. 6:6, 7, 8:3; Josh. 1:7, 8.

"Grieve not the Holy Spirit whereby ye are sealed to the day of redemption."—Eph. 4:33.

"Remember—*and repent;* or else I will come and will remove thy candlestick out of his place." Rev. 2:5.

"Take ye heed, *watch and pray!"* "Let him that thinketh he standeth, *take heed lest he fall!"* Mark 13:33, I Cor. 10:12.

---

[1] The tap-root of destructive criticism of the Holy Scriptures is the *evolutionary hypothesis,* which some of its former ablest advocatees, as Haeckel, and its opponents, as Virchow, have declared untenable and unprovable. In 1929 the President of the British Association for the Advancement of Science in South Africa, Prof. D. M. S. Watson, publicly stated in substance that he accepted the evolutionary theory *not* because it was *proved,* but because the alternative was *belief in Creation!* It might be well to remember the declaration of that great scientist, Lord Kelvin, who said: *"Scientific thought is compelled to accept the idea of a Creative Power."*

Liberal ministers of the Gospel and others who treat lightly the Word of God, and rashly adopt an unproved theory, should heed Lord Kelvin's rebuke: *"I marvel at the undue haste with which teachers in our universities and preachers in our pulpits are restating truths in terms of evolution, while evolution itself remains an unproved hypothesis in the laboratories of science!"*

Prof. J. D. Dana, of Yale University, a scholar of rare scientific attainments, wrote concerning the Genesis account of Creation, "I find it to be *in perfect accord with known science."*

Students who have teachers that speak slightingly of the Scriptures, should remember Prof. Dana's address to a graduating class in Yale: "Young men, as you go out into the world to face scientific problems, *remember that I, an old man,* who has given himself to scientific study all his life, say to you, that *there is nothing truer in all the Universe than the scientific statements contained in the Word of God!"*

Dr. Austin H. Clark, noted biologist of the Smithsonian Institute, Washington, D. C., says concerning the origin of man, "There are *no such things as 'missing links.'* 'Missing links' are *misinterpretations!"*

Dr. Etheridge, of the British Museum of London, bears the same testimony. He spoke emphatically, saying in substance, "If we examine carefully the countless specimens of human and animal life in this Museum, *we cannot find a single one to support the evolutionary hypothesis.*"

Well does the Holy Spirit through the Apostle Paul say, "The wisdom of this world is foolishness with God!" And God's inspired prophet 700 years before Christ reminds us of human frailty and need of humility: *"All flesh is grass, and the goodliness thereof is as the flower of the field. The grass withereth,* the *flower fadeth;* but the WORD OF OUR GOD SHALL STAND FOREVER!" Isaiah 40:8, I Peter 1:24, 25.

Chapter VII

THE SACRAMENTS

What is a Sacrament?

"A Sacrament is a holy ordinance instituted by Christ, wherein by sensible signs or symbols, Christ and His redemption are represented, sealed, and applied to believers." Matt. 28:19, 26:26, Westminster Shorter Catechism 92.

May a Church or its leaders, appoint sacraments?

No, they may not presume to do so. Because the Church belongs to Christ, only He as Head of the Church, could appoint them.

There Are Only Two Sacraments

According to Holy Scripture, how many Sacraments did our Lord institute?

Our Lord Jesus Christ instituted *only two sacraments,* Baptism, and the Lord's Supper. Matt. 28:19, 26:26, I Cor. 11:23-25.

How many Sacraments does the Papal Church have?

The Papal Church, contrary to Holy Scripture, presumes to teach that there are *seven* sacraments.

What proof does the Papal Church give for having seven sacraments?

Rome can give *no proof whatever* from Scripture. Having left God's Word, the papal church drifted about, uncertain as to the right number. Tertullian, obeying Scripture, names *but two.* Jerome, translator of the Vulgate (died 420), named *four.* Peter Damian (1072), twelve; Hugo St. Victor (1141), *thirty sacraments!* The Church of Rome at the Council of Florence in 1439, finally settled on *seven,* viz.: Baptism, Confirmation, the Eucharist, Penance, Extreme Unction, Orders, and Matrimony.

(90)

Why did the Church of Rome appoint seven sacraments?

Probably in order that it might *completely control the life* of its people by making them *absolutely dependent on the clergy.* The seven sacraments cover the most important events of human life, and the sacraments being controlled by the hierarchy, the laity are thus made absolutely dependent on the priesthood.

What grave error does the Church of Rome teach regarding the nature of the sacrament?

Rome teaches that the Sacraments confer divine grace *mechanically,* "by their outward action, as fire burns by its heat." This is called in Latin, *opus operatum.* Council of Trent, *Sess.* 7. Bellarmine, *de Effect. sacram.*, 1:9, 2:1.

What does the Word of God teach regarding the nature and operation of the sacraments?

The Word of God teaches *just the opposite* of the Roman dogma, viz.: that divine grace is *not* inherent in the sacraments, or in *him who administers them,* but is *bestowed directly by God the Holy Spirit* and is received by *a living faith.* I Cor. 12:8, 9, 11, Acts 10:45, Heb. 11:6, Eph. 2:8.

BAPTISM

What is Baptism?

Baptism is the application of water to a person in the name of the Holy Trinity. It is a sign or symbol *of the cleansing of the recipient's soul* by *the Holy Spirit,* through *faith in Christ as the Saviour.* It is also a sign and seal of the *dedication of the baptized person* to God and His service. Matt. 3:11, John 1:33, Acts 2:38, 18:8.

Should the children of believing parents be baptized?

Yes; and this is one of the *most precious, comforting truths of God's Holy Word.* Little children should be baptized by virtue of God's gracious covenant, which *includes the children with their parents,* "*The promise is to you and to your children.*"

There are many passages of Scripture which plainly show that children are *included with their parents* in God's everlasting covenant of grace and salvation. God promised Abraham, "I will establish My covenant between Me and thee, *and thy seed after thee* in their generations for an everlasting covenant to be a God to thee and *to thy seed after thee.*" Note that the inclusion of the children with their parents in the Covenant was stressed, for God *repeats the words,* "*and thy seed after thee.*" Gen. 17:7.

Peter at Pentecost called on those present to believe in Christ as their Saviour, and reminded them that God's covenant of salvation *included their children,* saying, "For the promise is to you and *to your children.*" Acts 2:39. The children, being thus included in the covenant, it was proper to administer to them the *sign and seal of the covenant,* viz.: baptism.

Again, Peter called on the people to repent and believe in Christ, saying, "Ye are the children of the prophets, and of *the covenant which God made with our fathers,* saying unto Abraham, "And in thy seed shall all the kindreds of the earth be blessed." Because they were children of the covenant, they had a *right to share in all the privileges of the covenant,* and *receive the seal of the covenant.*

The children of the covenant were promised that they should *all have the teaching of the Holy Spirit.* "And *all thy children* shall be *taught of the Lord;* and great shall be the peace of thy children." Isaiah 54:13. Again, "As for Me, this is My covenant with them, saith the Lord; My Spirit which is upon thee, and My words which I have put in thy mouth, shall not depart out of thy mouth, *nor out of the mouth of thy seed, nor out of the mouth of thy seed's seed,* saith the Lord, *from henceforth and forever.*" Is. 59:21.

"And it shall come to pass that I will pour out My Spirit upon all flesh, and your sons and your daughters shall prophesy," etc. Joel 2:28.

"Behold I, and *the children which God hath given me!*" Heb. 2:13.

Note carefully that the covenant must have a seal. *Under the* Old Dispensation *that seal was* circumcision, *which was symbolic of cleansing. What is the seal of the covenant* under the New Dispensation, *since circumcision was done away with?*

It was *baptism with water,* still symbolizing *the cleansing of the Holy Spirit.*

It is sometimes said that circumcision was a national or hygienic rite; but this is *an error,* for Scripture says plainly it had a *spiritual* meaning, it was a *"seal of righteousness by faith."* Rom. 4:11.

Again, "And they brought unto Him little children that He should touch them; and the disciples rebuked them. But when Jesus saw it, He was moved with indignation, and said unto them, 'Suffer the little children to come unto Me; *forbid them not;* for of such is the Kingdom of God.' And He took them up in His arms, and *blessed them,* laying His hands upon them." Mark 10:13-16.

Note that the disciples' objection to bringing little children to Christ for His blessing was *the same that some now make to baptizing little children,* viz.: that they are *too young to understand.* But Christ did *not think so,* for He rebuked the disciples, and *blessed the children.* Children are *never too young to receive Christ's blessing* or *the Holy Spirit;* for Scripture states plainly that John the Baptist was "filled with the Holy Ghost *from his very birth."* Luke 1:15. And so also was the prophet Jeremiah. Jer. 1:5.

It cannot be emphasized too strongly that just as circumcision, whose meaning was a spiritual one, "a seal of the righteousness of faith," was *administered to infants* under the covenant in the *Old Dispensation,* so *baptism is now administered* under the *New* Dispensation. To deny this is to hold that God's dealings with His people *under the Old Dispensation* was *more gracious and liberal than His dealings now under the New Dispensation,* which is clearly *not true.* If children were given the seal of the covenant under the Old Dispensation, why should they be *deprived of the seal of the covenant under the New?* Of course, they should *not be deprived of this privilege.* It is their birthright.

The fact that children *do not as yet understand the meaning of the covenant,* does not prevent the blessing which comes from the observance of the sacrament; for the parents *in faith* accept the terms of the Covenant and the Holy Spirit *graciously grants His blessing to both parents and children.* The special promises which God gives to the parents entitle them to believe that *if they do their duty in instructing the children and in praying with them* and *for them,* and throwing *all possible Christian influences around them,* that when the children come to the years of discretion the Holy Spirit will lead them *in faith* to *take upon themselves* the *sacred vows which their parents have in faith taken for them* in *their infancy.*

Those who oppose the baptism of children are waking up to the fact that they have been neglecting their children's nurture, for of late years we hear of parents dedicating their children. But does not the *same argument* that "children do not understand" apply to the *dedication* of children as to the *baptism* of children? It is not a matter of the children's understanding the sacrament, but of *parents having faith in God's holy Word,* and OBEYING HIS COMMAND. If parents believe in God's covenant of salvation for their children, of course, they ought to *give them the seal of that covenant.*

"Keep therefore the words of this covenant and do them; for ye stand this day all of you before the Lord your God, *your little ones,* your wives," etc.

"Therefore shall ye lay up my words in your heart and in your soul,—and ye shall *teach them your children,* speaking of them when thou sittest in thy house and when thou walkest by the way, when thou liest down, and when thou risest up—that your days may be multiplied and the *days of your children,* in the land which the Lord swore unto your father to give them." Deut. 11:18, 19.

"Now these are the commandments, the statutes and the judgments—that ye may do them, that thou mightest fear the Lord thy God, thou, and *thy son,* and thy *son's son, all the days of thy life*— And thou shalt *teach them diligently unto thy children* and shalt talk of them when thou sittest in thy house," etc. Deut. 6:1, 2, 7.

"O that there were such a heart in them that they would fear Me and *Keep all My commandments always* that it might be well with them and *with their children forever!"* Deut. 5:29.

"Thou shalt therefore keep His statutes and His commandments which I command thee this day, that it may go well with thee, and with *thy children after thee."* Deut. 4:40.

"The Lord said unto me, 'Gather Me the people together, and I will make them hear My words, that they may learn to fear Me all the days that they shall live upon the earth, and that they may *teach their children.'* " Deut. 4:10.

Notice the constant refrain, "Teach your children," "Thy sons and thy son's son," "that it might be well with them and with their children forever!" It shows that the children are included with their parents in the covenant, and therefore *have a right to the seal of the Covenant.*

"And ye fathers, provoke not your children to wrath, but bring them up in the nurture and admonition of the Lord." Eph. 6:4. The "nurture and admonition of the Lord" includes, of course, *prayer* and a *diligent use of all the means to lead the young to a saving knowledge of the Gospel.* If these are *faithfully used,* the Lord *promises to bless them to the salvation of the children.*

Does the benefit of baptism come from the water, or from him who administers the sacrament?

The benefit of baptism comes *neither* from the *water, nor* from *the minister;* it comes from the *blessing of the Holy Spirit,* and is received by the *believing soul* who through faith and prayer *lays hold of God's precious promises of grace.*

What grave error does the Church of Rome teach concerning baptism?

As seen above concerning the sacraments, Rome teaches the *mechanical efficacy* of baptism; that *without faith* or *conscious acceptance, "even while asleep,"* the baptized person's soul is regenerated and cleansed by virtue of the water of baptism! Bellarmine, *De Sac.,* 1, 9. But the Scriptures show that true baptism is of the *heart,* by the *inward working of the Spirit of God.* So St. Paul explained in his epistles. Rom. 2:25-29, 4:9, 10, I Cor. 7:19, Gal. 5:6.

Similarly, Eph. 5:26 states that Christ cleansed the Church "with the washing of water by the Word"; that is, *God's Word, is the instrument the Holy Spirit uses to cleanse the heart,* of which cleansing baptism with water is *the outward sign.* So also Titus 3:5. God our Saviour "saved us by the washing of regeneration and renewing of the Holy Ghost"; the washing of regeneration means the washing of the soul from sin, when regenerated by the Holy Spirit, of which the washing or baptism with water is the *outward symbol.* The Scriptures *nowhere teach* that baptism is *the means of regeneration.*

Regeneration is *always the work of the Holy Spirit,* who gives "the new heart," and cleanses the soul from sin. The *means* of regeneration is *the Word of God,* which water baptism represents. Ezek. 36:25, 26, John 3:3, 5.

What other distressing error does the papal church teach concerning baptism?

The Roman Church teaches that all who *die without baptism* are *eternally lost!* Bellarmine writes: "Those who die without baptism are adjudged to *condemnation and eternal death." De Amiss. Grat. et statu Pecc.,* 6:2.

What does the Reformed Church teach concerning little children who die unbaptized?

The Reformed Church teaches according to Scripture, that through the infinite mercy of God in Christ, those who have *not reached the age of responsibility,* as little children, are *included in the covenant of grace (regenerated by the Holy Spirit) and saved.* Matt. 19:14, Acts 2:39, Rom. 4:11, Jer. 1:5, Luke 1:15, Jonah 4:11.

THE LORD'S SUPPER, OR EUCHARIST

What is the sacrament of the Lord's Supper?

The Lord's Supper is a sacrament "wherein by giving and receiving bread and wine, according to Christ's appointment, His death is showed forth; and the worthy receivers are, *not after a corporal and carnal manner,* but by *faith,* made partakers of His body and blood *with all His benefits,* to their spiritual nourishment and growth in grace." Matt. 26:26-29, I Cor. 11:26, I Cor. 10:16, Eph. 3:17, Westminster Shorter Catechism, 96.

Our Lord Jesus Christ on the night of His betrayal, took bread and wine, and blessing them, broke the bread and poured out the wine, as symbols of his broken body and shed blood, and commanded His disciples to eat and drink them *in remembrance of His atoning death for their sins.* He also commanded His Church to celebrate this solemn memorial until He should return in power and glory to judge the world and take His people home to heaven. I Cor. 11:25, 26, John 14:3, Matt. 26:31, 34, Luke 22:14-20.

Did our Lord make any change in the bread and wine, or did these elements remain the same throughout the celebration of the sacrament?

The Scriptures clearly show that our Lord *made no change whatever in the elements:* the bread *remained bread,* and the wine *remained wine* throughout the sacrament.

What grave error does the Roman Catholic Church teach concerning the bread and the wine?

The Roman Church, directly contrary to the declarations of Holy Scripture, teaches that when the priest utters the words, *"This is my body,"* the bread and wine are *completely changed,* and *become the literal flesh and blood of Christ's body;* that the communicant eats *this literal flesh and blood,* and by it he is *made good* and *saved.* Rome asserts, that "after the consecration, there is *no more of the bread and wine* of the sacrament," but "that the substance of the bread and wine is *changed into the proper substance of the body and blood of Christ."* Rome's words are, "Jesus Christ is received *by the mouth of the body,"* that is, by the *mouth of the communicant.* Council of Trent, sess., 13:2, 4, 8. Bellarmine, *De Euchar.,* 3:18.

Anyone can see, if he examines Scripture carefully, that the Roman Church has committed *a great sin by falsely asserting* that there has been *a complete change in the substance of the bread and wine,* for Scripture speaks of the bread and wine *remaining the very same at the end of the sacrament.* There was *no change whatever.* The Roman Church has *presumptuously disregarded Holy Scripture,* and accepted in its place the *false assertions of men.*

CHRIST'S WORDS WERE FIGURATIVE

When our Lord said, "This is My body," "This is My blood," was He speaking literally, or figuratively?

The Scriptures give abundant evidence that He was speaking *figuratively, not* literally. He meant, "this bread *represents My body* broken on the cross for you." "This cup *represents My blood* shed for you." Notice that He *speaks figuratively* in using the word "cup" for the *contents of the cup,* the wine; this the Romanists also acknowledge.

THE BREAD AND WINE REMAIN UNCHANGED

What is the evidence that Christ spoke figuratively *and that the bread and wine* remain unchanged?

1. The fact that our Lord constantly used figures of speech, as the Jews did then, and as we do now. He said, "I am the Door"; "I am the Bread"; "the Vine"; "the Shepherd"; "ye are the branches"; "the salt"; "the light"; etc., etc. These were *all figurative statements,* and were well understood. When He said, "I am the Door," of course He did not mean a *literal wooden door,* with *lock* and *hinges!* When He said "I am the Vine, ye are the branches," He did *not mean* a *literal grape vine* with branches. He meant "this vine *represents Me,* and these branches *represent you,*" and "the oneness of the vine and its branches represents the *spiritual oneness* of you believers with Me, your Lord and Saviour."

Note that these statements are *not true,* if taken literally, and Christ's disciples had *no difficulty in understanding His figures of speech,* many of which He and the apostles frequently used.

2. The fact that our Lord made *no mention of a change* in the bread and wine, as *He surely would have done* had He meant us to believe that a change had actually taken place. He made no mention whatever of a change, and so *no one has a right to assert that there was a change,* for that would be disobeying the command that nothing be added to Scripture. Rev. 22:18, Deut. 4:2, 12:32.

3. After the prayer of consecration and the declaration, "This is My body," when the Church of Rome asserts a change took place, our Lord *still declares the elements* to be *bread and wine.* He says, "this bread," "this cup," showing that *no change into flesh and blood has taken place.* At the close of the sacrament, after they had eaten the elements, He again speaks of *"this fruit of the vine,"* showing that *the elements had remained the same,* that what they had drunk was *wine, not* blood. Matt. 26:29, I Cor. 11:26.

4. Again, when our Lord held the bread and wine in his hands, it is impossible that He meant they were *His literal body,* for at that very moment, *His whole body was sitting at the table before His disciples!*

5. The Church of Rome's assertion "that Jesus Christ is received by the mouth of body" *directly contradicts many Scriptures* which declare that Christ and His salvation are received *by faith alone.* "Justified by the faith of Jesus Christ," that is, "justified by trusting Christ as Saviour." "Live by the faith of the Son of God"; "Made children of God *by faith in Him";* "Christ dwelling in your hearts *by faith";* "without faith it is impossible to please Him"; "Whatsoever is *not of faith* is *sin."* According to Scripture *every blessing of salvation is received by faith,* and *never* "by *the mouth of the body."* Gal. 2:16, 20, 3:22, 26, Eph. 3:12, 17, Rom. 14:23, Hebrews 11:6. A discerning Spanish priest, Maldonate (Maldonado), was once explaining the expressions "Come to me," "Eating," etc., and said in homely language, "Do not prepare your teeth and your belly for it (the "bread of life"), but *believe in Him* and you have *eaten Him!"* John 6:35, 50, 51. The priest thus held the true Protestant doctrine, as taught in Holy Scripture!

6. Note also that the Roman Church's claim that a miracle is wrought by the change of the bread and wine into Christ's literal body and blood is wholly mistaken because it does *not agree with the real miracles of our Lord,* which were *all evident to the human senses.* Sight, touch, taste, smell, bore witness to the *genuineness of Christ's miracles,* when He fed the five thousand, stilled the tempest, raised the dead, and cast out devils. And so if a real miracle had taken place in the Sacrament, if the bread and wine had truly been changed into flesh and blood, *the senses would surely have perceived it.* But every communicant knows that the bread is *still bread,* and the wine *still wine,* because these look, taste, smell and feel like bread and wine, and *nothing else.* It is apparent to the communicant's *senses* that there has been *no change whatever.* To allege otherwise, as the Roman Church does, is clearly unreasonable and untrue, for it *rejects the testimony of the senses,* and *discredits the mighty miracles of our Lord.*

7. Another proof that what Christ gave His disciples to eat in the sacrament was simple bread and wine, and *not His flesh and blood is this,*—a literal interpretation, that what the priest gives the communicant to eat is actual flesh and blood makes the sacrament *a*

8

form of cannibalism—a thought too horrible and repulsive to dwell upon!

8. Note also that our Saviour rebuked the Jews *for misunderstanding His words,* just as the Church of Rome *now misunderstands them.* They took His words *literally* and imagined He said that *His very flesh and blood* were *to be eaten.* Christ then reproved them, and said in substance, "Even if you could eat the flesh and blood of My body, it would *do you no good.* It is the *spiritual* food that I give, the *saving truth of My words,* that *gives life.*" "It is the spirit that quickeneth, the *flesh profiteth nothing;* the *words* that I speak unto you, they are *spirit* and they are *life!*" *John 6:63.*

9. Again, *our Lord's bodily ascension to heaven* proves that His *literal* flesh and blood are *not eaten in the Sacrament.* Christ's sacred body is *no longer on earth.* It is *in heaven,* and *will not return to the earth* until He comes in majesty and power to judge the world, and take His people home to glory. Luke 24:51, Acts 1:9, 11.

If "flesh and blood" are not to be taken literally, what is the meaning?

"Flesh and blood" figuratively mean Christ's *atonement for our sins,* made by His *death on the Cross;* that *perfect redemption* which He wrought out *by His sufferings and death, as the sinner's substitute.*

Why does our Saviour use the figure of "eating" and "drinking" in partaking of the Sacrament?

To show that *faith is to the soul* what *eating and drinking* are to *the body.* By eating and drinking food is received, assimilated and *sustains the life of the body;* so *by faith* the saving truth of Christ and *His vicarious atonement for sin* are *received, made our own,* and *become the very life of the soul.*

Rome's Eucharist A Medieval Superstition

Was not the Roman Eucharist, including Transubstantiation and the Mass, a Medieval error which became a fixed dogma at a very late date?

The Roman dogmas of the Eucharist was a *medieval superstition,* intended to *impress ignorant people* and greatly *increase the power of the clergy,* by making the priest appear to *have miraculous power,* and the people *practically dependent on them for salvation;* for it is *falsely asserted* that in the sacrament they *repeat the sacrifice* which the *Son of God offered on the cross* to atone for the sins of the world. They also use the Greek name Eucharist for the sacrament instead of the simple Scriptural name of the Lord's Supper (I Cor. 11:20), in order to *throw a veil of mystery over it,* similar to their use of the Latin language in the liturgy. It did not become a formal doctrine *until the thirteenth century, A.D. 1215!*

Has not the Roman Church's monstrous teaching, that communicants in the sacrament eat the literal flesh and blood of Christ, *and that Roman priests have* power to change a wafer into Christ's body, *shocked many intelligent, earnest men, and* turned them away from Christ and salvation?

This gross heresy of the Church of Rome, acceptance of which is demanded of every communicant under threat of expulsion from the Church and *of eternal condemnation,* has driven many honest people, who saw that there was *no such doctrine in the Bible,* away from the Christian religion *into atheism!* How could it be otherwise, when men are forced to *accept as true,* what they know to be false? For if men think at all, they know that what the papal church requires them to believe in the Eucharist, under penalty of an eternal curse, is *a monstrous untruth.* They *know* they are eating a wafer (bread) and *not flesh and blood;* and they know that *no sinful human priest can offer a real atoning sacrifice for sin; only* the *Almighty Son of God can do that,* and He *actually did it on the cross,* "ONCE FOR ALL." Heb. 9:26, 10:10.

In celebrating the sacrament of the Lord's Supper, what other grave sin does the Church of Rome commit?

The Church of Rome refuses to *give the wine to the laity.* The pope and priests presume to *mutilate God's holy ordinance,* and deprive believers of *half the benefit of the sacrament,* thus committing the great sin of sacrilege. Rome asserts, "that Christian people for whom Jesus Christ hath shed His blood, *ought not to have the use of the cup.*" Council of Constance, *sess.* 13, Council of Trent, *sess.* 21, 12. Bellarmine, *De Euchar.*, 4:20.

Is not withholding the wine of the sacrament from the laity, and the celebrant appropriating it all for himself, a gross violation of Christ's command?

It is a *flagrant act of disobedience to the sovereign Lord;* for Christ commanded *all believers* to partake of the cup, saying, "All of you, drink of it," see the Greek, Matt. 26:27. And Mark records, "*They all drank of it.*" Mark 14:23.

The Council of Trent adds this threat: "If anyone saith that the Church of Rome was not moved by just causes to order that laity, and clergy who do not celebrate, shall communicate *only under the species of bread,* or that she hath erred therein, *let him be accursed.*" What audacity for any Council of sinful men to *claim "just causes"* to *forbid* what *Almighty God has clearly commanded!* Is not this a sure mark of *apostasy?* What awful impiety to curse those who humbly obey God's command given in Holy Scripture!

Was not the Church of Rome, in withholding the wine from the people, guilty of gross inconsistency, as well as guilty of violating God's command?

Yes, but this is only one of many inconsistencies in Roman Church practices. The Canon, requiring *Communion in one kind* (i.e., withholding the wine from the laity) was passed June 15, 1415, and at that time the Roman Church was *without a Head.* The same Council that enacted this decree had deposed pope John XXIII on *May 29, 1415,* and his successor was *not elected until November 11, 1417.* According to Church law therefore, the enactment of this Canon was *illegal,* because it was passed *without the sanction or authority of a pope.* And yet "infallible" popes have continued to observe this *illegal enactment* ever since!

It should be noted also, in passing, that according to high authority, the Roman Church is *uncertain* as to the *valid performance of its sacraments,* for Cardinal Bellarmine declared, "*No one can be certain* with the certainty of faith that he *receives a true sacrament,* because the sacrament cannot be valid *without the intention of the*

minister (celebrant) and *no man can know another's intention!"
Disput, Cont. de Justitia* III, 8, 5.

It follows inevitably from this, if Cardinal Bellarmine told the
truth, that *no* Roman Catholic *can be sure that he has ever* been
baptized, confirmed, absolved, or received communion, because he
cannot know the intention of the officiating priest! In contrast, how
precious is the true Scriptural and Reformed doctrine that sincere
believers *may surely know.* The validity of the sacraments does *not
depend on the intention of any priest,* but *on the* faithfulness of
Almighty God *and* His everlasting covenant of grace, which, to the
faith of the true believer, are *as sure as the eternal Rock of Ages!*
Matt. 24:35. Thank God, the teaching of God's Holy Word and
of the Protestant faith drawn from that Word, is wholly different
from that of the Church of Rome! The Bible clearly teaches that
believers may *surely know that they are saved.* St. John in his first
Epistle says: "These things have I written unto you that ye may
KNOW THAT YE HAVE ETERNAL LIFE."

*How does the requirement of the Roman Church, that communi-
cants* abstain from all food for hours before partaking of the sacrament, *appear in the light of Scripture?*

The requirement that communicants abstain from all food for
hours before partaking of the sacrament is nothing else than *a
harmful superstition;* for it *directly conflicts with Holy Scripture*
which represents the disciples as partaking of the Lord's Supper
immediately after they had eaten the Passover. Mark records, *"As
they did eat,* our Lord took bread, blessed it and broke it, and gave
to them," etc. Matthew's statement is similar, *"As they were eating,
Jesus took bread,"* etc. Therefore this rule of the Roman Church
requiring that the communicant fast for hours before eating the
Lord's Supper has *no authority in Scripture,* and is *directly contrary
to what Christ did in instituting the Eucharist, just at the close of
the Passover feast.* Mark 14:22, Matt. 26:26.

Was not withholding the cup from the laity not only contrary *to
Holy Scripture, but also to* the practice of the early Church?

Withholding the cup from the laity was indeed contrary to the
command of Christ and also *to the practice of the early Church.*

Leo I, bishop of Rome, denounced the Manichaeans for *refusing to take the cup in communion.* So also Gelasius I, bishop of Rome, 492 to 496, wrote of those who abstained from the wine of the sacrament: "Either receive the sacrament *in its entirety,* or be *excluded from* the sacrament *entirely,* because a division of the *mystery cannot take place* without *great sacrilege." Corp. Jur. Can. Decre* 3:11, 12.

Regarding the Communion, does not history show how popes contradicted one another, *each claiming to be "infallible"?*

History shows plainly that "infallible" popes and Church Councils contradicted each other concerning the matter of celebrating the Communion in one or both kinds.

The Council of Clermont, A.D. 1095, presided over by Pope Urban II, decreed in Canon 28 that "no one shall communicate at the altar unless he receive the body and blood of Christ *separately"* (that is, *in both kinds).* So also Pope Paschal II decreed A.D. 1118, "In receiving the Lord's body and blood, let the Lord's practice be *observed;* for we know that the bread was given *separately,* and the wine *separately by the Lord Himself,"* i.e., in *both kinds.* Four popes and a Council of 218 bishops and abbots decided for communion *with both bread and wine,* but at the Council of Constance in 1415 this was *reversed,* and a canon decreeing *half communion,* that is, *withholding the wine from the laity,* was passed instead! Into such strange confusion do leaders fall, who substitute *tradition* or *their own arbitrary opinions for the Word of God and the plain command of Christ! Letter* of Rev. H. A. Ironside, page 11.

Does the Reformed Church obey the divine command in administering both bread and wine in the sacrament?

The Reformed Church gladly obeys Christ's command and welcomes all true believers to partake of *both the bread and the wine.*

CHRIST REALLY PRESENT IN THE SACRAMENT

Does the Reformed or Protestant Church teach the real presence of Christ in the Lord's Supper?

The Reformed or Protestant Church does teach *the real presence of our Lord* in the sacrament; *not* His *bodily* presence, for *His body is in heaven;* but His *spiritual* presence. To the loving, believing heart our gracious Saviour is *truly present* to bless. Rev. 3:20.

Does not St. Peter, in another connection, teach the Reformed doctrine of Christ's presence; not bodily, but spiritual?

The Holy Spirit, speaking through St. Peter, *does teach* the Reformed doctrine of Christ's presence in those beautiful words: *"Whom having not seen, ye love; in whom though now ye see Him not, yet believing, ye rejoice with joy unspeakable and full of glory."* Here is Christ's *real, spiritual presence;* in this *we rejoice in the Lord's Supper.* I Peter 1:8.

THE ONE ATONING SACRIFICE FOR SIN

What is the only hope of guilty humanity for time and eternity?

The only hope of mankind for time and eternity is in the *perfect atoning sacrifice for sin* which the *Son of God offered on the cross of Calvary.* "Behold, the *Lamb of God,* which *taketh away the sin of the world."* John 1:29.

What did Christ intend the Lord's Supper to be, in relation to His atoning death on the Cross?

Christ declared that the Lord's Supper was intended to be *commemorative,* a *reminder* or *memorial* of His precious death on the Cross. Luke records His words: "This do *in remembrance* of Me." Luke 22:19. St. Paul repeats the words "this do *in remembrance of Me,"* as He gave them the bread, and also as He gave them the wine, "this do ye, as often as ye drink it, *in remembrance of Me."* I Cor. 11:24, 25. Then in order to show that the Lord's Supper was intended to be a *reminder of His death on Calvary,* He repeats the same thought in different words, "For as often as ye eat this bread and drink this cup, ye *do shew the Lord's death till He come!"* καταγέλλω "to *declare, announce* or *publish"* Christ's atoning death on the cross till He comes again in glory.

What fatal error does the Roman Catholic Church make concerning Christ's atoning sacrifice?

It presumes to teach that Christ's atoning sacrifice *can be repeated,* or *offered anew by men:* that a sinful human priest may offer it; and that in the so-called Mass the Roman priest does repeat, or offer again, *the same atoning sacrifice which our divine Redeemer offered on Calvary* 1900 years ago.

Does Holy Scripture teach that Christ's atoning sacrifice for sin could ever be repeated or offered up again?

Never. Scripture teaches that *no mere man* could *make atonement for sin,* and *no human priest* could *offer the sacrifice of Calvary: only the Son of God could offer it;* and He did offer this atoning sacrifice *only once* on the Cross—"ONCE FOR ALL." Hebrews 9:14, 13:20, 10:10.

What proof does the Church of Rome give for her blasphemous assertion *that her priests can repeat the atoning sacrifice of Christ?*

No real proof whatever; for this unholy dogma *contradicts many declarations* of God's Holy Word.

Is not the whole conception *of the Roman Mass* a fabrication of the Dark Ages, exalting the power of the priests *at* the expense of our Saviour, and His one ever-prevalent sacrifice for sin?

The *whole conception of the Roman Mass* was an *invention of Satan in the Dark Ages,* which falsely makes the priest appear to have power to offer a true atoning sacrifice for sin,—all of which is *directly contrary to the Word of God,* and *grossly dishonors the blessed Redeemer of men,* giving glory to the creature which *belongs only to the Creator.* Rom. 1:25.

What name do Romanists often give to the priest usurping the high position, honor and power *of the Creator?*

The Roman Church often *blasphemously calls* the sinful priest, *"alter Christus," "the other Christ." This horrible sin* St. Paul warns against as a mark of *apostasy,* calling the guilty party "that man of sin, the son of perdition, who opposeth and exalteth himself above all that is called God; so that he *as God sitteth in the temple of God,* shewing *himself that he is God."* Any man who allows himself to be called *alter Christus,* and *claims to repeat the divine sacrifice of the Son of God on Calvary,* is *guilty of this terrible sin.* II Thess. 2:3, 4.

THE DIVINE SACRIFICE OF THE CROSS CAN NEVER BE REPEATED

Does not the Word of God often declare that there is only one true *atoning sacrifice for sin; that the* Son of God offered it by His vicarious sufferings and death; *and that* this perfect Atonement for sin avails for all ages, *and will* never pass away?

The Word of God clearly teaches this. It is the *central theme* of the *Epistle to the Hebrews;* and to it the *whole Old Testament,* especially the *Levitical priesthood* and *sacrifices, directly pointed.* No less than *ten* times in Hebrews is it proclaimed that Christ, the *one and only* great priest of His people, has offered the *one and only Sacrifice for sin* under the New Covenant; and that *this divine sacrifice the Son of God Himself offered* ONCE FOR ALL *time,* and *it could never be repeated.*

What are these ten passages which show the perfection and finality of Christ's one atoning sacrifice?

Scripture declares, both negatively and positively, that the Son of God's sacrifice, *unlike* the Old Testament sacrifices, was offered:

1. *"Not* daily." Heb. 7:27.

2. *"Nor* often." Heb. 9:25.

3. *"Nor often times."* Heb. 10:11.

4. "But *once only.* 'This He did *once,* when He offered up Himself.'" Heb. 7:27.

5. "He entered in *once* into the Holy Place, having obtained eternal redemption for us." Heb. 9:12.

6 and 7. "And as it is appointed unto men *once* to die, but after this the Judgment; so Christ was *once* offered to bear the sins of many." Heb. 9:27, 28.

8. "By the which will we are sanctified through the *offering of the body of Jesus Christ once for all."* Heb. 10:10. The Greek ἐφάπαξ means *once for all,* "once and no more."

9. "But this man after He had offered *one* sacrifice for sins *forever,* sat down on the right hand of God." Heb. 10:12.

10. "For by *one* offering He hath *perfected forever* them that are sanctified." Heb. 10:14.

It seems impossible to find language more clear and explicit, repeatedly declaring that there is *only one atoning sacrifice for sin*, which can satisfy divine justice. That our Lord Jesus Christ *offered this on Calvary once for all;* and that for this divine sacrifice there can *be no substitute,* and of it there *can be no repetition.*

No human being could offer the divine sacrifice, only the *eternal Son of God could do that.* And to claim as the Roman Church does, that her priests do offer it, is the *great sin of blasphemy against God,* and a *gross disparagement of the glorious Saviour,* the Son of God.

If a Roman priest were literally repeating in the Mass the sacrifice of Calvary, as is falsely claimed, would he not *be* guilty of an unpardonable sin?

Yes, he would, for he would be *"crucifying the Son of God afresh,"* which in Hebrews 6:6 is given as the *sin of apostates.*

And if the theory of the Mass were really true, would not Roman priests, saying thousands of Masses all over the world, be torturing the Saviour afresh with the agonies of the Cross?

Yes, that is true; though the thought is *too awful to dwell upon.* But thank God the Roman Mass is *not true;* for Holy Scripture declares that our gracious Redeemer no longer suffers for sin—He *"dieth no more,"* but is now *highly exalted in heaven, triumphant over sin and suffering, death and hell.* Rom. 6:9, 10, 8:34, Phil. 2:9-11.

How does the Church of Rome try to evade the shocking consequences of her mistaken doctrine of the Mass, *that the priest* repeats Christ's sacrifice of the Cross?

The Church of Rome declares that the sacrifice the priest offers in the Mass is a *"bloodless sacrifice."* But if "bloodless," then it is *not a real sacrifice;* for God's Word declares, "It is *the blood that maketh atonement,"* and, *"without shedding of blood is no remission."* Levit. 17:11, Heb. 9:22.

What fact shows that the so-called Sacrifice offered in the Mass *is* counterfeit *and can* never save sinners?

The fact that Christ's perfect atoning sacrifice offered on Calvary is *not* held *to be sufficient,* but that it is *necessary also* to have *a*

Roman priest repeat that sacrifice in the Mass. Unless the priest repeats the sacrifice in the Mass, *the sacrifice of Christ cannot avail,* that is to say, is *incomplete!* In other words, according to the teaching of the Church of Rome, atonement is *in part* made by *the death of Christ* and *in part* made by what *the priest does;* which directly *contradicts the Word of God, dishonors the Saviour* and *can never save men.*

What does a careful survey of Holy Scripture show concerning the Lord's Supper?

Scripture shows that the Reformed doctrine of the Lord's Supper is the *true apostolic doctrine;* that the whole theory of *the Roman Mass,* and of *priests repeating Christ's sacrifice of Calvary* is *directly contrary to Holy Scripture* and *dishonors the great Redeemer.* Moreover the Reformed doctrine is *full of comfort and strength* to *the believer;* Christ is *truly present in the sacrament* and *fills our hearts with joy and peace,* and this doctrine renders, as is justly due, all *glory and praise to the crucified and risen Saviour,* and *not* to a sinful human being. For it cannot be repeated too often, the Roman heresies of Transubstantiation and the Mass are *a gross perversion of Holy Scripture, offering a counterfeit atonement* which *can never take away sin,* but like a broken reed will pierce the hand that leans upon it, and will *utterly fail the sinner in the Day of Judgment.*

CHAPTER VIII

THE MEDIATOR AND THE FORGIVENESS OF SINS

How many Mediators are there between God and men?

The Word of God declares there is *only one Mediator and Advocate,* the Lord Jesus Christ. "There is one God, and one Mediator between God and men, the man Christ Jesus." I Tim. 2:5. He is the Mediator of the New Covenant. Heb. 9:15, 8:6. "Ye are come to Jesus, the Mediator of the New Covenant." Heb. 12:24.

The Lord Jesus Christ is also the *only Advocate for sinners.* "No man cometh unto the Father but by Me." "If any man sin, we have an Advocate with the Father Jesus Christ, the righteous; and He is the propitiation for our sins, and not for ours only, but also for the sins of the whole world." I John 2:1, 2. *"As Mediator and Advocate, Christ ever lives to make intercession for all who come unto God by Him."* Heb. 7:25, 9:24, Rom. 8:34.

Why is Christ the only *Mediator and Advocate for all mankind?*

Our Lord is the only Mediator and Advocate for all men, because He alone has both *a divine* and *a human nature,* standing between the holy God and sinful men; and also because of the perfect atoning sacrifice for sin which *He alone as the Son of God could offer,* and *did offer, on the cross.* Through Him alone our unworthy prayers, praises and service become acceptable to the Father; and through Him alone All grace and blessing are conveyed from the Father to us. "Through whom we have access by one Spirit unto the Father." Eph. 2:18. "By whom we have access by faith into this grace wherein we stand." Rom. 5:2, Heb. 4:15, 16. "Accepted in the Beloved." Eph. 1:6.

What does the Roman Church teach concerning mediators?

The Church of Rome, *directly contrary to Holy Scripture,* teaches "That there are *other mediators* beside the Lord Jesus Christ.

(110)

Bellarmine *De sanct., beat.* I, 20. So also Council of Trent. Such supposed mediators are Joseph, Mary, saints and angels, etc.

Does not the Church of Rome, in teaching that there are other mediators beside the Son of God, commit a great sin?

The Church of Rome, in teaching that there are other mediators beside the Son of God, *commits a great sin,* not only *in directly contradicting the Word of God,* but also in *making sinful beings usurp the position which belongs to Christ alone.*

The Roman Church also contradicts Holy Scripture in *falsely asserting* that "*the departed saints know our hearts and secret thoughts.*" Bellarmine *De sanct. beat.* I, 20. Note that the Word of God *declares exactly the opposite.* "Thou, Lord, who knowest the hearts of all men." Acts 1:24. "For Thou, *even Thou only,* knowest the hearts of all the children of men." I Kings 8:39. "*For Thou only* knowest the hearts of the children of men." II Chron. 6:30.

Did the early Christian Church hold that there was any other Mediator but Christ, or did they worship or invoke saints, angels and Mary?

No, they *did not.* The Fathers of the early Church *opposed all such worship and invocation.* There are only 4 instances in the New Testament of acts of reverence being offered to saints and angels, and *in all of these reverence and worship were promptly rejected and forbidden as disloyal to God.* Cornelius the Centurion wishing to worship Peter, the people of Lystra intending to sacrifice to Barnabas and Paul, and twice in Revelation John wished to worship the angel who showed him great things, but they all refused to allow it, and the angel said twice, *Worship God.* Acts 10:25, 26, 14:13-15, Rev. 19:10, 22:8, 9.

Irenaeus, A.D. 180, said, "The Church *does nothing by invocation of angels,* but by directing her prayers *to God in the name of the Lord Jesus Christ.*" So also St. Clement.

Origen, A.D. 230, declared, "*Every prayer and supplication,* intercession and thanksgiving is to be *sent up to God.* It is *not reasonable to invoke angels.* If they knew, they *would not suffer us to pray to any other but God.*"

Similarly, Athanasius *opposed* calling *on any created being in prayer.* A.D. 370.

St. Augustine, A.D. 389, taught, "Let not our religion be a cultus of *dead men.* The saints are to be honored by way of imitation, *not worshipped by way of religion."*

The Council of Laodicea, A.D. 360, decreed, "Christians *ought not to invoke angels.* To do so is to *forsake Christ* and be *guilty of idolatry.* Let such a one be *anathema."*

FORGIVENESS OF SINS

According to the Word of God, who can forgive sins?

Only Almighty God can forgive sins, for He alone is Judge and lawgiver. It is His holy law we have broken. The Lord Jesus Christ *has power to forgive sins* because He *is God.* Psalm 51:4. Is. 33:22, Micah 7:18, 19, Mark 2:7, 10.

According to the Church of Rome, who can forgive sins?

The Church of Rome *falsely teaches* that *its priests can forgive sins.* It further declares, "that they pardon sins, not only as ambassadors of Jesus Christ, but *as Judges,* and *by way of jurisdiction!"* Bellarmine, *De Poenit.,* 3:2.

Note that in this declaration the Roman priest *not only usurps God's prerogative* of pardoning sins, but also *usurps His place as Judge!*

The Council of Trent in 1557 declared in its 14th session, Canon 9, "Whoever shall affirm that the priests' sacramental absolution is *not a judician act,* but only a ministry to pronounce and declare that the sins of the person confessing are forgiven, so that he believes himself to be absolved *even though the priest should not absolve seriously,* but *in jest;* or shall affirm that the confession of the penitent is not necessary in order to obtain absolution from the priest,— let him be *accursed."* Again, Canon 10, "Whoever shall affirm that priests who are *living in mortal sin,* do *not possess the power* of 'binding' and 'loosing' (that is, of condemning, or forgiving sin) — let him be *accursed."* What a repulsive dogma this is, *insulting to a holy God!* that absolution even when given *hypocritically,* or *"in jest"* is still efficacious, or the case of a *priest living in mortal sin,* that is, himself *destitute of divine grace,* yet is still *supposed* to have *the power of God to forgive sins*[1]—does not such doctrine prove that the Church which declares it is *apostate?*

Does Holy Scripture anywhere countenance such teaching?

God's Holy Word *nowhere gives any ground for such sinful teaching.* According to Scripture, *no human being can forgive sins,* and *no* human being *can act as Judge.* All such power belongs *to God alone.* It is the height of folly and impiety thus to put a sinful priest *in the place of God!*

GOD ALONE CAN FORGIVE SINS

If a human priest cannot forgive sins, what is the meaning of *"the keys,"* of *"binding and loosing,"* or of *"remitting and retaining sins?"* Matt. 16:19, John 20:23.

These expressions indicate a DECLARATIVE POWER ONLY; the right to *proclaim in Christ's name and with His authority,* that all who truly repent of sin and trust in Him for pardon and salvation, shall *surely be forgiven and saved.* But it is *Christ alone,* and *not* the minister, *who forgives.* According to God's Word, the minister is only *a herald to announce what the King will do,* on condition of the faith and repentance of the sinner. This was the teaching of the

---

[1] Roman Catholic writers often praise the priest, as if he had the power to forgive sins, forgetting that *as they exalt the sinful human agent* they *disparage the majesty and power of the Divine Lord,* who *alone can forgive sins* and *grant eternal life.* The bishop of Pelotas in Southern Brazil says, "Behold, my children, the power of the priest! The tongue of the priest *makes a God out of a piece of bread!* This is *far more than to create a world!* Some one says, 'Why does St. Philomena obey the Curate of Ars?' *Certainly she may well obey Him,* since *God obeys him!"* What *horrible falsehood and blasphemy!* To say that the tongue of a priest makes a God out of a piece of bread is both *false and blasphemous,* as it is also to say that *Almighty God obeys a sinful priest!* Liguori, in his book *"The Dignity and Duty of a Priest,"* declares, "In the matter of giving or refusing absolution, of pardoning or condemning, *God Himself,* is *obliged to abide by the judgment* of His priests!" What folly and impiety for Roman priests thus to boast of a power which they do *not possess,* and *grossly dishonor the Creator of heaven and earth!*

A leading Brazilian once rightly said, "The Roman Church, by her numerous mediators, *blocks the way to Christ,* and *interposes herself and her priesthood between the sinner* and *his Saviour!" An Open Door in Brazil,* page 49.

apostles, and of the early Church, before papal followers had corrupted it.

Remember Tertullian's declaration in the third century, that *all Christians have, like Peter,* the "power of the Keys," to *proclaim* forgiveness and salvation through the Lord Jesus Christ. And this has always been the doctrine of the Reformed Church.

The liturgy of the Church of England, after the general confession of sin, rightly declares, "HE pardoneth and absolveth all who truly repent and unfeignedly believe His holy Gospel," showing plainly that it is *Christ alone who pardons* and *absolves, not* the minister.

What other Scriptures show that the power of the apostles and of all Christ's ministers was declarative only?

Many texts which show that forgiveness and cleansing are *God's prerogative.* "There is forgiveness with *Thee,* that Thou mayest be feared." "My soul waiteth for *the Lord*"; "Let Israel hope *in the Lord*"; "and *He* shall redeem Israel from all his iniquities." Psalm 130, the whole Psalm. Rev. 1:18 and 3:7, show that *only Christ* "*opens*" and "*shuts*" *the door of mercy and of heaven. He alone* can forgive, *He alone* can condemn.

Did the apostles ever claim the power to forgive sins?

Never. They spoke of themselves merely as *Christ's messengers.* St. Peter expressly exhorted Simon Magus to *pray to God for forgiveness* of his great sin. "Repent therefore of this thy wickedness, and *pray God* if perhaps the thought of thine heart may be forgiven thee." Acts 8:22-24. St. Peter thus declares it was *God alone who could forgive sins.* So also St. Paul. "Who is Paul, or who is Apollos, but ministers?" So then neither is he that planteth anything, neither he that watereth, but *God that giveth the increase.*" This is as much as to say: "We are *nothing* God is *everything;* all power and grace, forgiveness and salvation are His alone." I Cor. 3:5-7, II Cor. 5:18, II Peter 4:11. Forgiveness is *all of God alone.*

THE GROUND OF FORGIVENESS OF SINS

What is the ground on which sinners may receive forgiveness of sins?

The Word of God teaches that *the only ground or plea* on which sinners may *receive forgiveness and acceptance with God*, is the *perfect atonement of the Lord Jesus Christ*, who bore our guilt, paid our debt, fulfilled the righteousness of the law for us, and *set us free from condemnation forever*. John 1:29, 5:24, Rom. 8:1, Phil. 3:9, I Peter 2:24.

What does the Church of Rome declare to be the ground on which sinners may receive forgiveness?

The Church of Rome teaches that not only is Christ's merit and atoning death, but *also the merit and good works of saints*[1] *and the Virgin Mary* are the ground of forgiveness. These works are called *"super-abundant satisfactions,"* or *"works of super-erogation."*

What is meant by "super-abundant satisfaction," or "works of super-erogation"?

The papal Church teaches that the saints have *"done works more perfect than God's law requires";* and that *"good works merit eternal life."* Bellarmine, *De Indulg.*, 3:2, 3. *Tolet. De Instruct. sacerdot.*, 6:21. On the other hand, God's Word declares that *no man has merit, or can win eternal life.* "All our righteousness (our *imagined meritorious works*) are *as filthy rags.*" Isa. 64:6. "So likewise ye, when ye shall have done all these things which are commanded you, say: 'We are *unprofitable servants;* we have *done that which was our duty to do.'*" Luke 17:10.

---

[1] In the Roman service commemorating Thomas Becket is found this petition; "O good Jesu, forgive us our debts *through the merits of Thomas,* and raise us up from the three fold death. O good Jesu, release us from our sins that bind us, *through Thomas' wounds.* All things give place and obey Thomas—pestilences, diseases, death and devils; fire, air, earth and the seas. Thomas filled the world full of glory. He maketh the lepers clean. He looseth them that are bound from the bonds of death." It would be difficult to find elsewhere, in the same compass, *more nonsense and falsehood* than these words contain! St. Peter exhorts all Christians: "Submit yourselves to *every ordinance of man* for the Lord's sake, whether it be to *the King as supreme,*" etc. I Peter 2:13. Thomas Becket was *guilty of grave disobedience and rebellion against his King,* breaking both the *law of God* and *of the realm.* How then can *a criminal* be *worshipped as a saint,* and how can it truthfully be said that "Becket filled the world with glory" when he really *filled it with shame and crime?*

9

SALVATION BY GOD'S FREE GRACE ALONE

Human merit and good works are *the opposite of God's free grace* which *is found in Christ alone*.

Only by His perfect merit and righteousness can men be saved. "By the deeds of the law shall no flesh be justified." Rom. 3:20. "*Not by works of righteousness which we have done,* but according to His mercy He saved us—being justified by His grace through Jesus Christ our Saviour." Titus 3:5-7. "By *grace* ye are saved through faith; and that *not of yourselves,* it is the *gift of God; not of works, lest any man should boast.*" Eph. 2:8, 9. "He hath saved us—*not according to our works,* but according to His own purpose and grace, which was given us *in Christ Jesus* before the world began." II Tim. 1:9, Rom. 3:24, 26, 6:23, Gal. 2:16, 21, 3:10, 13.

The Apostle Paul repeatedly points out the *irreconcilable antagonism there is* between *human merit* and *divine grace;* between *trusting to one's own good works* for salvation, and *trusting in the righteousness of Christ.* These are *mutually exclusive;* salvation *cannot* be *partly by human merit* and *partly by Christ's righteousness.* It must be *wholly by Christ's death and righteousness,* or *not at all.* Rom. 4:4, 5, 11:6, Gal. 1:6-8, 5:4.

What other grave errors *does the Church of Rome teach in this connection, which are* entirely opposed to the true Gospel?

The Church of Rome teaches:

1. "That men may satisfy the justice of God by their sufferings." Council of Trent, *sess. 4.* Bellarmine, *De Indulg.,* 1:2, *De Poenit,* 4:7.

2. "That there are persons who endure *more punishment than their sins deserve.*" Bellarmine, *De Indulg.,* 1:2.

3. "That men's good works *do merit eternal life,*[1] not only by the promise of God, but also by *their own worth and dignity!*" Bellarmine, *De Justif.,* 5:7.

---

[1] "The service of God, according to the monks was a thing of desert and reward. So many good works done, so much to the right page in the Great Book; where the stock proved insufficient, there was the reserve fund of *the merit of the saints,* which the Church *dispensed for money* to those who needed." "Merit!" thought Luther, "what merit can there be in such a poor caitiff as man! The better a man is, the *more clearly he sees how little he is good for,* and the *greater mockery it seems to*

4. "That men may *merit not only eternal life,* but also an *increase of glory.*" Council of Trent, *sess.* 6. Bellarmine, *De Justif.,* 5:20.

5. "That there are men *perfectly righteous in this life.*" Bellarmine, *De Justif.,* 4:10, 12, 13.

HUMAN MERIT AND GOOD WORKS ARE "FILTHY RAGS"

What Scriptures show that the Church of Rome's whole position regarding human merit and good works is vicious, *and that everyone of these points is* opposed to the true Gospel?

The Bible plainly states that *the best of men have sin: none* are *perfectly righteous.* "There is not a just man on earth that *doeth good and sinneth not.*" There is *none righteous, no, not one.* Eccles. 7:20, Prov. 20:9, Rom. 3:10, Phil. 3:12.

"If we say we have no sin, *we deceive ourselves* and *the truth is not in us.*" I John 1:8, Jas. 3:2.

"We are all as an unclean thing, and *all our righteousness* are as *filthy rags.*" Isa. 64:6.

So far from men suffering more than their sins deserve God's Word says: "Thou our God hast punished us *less than our iniquities deserve.*" Ezra 9:13. "Know therefore that God exacteth of thee *less than thine iniquity deserveth.*" Job 11:6. To trust in any degree to human merit or one's own good works is a *false hope* that will *lead to eternal ruin;* it is the "wood, hay and stubble," that will burn up before our eyes in the Day of Judgment! If salvation is sought *in any degree by works,* then it is *not of grace.* Rom. 11:6. Trust in good works or human merit *makes the cross of Christ of none effect.* Gal. 5:4.

---

attribute to him the notion of *having deserved reward.*" "Miserable creatures that we are! We earn our bread in sin. Till we are seven years old, we do nothing but eat and drink, sleep and play; from seven to twenty one we study four hours a day; the rest of it we run about and amuse ourselves; we work until we are fifty, and then grow again to be children. We sleep half of our lives; we give God *a tenth of our time;* and yet we think that with *our good works we can merit heaven!*" Ah, "enter not into judgment with Thy servant, O Lord!" "A perpetual struggle! Forever to be falling, yet to rise again, and stumble forward with eyes turned to Heaven—this was the best that would ever come of man. It was accepted in its imperfection by the infinite grace of God, who pities mortal weakness, and accepts the intention for the deed; who, when there is a sincere desire to serve Him, overlooks the short-comings of infirmity!" Luther's *Table Talk. Times of Erasmus and Luther.* Froude.

Does the Reformed Church teach this great Gospel truth, of the utter failure of human merit and good works, and that salvation is received only through the atoning death and perfect righteousness of Christ, which is "imputed to the sinner, and received by faith alone"?

The Reformed Church does *joyfully proclaim this blessed truth,* just as the Apostolic Church proclaimed it in the *first century;* Augustine in the *fifth century;* Bernard in the *12th century;* and Luther in the *16th century,* proclaimed it. We dare not proclaim any other Gospel, for that would be *treason to our Lord;* it would make *His cross "of none effect,"* and would by *false hopes* lead multitudes down the *broad road to perdition.* Gal. 1:8, 9, I Cor. 1:17, II Peter 2:1.

Good Works Necessary as Evidence of Saving Faith

Does the Scripture doctrine that we are saved solely by what Christ has done for us, *and* not *by our own merit, imply that good works are not vitally important?*

By no means. Good works are indispensable, *not* as the *ground of forgiveness and salvation,* but as *the evidence of it.* "Faith without works is *dead,"*—is a hollow, spurious faith. Good works show that we *truly believe and obey God;* without them, a profession of faith is *empty and useless.* Christ redeemed us that we shall be a people *"zealous of good works."* After declaring that men are saved *"not* by works of righteousness which we have done," St. Paul adds, that "they who have believed in God should be *careful to maintain good works";* and later repeats: "and let ours also (Christian believers) *learn to maintain good works*—that they be not unfruitful." Titus 2:14, 3:8, 14, I Tim. 2:10, 5:10, 6:18, II Tim. 2:21, 3:17, Jas. 2:17, 20, 26.

John Calvin admirably said: "It is *faith alone* that *justifies;* and yet the faith which justifies is *not alone.*"

Thus Holy Scripture reveals that Christ is the *only Mediator* between God and men; that *God alone can forgive sin;* and that *the ground of His forgiveness* is *not* human merit or good works, but the *atoning death of the Son of God* upon the cross, and *His perfect righteousness fulfilling the law of God for us.* Gal. 2:16, Rom. 11:6.

CHAPTER IX

CONFESSION OF SIN, PENANCE, AND INDULGENCES

Is it the Christian's duty to confess his sins? If so, to whom should he confess them?

The Word of God teaches that it is the duty of every Christian humbly to confess his sins, and that confession should be made *to God*. Confession should be made to God, because He is our Creator, and Redeemer, and *will be our Judge.* He alone is Lord of the conscience, and searches the hearts of men; it is *against Him* that we *have sinned,* for it is *His holy Law that we have broken.*

David, through the Holy Spirit, confessed His sins to God, saying, "Against Thee, *Thee only,* have I sinned, and done this evil in Thy sight." Ps. 51:4. "Search me, O God, and know my heart; try me and know my thoughts"; implying, that I may know my sins, and *humbly confess and forsake them.* Ps. 139:23, 24.

"I acknowledged my sin unto *Thee,* and mine iniquity have I not hid. I said I will confess my transgressions *unto the Lord,* and *Thou* forgavest the iniquity of my sin." Ps. 32:5. David had a High priest and many other priests, but he did not confess his sins *to them;* he confessed them *to God, the Searcher of hearts.* Hezekiah and his people, the record declares, confessed their sins to God, not to priests. II Chron. 30:22.

Confession of sin is prerequisite to pardon: unless men confess their sins they *cannot expect forgiveness.* "He that covereth his sins shall not prosper, but whoso confesseth and forsaketh them shall have mercy." Prov. 28:13. "If we confess our sins, He (Almighty God) is faithful and just *to forgive us our sins,* and to *cleanse us from all unrighteousness."* I John 1:9.

In every case confession of sin was made *to God,* because He is Lord, and He alone can grant forgiveness.

*What is the teaching of the Roman Church concerning confession
of sins?*

The Church of Rome, here as elsewhere, goes *directly counter to
God's Word.* It requires auricular confession; that is, confession
made in the ear of a Roman priest. An authorized catechism[1] says:
"To receive the sacrament of penance worthily, we must confess
our sins[2] *to the priest.*" After asserting that priests of the Church
have power to forgive sins, it is said, "Confession is the telling of our
sins to a duly authorized priest for the purpose of obtaining forgiveness."[1]

SINS SHOULD BY CONFESSED TO GOD, NOT TO A PRIEST

*Is there anything in Holy Scripture that justifies the Roman con-
fessional, requiring believers to confess their sins to a priest, and
not directly to God?*

There is *nothing whatever* in Holy Scripture that justifies the
requirement that confession of sins be made to a Roman priest, and
not directly to God. The confessional was a medieval imposition,
and did not become a regular dogma of the Church of Rome until
the year 1215. It is an unwarranted addition to the Gospel of Christ
which the popes presumed to make, and *directly disobeys God's
command,* that nothing is to be added to His holy Word.[2] Deut.
4:2, 12:32.

What is wrong about confessing sins to a Roman priest?

As already stated, it disobeys God's command by *adding* something which is *not warranted by Holy Scripture.* Moreover, in the
confessional the priest commits the great sin of *usurping the place
of God.*[2] God alone is the Searcher of hearts and the Judge; there-

---

[1] A catechism of Christian Doctrine, prepared and enjoined by order of the Third
Plenary Council of Baltimore.

[2] John Chrysostom, eminent leader of the Greek branch of the Christian Church
(died A.D. 407) was true to the Gospel when he said; "I beseech you to confess
your sins continually to God. I do not bring thee unto the theater of thy fellow
servants, nor do I compel thee *to uncover thy sins to men.*" This shows plainly that
confession of sins to a priest was *not* the practice of the Christian church early in
the 5th century.

fore, no human being may dare to occupy the position which belongs to Him alone, nor to pry into the secrets of a man or woman's soul. I Chron. 28:9, II Chron. 6:30.

It is the solemn duty of every individual to realize his *direct responsibility to God,* to cultivate *a sense of His presence,* and it is his privilege to have *direct access to God;* therefore, no priest nor human being may come in between the soul and its Maker. This is the *very heart of true religion; constantly to maintain a sense of nearness to God,* to strive *to live in His presence,* and cultivate a sense *of direct responsibility to Him,* before whom we must finally give an account for the deeds done in the body. The practice of confessing sins to a priest *destroys this direct relationship to God* and *substitutes a sinful human being* for Him "unto whose eyes all things are naked and opened," and with whom alone "we have to do." Heb. 4:13.

Does not the form of absolution used by the Roman priest in forgiving sins show how totally different Romanism is from the true Gospel?

It does show that Romanism and the true Gospel of Christ are *entirely different;* for the person confessing is supposed to say: "I confess to Almighty God, to the blessed Virgin Mary, to blessed Michael the Archangel, to blessed John the Baptist, to the holy Apostles Peter and Paul, to all the saints and to you, Father, that I have sinned," etc. Then the priest is supposed to say, *"Absolve te"* (*I* forgive you). "The passion of our Lord Jesus Christ, the merits of the blessed Mary and of all saints, whatever *good you have done,* and *whatever evil you have suffered,* be unto you for the remission of sins," etc.

Why mention the Virgin Mary, Michael the archangel, John Baptist, Peter and Paul and the rest who *have nothing to do with confession of sins to God.* Were they not sinful, erring human beings, saved *not by their merit,* but by the free grace of God? It is a *great* sin thus to put them *on a level with the Almighty Creator.* Note also that contrary to Holy Scripture, forgiveness of sins and salvation are *falsely made to depend,* not on the merit and righteousness of *Christ alone,* but also *on the merit of sinful human beings, and even on the sufferings and supposed merit of the penitent himself!* What a *total perversion of God's salvation* this is! See also the arrogance of the priest; he does not say as he should, *God* forgives you; but says, *I* forgive you! Is not this a clear proof of apostasy?

History shows, as Roman Catholics have acknowledged, that the Roman Confessional has led to *scandalous abuses,* and to the commission of many crimes, fulfilling the Scripture warning of II Tim. 3:6. The Romanist scholar Erasmus wrote[1]: "The stupid monks say mass as a cobbler makes a shoe. They come to the altar *reeking from their filthy pleasures.* Confession with the monks is a cloak to steal the people's money, to rob girls of their virtue, and commit other crimes too horrible to name." Erasmus' *Letters.*

Shamefully indecent questions have been prescribed by Church authorities to use in asking women as well as men in the Confessional, questions which by injecting impure suggestions into innocent minds have led to temptation and moral ruin! See Den's *Theology,* containing questions in Latin to be used by priests in the Confessional, which, if translated into English, would render the author or confessor liable to prosecution. Women who were converted to the Protestant faith have declared that what convinced them that the Roman Church was *not* the true Church was the indecent questions the priest had asked them in the Confessional! Lord Acton, a Roman Catholic, wrote: "There are many opinions not only sanctioned, but *enforced,* by the authorities of the Church of Rome which *none can adhere to without peril to the soul.*" He cites as examples, "the *ungodly ethics of the papacy,* the *Inquisition,* and *the Casuists.*" *Letters of Lord Acton, edited by Herbert Paul, Letter* of March 4, 1882, page 127.

Romanists quote James V:16 in an attempt to justify the Confessional. Does this text at all apply to confessing sin to a priest?

No. This text has no reference whatever to auricular confession. "Confess your faults one to another" is a command to *all* believers, and expresses a reciprocal action of Christians acknowledging their

---

[1] Remember that this was not the statement of a non-Catholic, but of *a member of the Roman Church.*

faults, *not* to a priest, but *to "one another."* Whenever an injury has been done, it is the duty of the offender humbly to acknowledge his fault, and ask forgiveness of the injured party. If A has done wrong to B, it is A's duty to acknowledge his fault to B, and ask B's forgiveness; and where B has injured A, it is B's duty to confess his wrongdoing, and ask pardon of A. Of course, what is most important, both A and B should confess their sin *to God,* and *seek His forgiveness.* But there is *nothing whatever* in this Scripture to *justify the Roman Confessional.*

If the Roman Confessional had no sanction in the Word of God, how did it ever come to be established in the Christian Church?

Because the Confessional enormously increased the power of the pope and the priesthood. The priests thus obtained knowledge of the secrets of men, from the Emperor down to the humblest peasant, and all classes of society were placed in the power of their confessors, whom they did not dare to disobey or offend. Not only were the sins and scandals of each individual's private life, and that of families, laid bare, but all the intrigues of State and the political schemes of the rulers of Europe were in the possession of the Confessor, who could use his knowledge for the advantage of the Church, or to help a political party in which he was interested.

What greater intellectual and moral bondage for human beings could be imagined, or what more dangerous power could be wielded than that of the Roman Confessional? History furnishes many impressive warnings; see Charles IX of France and the massacre of St. Bartholomew; or Louis XIV and the cruel Revocation of the Edict of Nantes in 1685.

REPENTANCE, NOT PENANCE

What does God's Word declare is the condition on which one may receive forgiveness of sins?

The Word of God declares that the sinner must truly repent of his sin and *forsake it; without sincere repentance* there *can be no forgiveness.* "Repent ye, for the Kingdom of heaven is at hand." Matt. 3:2. "Repent ye, and believe the Gospel." Mark 1:15. "Except ye repent, ye shall *all likewise perish.*" Luke 13:3, 5. "They glorified God saying, 'Then hath God also to the Gentiles granted *repentance unto life.*'" Acts 11:18.

What does Holy Scripture mean by "repentance unto life"?

It means repentance *that leads to salvation.* It is the work of the Holy Spirit in the sinner's heart, showing him the heinousness of his sin, and the infinite mercy of God in Christ, leading him to be *truly sorry for his sin,* to *forsake it,* and turn to God, resolved *in Christ's strength* to obey His commandments and *sin no more.* Luke 22:61, 62, Ezekiel 36:31, II Cor. 7:10, 11, I Kings 8:47, 48, 50.

True repentance is the opposite of *remorse.* David and Saul of Tarsus had repentance unto life; Judas had *remorse* and *committed suicide.* The first is "the godly sorrow which worketh repentance to salvation, not to be repented of"; the second is "the sorrow of *the world that worketh death.*" II Cor. 7:10.

What does the Church of Rome teach?

The Church of Rome teaches *penance,* instead of Gospel repentance. The Roman Catechism[1] declares, "Penance is a sacrament, in which the sins committed after Baptism are forgiven by means of the absolution of the priest." It is a kind of punishment for sin, inflicted by the priest: the catechism says, "The priest gives a penance after confession that we may satisfy God for the *temporal punishment due to our sins.* We must accept the penance which the priest gives us." Punishments imposed by the priest are, repeating certain prayers many times, fastings, vigils, pilgrimages, wearing sackcloth, in old times scourging, and other means of causing pain or discomfort to the body.

Note that penance is a wholly different thing from Gospel repentance; it is a *counterfeit* repentance just as the sacrifice offered by the priest in the Mass is a *counterfeit* atonement. Penance is an *outward act;* repentance is of *the heart.* Penance is imposed by a *Roman priest;* repentance is the work of *the Holy Spirit.* Penance is supposed to make satisfaction for sin; but *nothing* that any human being can do or suffer could *really satisfy divine justice.* Only the

---

[1] "A catechism of Christian doctrine, prepared and enjoined by order of the Third *Plenary Council of Baltimore.*"

Lord Jesus Christ, *as the Lamb of God who taketh away the sin of the world, can do that,* and He did it *once for all* when He made atonement on the cross, and completely satisfied the divine law. Trusting to penance imposed by a priest is a *false hope,* for the penitent may do and suffer many things, yet his heart remains the same *without true repentance.* The Church of Rome's error is like that of heathen religions, seeking to win forgiveness or deliverance from sin by *self-inflicted* or *priest-imposed punishment,* like the tortures of Buddhist and Hindu devotees. Martin Luther found out this great difference when he was ascending the *santa scala,* the "sacred staircase" in Rome, trying to *do* something instead of *trusting the atoning sacrifice of Christ,* when the Holy Spirit enlightened his mind with the great truth, THE JUST SHALL LIVE BY FAITH, and he became a "new creature" in Christ Jesus.

Does the scripture, "Bring forth fruits meet for repentance," give any support to the dogma of penance? Matt. 3:8.

Not at all. This text does *not refer to punishment,* either self-inflicted or imposed by a priest. It means that a Christian should *give evidence by his outward conduct* that he *has truly forsaken his sin* and in the *power of the Holy Spirit,* is leading *a new life of obedience to God.* What God desires in the sinner is not punishment of oneself for sins, *but a change of heart,* a *real forsaking of sin,* shown by a new life of obedience to God's commandments.

RESTITUTION IS NOT PENANCE

Restitution, which Scripture enjoins, is also very different from penance. Restitution is the *restoring of property to the rightful owner,* of which he has been deprived, or the *making good of any loss or injury* which one has caused another. It is *not* an act of penance, *punishing oneself;* but an act of *justice and honesty* restoring to another what rightly belongs to him. See the case of the tax-collector Zaccheus. Luke 19:8. Also Exod. 22:1.

In short, as already said, penance is a *counterfeit* repentance. It is the work of *man on his body;* true repentance is the work of *God in the soul.* The Divine Word commands: *"Rend your heart, and not your garments."* Joel 2:13. Repentance is "rending the heart," the heart that is *"broken and contrite" for sin through* the *working of the Holy Spirit.* Penance is "rending the garments"; an outward form without inward reality, which Christ warns His people carefully to avoid.

FASTS

It should be noted that the Fasts appointed by the Church of Rome are quite different from the fasting taught in Holy Scripture. The Church of Rome's fasts are largely *mechanical, not* spiritual, simply observing certain times appointed by popes to abstain from certain food; they are *not necessarily* connected with prayer or other religious exercises. The statements of the catechism, and also the wild revelry[1] and feasting, and drinking which precede Lent and other occasions in Roman Catholic communities, as *Mardigras,* show this. A Catechism defines fast days as 'days on which we are allowed but *one full meal*'; days of abstinence are those 'on which we are *forbidden to eat flesh-meat,* but are allowed the usual number of meals. Cardinal Bellarmine remarks, "that upon certain days ordained and appointed by the pope, one ought to abstain from certain meats." *De bonis operibus,* 2:14, 15. This is one of the "good works," which in part *procure salvation!* Observe that the rule is *not* based on what *God ordains,* but on what *the pope* ordains. How different was the fasting of the apostles and early Church! With them fasting was not mechanical, abstaining from one meal or three meals, or from "flesh-meat" merely, while enjoying an abundance of every other kind of food and drink![1] but it was a *spiritual* exercise uniformly associated with prayer, in preparation for some important work, as the *appointing of missionaries, ordination,* etc. "As they ministered to the Lord and fasted, the Holy Ghost said, 'separate Me Barnabas and Saul for the work whereunto I have called them. And when they had fasted and prayed and laid their hands upon them, they sent them away.'" Acts 13:2, 3. "And when they had ordained them presbyters (elders) in every church and had prayed with fasting, they commended them to the Lord." Acts 14:23. Daniel sought a blessing by prayer and fasting. Dan. 9:3. God

---

[1] The Roman Catholic scholar Erasmus, in addition to profound learning, had keen discernment. He once remarked that "Luther had committed two sins; he had touched the pope's crown, and *the monks bellies!*"

called upon His people to turn to Him *with fasting and weeping.* Joel 2:12. In time of great danger King Jehoshaphat and the people of Judah fasted and prayed. II Chron. 20:3.

True fasting is always a *spiritual* exercise, connected with prayer, repentance or spiritual service. It is *never mechanical,* or *performed to make merit.* Mere routine fasting is *denounced in Scripture* as an *abomination.* God spoke through Jeremiah reproving the great sins of His people, saying, "Pray not for this people; *when they fast,* I will *not hear their cry.*" Jer. 14:12. The fast that pleased God was to *abstain from sin,* and *live a life of obedience to Him,* of which abstinence from food was a *symbol.* Isa. 58:5-7. Christ reproved the Pharisees because they were *careful to fast,* but *neglected righteousness of life.* Matt. 6:16, 9:14, 24:23.

The apostle Paul warned against asceticism, penances, and abstaining from meats as *a mark of apostasy.* Col. 2:16, 20-23, I Cor. 8:8, I Tim. 4:1-5.

PAPAL INDULGENCES A BARTERING OF GOD'S SALVATION

What is meant by papal Indulgences?

A Roman Church catechism defines an Indulgence to be "a remission of that *temporal punishment* which *even after the sin is forgiven,* has *yet to be suffered* either here or in Purgatory." This remission of punishment is said to be made "by an application *of the treasure of the Church* on the part of a lawful superior," that is, the pope. But before the Reformation the meaning was much broader than that. It was generally believed that Indulgences *provided entire deliverance from the punishment due to sin.*[1] Alexander VI, pope from 1492 to 1503, officially declared that *papal Indulgences delivered souls from Purgatory.* Ranke, *History of the Popes,* Book I, ch. 2, page 55.

---

[1] A well-informed historian remarks: "Indulgences and Dispensations! Dispensations to eat meat on fast-days; to marry one's near relative; dispensations for anything and everything which the faithful might wish to purchase, who desired forbidden pleasures. The dispensations were *simply scandalous.* Some say, indulgences are "the remission of penances which the Church inflicts upon earth." But it is certain they would have sold cheap if the people had thought that this *was all that they were to get by them.* As the thing was represented by the spiritual hawkers

There can be no reasonable doubt that at the time of the Reformation the people were assured by the pope's emissaries that Indulgences *covered all sins,* and provided *complete deliverance from punishment.* There can be little doubt that the majority of the Roman Catholic laity, unaccustomed to papal theological *hairsplitting, still believe it.*

PAPAL INDULGENCES ARE BASED ON THE FALSE FOUNDATION OF THE MERIT OF THE SAINTS

What is the foundation of the doctrine of papal Indulgences?

Two grossly false propositions form the crumbling foundation of papal indulgences. One is that the "superabundant merit" and "good works" of saints and martyrs *form a rich Treasury or storehouse,* sufficient to supply needy sinners; the second is, that the pope has power, by dispensing this "superabundant merit," *to forgive sins.* See Bellarmine, *De Indulg.,* 3:2, 3; Tolet, *De Instruct. sacerdot.,* 6:21.

The Church of Rome also declares, "that holy men may in some sort redeem, or *buy off,* our sins *by their sufferings."* Again, "the sufferings of the saints are *just compensations to redeem us* from the *punishments which we owe to God."* Bellarmine, *De Indulg.,* 1:4.

What a shocking perversion of the Gospel, and flat contradiction of Holy Scripture all this is! For we are not redeemed by the sufferings of holy men or saints, but *by the precious blood of Christ,* by the sufferings and death of the *Son of God alone!* No true Christian would dare to trust to the sufferings of saints, for God's Holy Word warns, *"Cursed be man that trusteth in man,"* "Neither is there salvation *in any other." Christ alone* is *our salvation; He* is *our perfect Righteousness: He alone* can *redeem.* "And this is the name whereby she (the Church of God) shall be called,—"THE LORD OUR

who disposed of these wares, Indulgences were *letters of credit on Heaven!"* When the Great Book was opened, the people believed that the finding would be thus; "Debtor, so many murders, so many robberies, lies, slanders, debaucheries. Creditor, the merits of the saints placed to the account of the delinquent by the pope's letters in consideration *of value received.* This is the way in which the pardon system was practically worked; this is the way in which it is *worked still,* where the same superstitions remain." Prof. J. A. Froude.

RIGHTEOUSNESS." Jer. 23:6, 33:16, Is. 12:2, Acts 4:12, I Peter 1:18, 19.

The Bible shows there is no such thing as a storehouse or Treasury of "superabundant merit" and "good works" of saints; for God says plainly, *"All our righteousness are as filthy rags."* Is. 64:6. "So likewise ye when ye shall have done all these things which are commanded you, say: "We are *unprofitable servants;* we have done that which *was our duty to do."*

Can a pope or church or any human being forgive sins, or remit any part of the punishment due to sin?

No Church or human being has the power to forgive sin, or to remit any part of *the punishment due to sin.* To claim this power is an *impious falsehood,* for which the popes and the Roman Church will *have to give an account to God at the Judgment Day.* Only Almighty God can forgive sin and deliver from the punishment of sin. Indulgences are a *wicked invention to deceive men,* and are *contrary to the whole plan of salvation* as revealed in Holy Scripture. They moreover make sinful man *usurp the prerogative of the holy God,* who alone is *Redeemer and Judge,* and will surely "render to every man according to his works." Is. 40:10, Rev. 22:12.

THE GRAVE SCANDAL OF PAPAL INDULGENCES

It is difficult now for any one to conceive the shameful demoralization and vice which resulted from the sale of Indulgences at the time of the Reformation. A testimony to this deplorable fact is seen in the action of the Roman Catholic princes of Germany, who tried to stem the flood of corruption throughout the Empire by assembling in the Diet of Nuremberg, 1523, and addressing a petition to pope Adrian VI for the remedy of *"A Hundred Grievances of the German Nation."* Some of the grievances stated were: No. 5, "How license to sin with impunity is *granted for money."* No. 67, "How *more money than penitence* is exacted from sinners." No. 91, "How bishops *extort money* from *the concubinage of priests."* Claude d'Espence denounced Indulgences at the Council of Trent, and Grosseteste, bishop of London, protested to the pope against purchasable pardons. Julius II sold Indulgences, and Paul III drew revenue from brothels. The princes declared also that vendors of Bulls of Indulgence certify by these purchasable pardons, *not only past and future sins are forgiven,* but also *the sins of those who are in the fires of purgatory!* Everyone, in proportion to the price paid for these wares, was promised *impugnity in sinning.*" Popes could *not deny* these horrible charges for the book entitled "Taxes of the Sacred Apostolic Penitentiary" is *still extant,* with a *regular tariff for absolution from all kinds of sins.*

Sins Commercialized by the Published Papal Rates for Absolution

In the book of Religious Rates for Absolution registered at the Court of France in the year 1699 are these items:

Absolution for Apostasy	80 livres
Absolution for Bigamy	1050 livres
Absolution for Homicide	95 livres
Dispensation from vows of chastity......	15 livres

Preface of Laçon, by C. C. Colton, London, 1820.

What should be the attitude of all true Christians toward Papal Indulgences?

All true Christians should *utterly abhor papal Indulgences* because:

1. Indulgences are *directly contrary to the Word of God* and to His whole scheme of salvation, which cannot be earned by human merit, *nor can be bought or sold for money.*

2. Indulgences are *contrary to the practice of the early Church,* and to the testimony of the Fathers. Antoninus, Archbishop of Florence, declared, "We have *no testimony in Scripture* nor among *the Fathers, in favor of Indulgences." Sum. Theol.,* 1, 3.

3. Indulgences greatly dishonor the Holy Trinity. The pope in granting them, *usurps the place of Almighty God,* who *alone can pardon sin;* and they *dishonor the Saviour* by offering a *counterfeit* substitute for *His real atonement.*

4. Indulgences are *false,* because there is *no treasury filled with human works* and *merit,* which can be put to *the credit of another,* like transfer of a bank account. The so-called "super-abounding satisfactions" of the saints have *no real existence* but are a *vain*

delusion. They are *the "filthy rags" of human righteousness,* the "wood, hay and stubble," which will be *burned up in the fires of Judgment.* I Cor. 3:12, 13, Rom. 3:20, Gal. 2:16, 21, Is. 64:6.

5. Indulgences blind men's consciences to *the awful nature of sin* and its *dreadful consequences;* to their *responsibility to God,* and to the *only way of escape from condemnation,* viz.: by true repentance and faith in the perfect merit and righteousness of the Lord Jesus Christ. Phil. 3:7-9.

6. Indulgences *embolden men to sin,* because they are *supposed* to provide *an easy way to escape* the consequences of sin.

7. Indulgences have cruelly deceived and *robbed the poor;* who, while spending all they possess to obtain deliverance, are through a *false hope,* left to *perish in their sins!*

8. Papal Indulgences have caused grievous scandal among Christians and unbelievers and have *brought ridicule and contempt on God's holy religion.*

9. Indulgences are a form of the mortal sin of *Simony* (Acts 8:18-24), that is, of *selling the free grace of God,* and *making merchandise of the precious blood of Christ.* The apostles solemnly warn against this sin. Jude 11. St. Peter also foretold *this mark of apostasy* in the Church: that "false teachers should bring in damnable heresies, denying the Lord that bought them: who *through covetousness should make merchandise of you;* whose judgment now of a long time lingereth not, and *their damnation slumbereth not.*" II Peter 2:13, 15.

To Simon Magus, St. Peter said: *"Thy money perish with thee,* because thou hast thought that the gift of God may be purchased with money!" If this is true of an ignorant man who would buy God's gift, how much more is it true of supposed *Church leaders who sell God's salvation by Indulgences!*

No wonder that Martin Luther, the Roman Catholic princes of Germany who appealed to Adrian VI, and thousands of the common people of Europe who were *horrified* at *the abuses which attended the sale of the Pope's Indulgences,* were shocked at the brazen effrontery of the monk Tetzel as he shouted to the people in the market place, "Pour in your coin! *Whatever crimes you have com-*

10

mitted, or *may commit,* are *forgiven.* The souls of your kindred will *fly out of purgatory the moment your money rattles at the bottom of the coffer!"* White's *Eighteen Christian Centuries.*

If Indulgences are such a soul-destroying sin, so clearly opposed to the Gospel of salvation, why did the popes persist in selling them, and why do they now uphold the practice?

Because Indulgences have been a source of *enormous revenue* to the Vatican[1]; by appealing to the superstitious fears of their people, high and low, the popes have *filled their empty coffers with gold.* The great cathedral of St. Peter's at Rome and many other expensive churches were built by Pope Leo X and other popes by *money largely obtained from the people* by *false promises of forgiveness and deliverance from purgatory.* This evil dogma became fixed in the Church as late as the twelfth century, about 1190.

---

[1] "It was money, ever money. Money, not charity, covered the multitude of sins. If a man committed sins, he was prescribed penances, which could be commuted for money. If he was sick or troubled in mind, he was sent on a pilgrimage to a shrine or some wonder-working image, where for due consideration, his case was attended to. But it was no *use to go to a saint empty-handed.* The rule of the Church was, *nothing for nothing.* When indulgences were offered for sale by Tetzel, the pope bought the support of the Archbishop of Mayence, by promising *half the spoil gathered in his province.* (This was the same Archbishop who as one of the seven electors to choose the new emperor, took bribes *six times alternately from both the candidates!*) At a chapel in Saxony, there was an image of a Virgin and Child. If the worshiper brought a handsome offering, the child *bowed and was gracious;* if the present was meagre, it turned away its head, and withheld favors till the *purse strings were untied again!* There was a great rood or crucifix of the same kind at Bexley in Kent, where the pilgrims went in thousands. This figure used *to bow,* too, when *it was pleased;* and a good sum of money was sure to secure its good will. When the Reformation came, it was found that *the images were worked with wires and pulleys!* The German lady was kept as a curiosity in the cabinet of the Elector of Saxony. Our Bexley rood was brought up and exhibited in Cheapside, and was afterward *torn in pieces* by the people!" Froude's *Times of Erasmus and Luther.*

CHAPTER X

THE FUTURE STATE, PURGATORY, AND MASSES FOR THE DEAD

What does the Word of God teach concerning man's future state after death?

The Word of God teaches that after death there is a *glorious heaven,* where the righteous shall forever dwell with the Lord in joy and peace; and an *awful hell,* where the wicked shall forever dwell, receiving the just punishment for their sins. To the righteous our Lord Jesus Christ, the Almighty King, shall say: "Come ye blessed of My Father, inherit the Kingdom prepared for you from the foundation of the world." To the wicked He shall say: "Depart from Me, ye cursed, into everlasting fire prepared for the devil and his angels." "And these shall go away into *everlasting punishment,* but the righteous into *life eternal.*" Matt. 25:34, 41, 46.

Though sinful men in their folly wish to deny that there is a hell, yet the awful fact remains the same; for God, who cannot lie, declares it. The clearest statements of eternal punishment are made by the loving Saviour, who "gave His life a ransom for us." And He made them to warn us to "flee from the wrath to come," and lay hold on eternal life. No man, however great a sinner, need go down to eternal darkness; a way of escape has been provided through Christ's precious blood; "believe on the Lord Jesus Christ, and thou shalt be saved." If any man fails to be saved, it is *his own fault,* because he has *rejected God's offer of mercy in Christ.* And at last every lost soul will confess that God is good, and that *his own condemnation is just,* because he *refused Christ's blood-bought redemption.* John 3:16-19, 36; 5:24, 29; Matt. 13:41, 42, 49, 50; Heb. 2:3.

There Is No Intermediate State, No Purgatory

Does the Word of God teach that after death there is any other place beside heaven and hell?

The Word of God teaches that after death there is a heaven and a hell, and *no other place*. There is *no intermediate State;* all men must go either to heaven or to hell. Matt. 25:46, Rom. 2:5-10, Luke 16:22, 23.

Does the Church of Rome teach these plain declarations of the Word of God?

It does *not;* for it teaches that beside heaven and hell there is a place called Purgatory. This is said to be a *place of torment,* to which *good people* who have been *redeemed by Christ must go after death,* to *suffer punishment in part for their sins!* The Church of Rome falsely declares that our Saviour Jesus Christ "hath delivered us from the guilt, but *not from all the punishment* that was due to our sins." Also, "that beside the blood of Jesus Christ, there is a *Purgatory* for the *expiation of our sins;* and that the *souls of the children of God,* when they go out of the body, *go to this place of torment";* and "that whoever does not believe this, shall be damned." Council of Trent, *sess.* 6, 30. Bellarmine, *De Purgat.,* 1:10-15, and the Council of Florence.

What Scripture proof does the Church of Rome give for this horrible dogma?

No real proof whatever. On the contrary, this teaching *conflicts with many passages of the Word of God.*

Why should true Christians wholly disbelieve Purgatory?

1. Because Purgatory has *no Scripture foundation,* and because God's Word warns of the *great sin of adding anything whatever* to the doctrines He has revealed. Deut. 4:2, 12:32, Rev. 22:18.

2. The doctrine of Purgatory *greatly dishonors the Saviour,* by *belittling His glorious redemption* as only partial and incomplete, whereas Scripture everywhere represents it as *perfect and complete.* If, as the Church of Rome alleges, *good Christians* must *suffer torment* in Purgatory to expiate their sins, then Christ's salvation is *only partial* and *defective.* But thanks be to God, Christ paid the sinner's *whole debt,* and completely delivers from *all punishment forever.*

3. Many Scriptures declare that the believer is *fully justified*, and therefore "there is now no condemnation." Rom. 8:1, Rom. 3:24-26. Scripture says plainly *no accusation* can be laid *against those whom God has redeemed*. "Who shall lay anything to the charge of God's elect? It is God that justifieth." "Who is he that condemneth? It is Christ that died," and therefore *full atonement for sin has been made*. Rom. 8:33, 34, Rom. 5:20, 21. Again, "He that believeth shall not come into condemnation, but is *passed from death unto life*. John 5:24. Note carefully the passing is *not to torment in purgatory*, but to *life, eternal life!* Further, since Scripture assures us that the precious blood of Christ cleanseth from all sin, that the soul of the believer is made "whiter than snow," then there is *no need of the "purifying fires of torment."* I John 1:7, Ps. 51:7, Is. 1:18, Heb. 1:3.

4. Any intermediate State is disproved by the many Scriptures which show that man's destiny is eternally *fixed at death;* thereafter there can be *no hope of cleansing* or *deliverance*. "*Now* is the accepted time; *now* is the day of salvation." II Cor. 6:2, *Today*, while life lasts, is the time for repentance, to "make our calling and election sure." "*Today* if ye will hear His voice, harden not your hearts." The word "Today" is repeated *five times* in the third and fourth chapters of Hebrews, showing that the present life, the immediate present, is the *time to seek deliverance from sin* and find *complete salvation in Christ*.

Many texts exclude purgatory or any intermediate state, by showing that there is *no interval between death* and *the soul's award*, its entrance into the eternal state, whether of happiness or misery. The transition from this world to heaven or hell is *immediate*. St. Paul said, "To me to live is Christ, to die is gain"; death would at once bring the eternal award. But death would not be gain, if Paul had first *to go to torment!* Phil. 1:21, 23.

Again, "absent from the body, present with the Lord." II Cor. 5:1, 6-8. Simeon having seen the infant Christ, prayed, "Now lettest Thou Thy servant depart in peace"; but his prayer was *mistaken*, if he were *going to torment in purgatory* and *not* to heaven. Our Lord said of Lazarus that he was "comforted in Abraham's bosom"; but this would not have been true, if he went *to purgatorial torment.* Of Dives it is said, "the rich man died and was buried, and *in hell* he lifted up his eyes, *being in torments*"; the connection shows that his death and burial were immediately followed by his suffering the torments of hell. Luke 16:23, 25.

5. When the thief on the cross prayed in repentance, Christ replied, *"Today* thou shalt be with Me in Paradise," that is, *in heaven.* If purgatorial fire really existed, one would surely expect it in the case of this man; but Christ in mercy took him *that very day to heaven.* Scripture declares God's children die "in Christ." I Cor. 15:18, and those who thus "die in the Lord" are said to *rest from their labors."* Rev. 14:13. But this could *not* be true if they went *to the torments of purgatory.*

There are a multitude of other texts which clearly disprove the odious doctrine of Purgatory. See the great number of texts which speak of the *blessedness of the righteous,* of all those who trust in Christ for salvation. Reference is made to these *12 times* in Matthew and *12 times in Luke's Gospel,* 7 times in Revelation, and often in other places.

"Blessed are the poor in Spirit; for theirs is the Kingdom of heaven."

"Blessed are the pure in heart; for they *shall see God"* (*not torment*).

"Blessed is that servant whom his Lord when He cometh shall find so doing" (*watching and waiting for His coming*).

"Blessed are the dead who die in the Lord; yea, saith the Spirit, that they may *rest from their labors,* and their works do follow them." They enjoy the *blessed rest of heaven,* and do *not suffer the torments of fire.*

"Blessed are they that are called to the marriage supper of the Lamb." They enjoy the glorious marriage feast in heaven! See also the number of texts which assure faithful believers that at death there will be *an end to all the trials and sorrows of earthly life;* "And there shall be *no more death* neither *sorrow, nor crying;* for the former things are *passed away."* "They shall hunger no more, neither thirst any more,—for the Lamb who is in the midst of the throne shall feed them, and shall lead them unto living fountains of waters; and *God shall wipe away all tears from their eyes!"*

So far from punishment and torment being the lot of the righteous dead, God's Word represents Christians *entering heaven, "clothed in the white robes of Christ's righteousness,* and *palms of victory in their hands, shouting Hallelujah!"* "Blessing and honor, glory and power unto Him who sitteth upon the Throne and unto *the Lamb forever!* Unto Him who loved us and washed us from our sins in His own blood, unto Him be glory *forever and ever!"* No. Thank God there is *no dark Purgatory of suffering and torment* awaiting the *true Christian,* but *only rest, peace and joy with Christ forever.* It is a shame that covetous men for the sake of wealth should *blacken and misrepresent the Glorious Gospel of Christ* by such *false teachings as Purgatory,* in order to work on the feelings of bereaved souls with the *harrowing fear of torment,* and thus *make gain!*

Roman priests quote I Peter 3:19 to support their dogma; does this text prove that there is a purgatory?

This text gives *no ground whatever* for asserting that there *is such a place.* The Church of Rome's mistaken notion is, that while Christ's body lay in the grave after His crucifixion, His soul *went to purgatory to preach to the lost.* They were lost, were condemned, because they were *"disobedient";* they *had rejected God's warnings and offers of mercy* through Noah, "for 120 years." But this *contradicts the Roman theory,* for "the lost" do *not go to Purgatory, only Good Christians* are supposed to go to Purgatory, *the lost go to hell!* The word "prison" refers to *hell,* for in Rev. 20:7, Satan is spoken of as "loosed" from "his prison," and Jude 6 and II Peter 2:4 both speak of *the angels in hell, in "everlasting chains."* The expression "spirits in prison" means the spirits who are NOW in prison or hell; they were *not in prison at the time they were preached to.* The natural interpretation is, that Christ, *through His servant Noah,* preached to unbelievers before the flood, but they *refused to repent, rejected His offers* of mercy and, as a result, are *now in the prison of hell.* The text is a warning against disobedience to God and rejection of the Gospel. Compare II Peter 2:5, where Noah is spoken of as "a preacher of righteousness." Similarly in I Peter 4:6, the Gospel was preached to the ancients who are *now dead,* who suffered persecution from men in the flesh, that they might be *led to repent-*

ance and *live unto God in the Spirit.* Compare Gal. 3:8, where it is said the Gospel was *"before-preached to Abraham."*

The Papal dogma of Purgatory is not only contrary to Scripture, dishonors the holy character of God, His mercy, justice, and love, but also *contradicts the testimony of early Christian leaders,* who rejected this *false dogma.* The Roman Church now teaches that *"pious and justified souls"* who departed this life in a *state of grace"* *must go to Purgatorial torments! Catechism of Trent,* I, v. 5. Perrone, *Prael. Theol.* The pains of Purgatory, both physical and mental, are the same as the pains of hell, except as regards duration. Benedict XIV, *De Sacrif. Missae,* II, ix, 3, 6; xvii, 3.

This directly contradicts what the Book of Wisdom, which the Roman Church accounts canonical, declares: "But the souls of the righteous are in the hands of God, and there shall *no torment touch them.* Their departure is taken for misery, and their going from us as utter destruction, but *they are in peace."* Wisdom iii, 1-3. Though the dead are justified souls, which according to the Council of Trent, includes *sanctification, union with Christ and the full enjoyment of faith, hope and charity* (Conc. Trident VI, vii) yet the Catholic Church represents them as *pursued by "the wrath, anger and vengeance of God!"* (Cardinal Wiseman, *Lecture* ii.)

PURGATORY CONTRADICTS OTHER ROMANIST DOCTRINES

Venial sins are declared to be punished in Purgatory although it it also declared that venial sins are *so trifling that no one is bound to confess them at all!* St. John Chrysostom took the Protestant or true Scriptural view, saying, "Where there is *grace,* there is *remission;* where there is *remission,* there *is no punishment."* *Hom.* VIII, *in Epist. ad Rom.* St. Bernard declared: "God acts with *liberality;* he forgives *entirely."* *Serm. de Fragmentis.* Leading authorities testified against Purgatory and Indulgences. "We have *no testimony in the Scriptures, nor among the Fathers, in favor of Indulgences,* but only the authority of some modern authors." St. Antoninus, Archbishop of Florence, 1459. *Summ. Theol.,* I, 3.

Cardinal Fisher, 1535, wrote: "Since it was so late before Purgatory was admitted into the Universal Church, who can be surprised that in the earlier period of the Church, *no use was made of Indulgences?*" Fisher, *Adv. Luter*, 18.

Thus the overwhelming testimony of Holy Scripture and of the Fathers proves that the dogma of Purgatory is *utterly baseless;* there *is no such place*. Purgatory was *an invention* of the Roman priests in the Dark Ages, and became a fixed dogma of the Church of Rome *as late as the year 1438,* that is, less than a century before the Protestant Reformation. Think of it taking popes and priests *14 centuries* to *find out that there was a place called Purgatory!* Could anything be imagined *more false and repulsive* than this dogma? The Priest called to the bedside of a dying man, administers what is called "extreme unction," and pronounces *"full and final absolution."* And yet the man is hardly buried before money is *cruelly demanded from his mourning relatives* to *pay for masses* to be said "in order to *shorten the period of his torment in purgatorial fires!"*

So shameless was the rivalry of shrines in France, in offering special bargains for Masses that the Roman Church was called *La réligion d'argent,* "the creed of money." St. Peter gives a special mark by which to recognize false teachers in the Church, "Through *covetousness* shall they with feigned words *make merchandise of you."* II Peter 2:3.

What is the doctrine of the Reformed Church regarding the State of believers after death?

The Protestant doctrine is the *apostolic doctrine of Holy Scripture,* simply and beautifully stated in the Westminster Shorter Catechism, No. 37: "The souls of believers are at their death made perfect in holiness and *do immediately pass into glory;* and their bodies, being still *united to Christ,* do rest in their graves till the Resurrection." I Thess. 4:14, Rom. 8:23, II Cor. 5:6-8, I Cor. 15:51-57. Thus the Reformed Church believes there is a heaven and a hell, but *no intermediate place, no purgatory. We thank God for the unspeakable comfort and hope which the Reformed doctrine gives to thousands, as they stand by the open grave of their beloved dead!* Rev. 14:13.

If the dogma of Purgatory is directly contrary to Scripture, as we have seen, and so repulsive to right-minded people, why does the Church of Rome persist in teaching it?

Because the Papal hierarchy *love money,* and the fear of purgatorial torment is a *great source of revenue.* Belief in purgatory is the *false foundation of Masses for the dead.* The laity are taught that their beloved dead are suffering the torments of fire, but that release may be had by *liberal payment for masses.* The secular press in Romanist countries often contains notices of bequests for masses and advertisements of lotteries or raffles *"for suffering souls in purgatory,"* saying, "Will you for the small sum of one dollar leave your loved ones in torment?"

A Roman Church in Mexico not long ago published this announcement of a lottery, "At the last drawing the following numbers were successful, and their purchasers may be assured that their well-beloved ones are *now delivered from purgatory:* No. 841. The soul of the lawyer, James Vasquez, is released, and is now in heavenly joy. No. 43. The soul of Signora Calderon has been rendered happy forever. No. 762. The soul of the aged widow, M. de Parras, has been forever set free. A new drawing will take place in this Church of the Virgin, and for four successful lots *four tortured souls will be transported from purgatory to heaven!* Tickets at *five francs each* may be procured from the priest. *Will you leave your beloved to languish eternally in purgatory to save yourself five francs?"*

Sir Hiram Maxim related this actual occurrence in Ireland. A Roman Church member died and left a will, in which there was the usual bequest for masses to be said for the dead man's soul in purgatory. The local priest called and *demanded £100* to say the masses. The executor asked how many masses would be said for that sum, and being informed, told the priest to return in two weeks. When he returned, the executor informed him that he had written to the Vatican where the masses had been said *for £20,* and showed *the Vatican's receipt and certificate.* The priest left in anger, but the grieving relatives of the deceased were kept, at least in part, from being *swindled by an avaricious priest!*

As the Gospel of God's free grace, which the Roman Church professes to believe, is bestowed *"without money and without price,"*

THE FUTURE STATE, PURGATORY, AND MASSES FOR THE DEAD

one might reasonably suppose that the ordinary dictates of humanity would lead Roman priests to perform services for the dead without charge. But alas, it *is not so!* Ordinarily it is, *no payment, no masses,* and therefore, *no "repose for the soul."* Mercenary leaders saw in this invention *an opportunity to amass wealth too great* to let slip! The harrowing appeal to the fear and affection of relatives to *deliver their dead from torment* is rarely made in vain. And so the *cruel delusion of masses for the dead,* like Indulgences, continues to be practiced, *casting a blight on those who ought to rejoice in the full salvation of God,* and *bringing reproach on the Holy Name,* which is above every name, because *merchandise is made of His precious atonement!*

No one can prevent the Roman hierarchy from making gain of the fears and sorrows of their people, but one should protest with all the energy of his soul against their dishonoring the Christian religion by calling this false and ignoble superstition a part of its God-given doctrines!

THE GRAVE ABUSE OF INDULGENCES STILL CONTINUES

Surely in later times the Church of Rome must have perceived this grave error, and wished to abolish it?

Alas, no! Although the popes knew that Indulgenes were *wholly contrary to Scripture,* and *conducive to bad morals,* they could not resist the temptation to *make easy money by the sale of them.* The *demoralization* which resulted from this practice was *terrible,* and *spread like poison through the Church.* In 1250, Grosseteste, bishop of London, England, protested to the pope that the *low morality of the priesthood* was due to *purchasable pardons.* "Rome was a fountain of pardons for all violations of the decalogue." Flick, page 590. Schick, a Roman Catholic writer, records that pope Paul III drew revenue *even from brothels in Rome!* A commission of Cardinals reported to him that pardons and dispensations *produced indescribable scandals,* and begged him by the *blood of Christ to put an end to them!*

At the Council of Trent, Claude d'Espence said of the Papal Court: "the sins of men are *her golden harvest,* the evidence of which is *her super-abundant wealth*. When money is the object, *everything is permitted;* there is no crime for which one *cannot buy a dispensation at Rome!* As soon as the money is paid into the chest the *sin is forgiven.* The only unpardonable offence is *to be poor!* It was reported on good authority that pope Pius IV (died 1565) in six years amassed a fortune of *six million scudi,* or about *6 million U. S. dollars!*

Of pope Pius VI (died 1799) and his Court, Bishop Ricci wrote: "Rest assured *no one* in Rome *knows what religion is.* The pope is near Florence; the scandals of his entourage help much to destroy him in the eyes of the people."

Even in this "enlightened" 20th century, the popes still issue Indulgences and Dispensations, for the practice is very profitable. Indulgences are not openly sold as in the time of the Reformation, but it is well understood that "the faithful" must *not come empty handed!* At Easter, 1926, the *pope offered Indulgences* to all who came on pilgrimage to certain Churches in Rome, and a cardinal was sent to dispense them. The writer saw him sitting with a rod in his hand, and a long line of people passed before him. Each one in the line was *tapped with the rod,* and thereby was supposed to *receive the papal Indulgence.* The Cardinal apparently did not know whom he was tapping, and it seemed to be equally a matter of indifference to the careless crowd who were supposed to receive the Indulgences!

Again in 1933, Pius XI proclaimed a "holy year" and urged the faithful to come on pilgrimage to Rome, promising indulgences to all who visited certain Churches, and repeated certain prayers. While no sale was announced, it was generally understood that *pilgrims must not be unmindful of "Peter's pence."* The outward form of Indulgences may be changed, but *the same God-dishonoring practice remains in principle,* a practice with which *true religion cannot coexist. Watchful* Rome, where wealth and worldly advantage are concerned; but *sleeping* Rome concerning *Spiritual truth and forsaking error!* O, that God would raise up another Luther to awaken the sleeping church, and to proclaim again with trumpet tones *the free grace of God in Christ,*—

THE JUST SHALL LIVE BY FAITH!

CHAPTER XI

THE CELIBACY OF THE CLERGY

According to the Word of God, does holiness inhere in any outward condition or state, as of marriage or celibacy?

According to Holy Scripture, holiness does *not* inhere in any outward state or condition. Holiness is a matter *of the heart,* which is *renewed by the Holy Spirit* and is *wholly yielded to God to do His will.* There are many holy men and women *in* the marriage state, like John Wesley's father and mother, and there are many *unholy men and women* who are *celibate.* I Sam. 16:7, Matt. 5:8, Eph. 4:23, 24, I Peter 3:15.

What is the teaching of Holy Scripture concerning marriage?

Scripture declares that marriage, though *not* a sacrament, was originally *ordained by God at the creation.* Gen. 2:18, 24; also that "marriage is *honorable in all.*" Heb. 13:4, Ps. 128:1, 3, 6. The Holy Spirit uses marriage as a type of that most sacred of all relations, the union of the Church and the believer with their Lord. Eph. 5:23-33.

What does the papal Church teach regarding the marriage of Churchmen?

The papal Church presumes to assert "that the marriage of Churchmen is a *"pollution and a sacrilege!"* It makes celibacy compulsory for all clergy, monks and nuns. Bellarmine, *De Monach,* 2:30. *Decret-Gratian,* 82. Many Roman writers extol the celibate state as peculiarly holy.

What warrant from God's Word does the Church of Rome give for this opinion?

No warrant can be given, for God's Word clearly opposes this whole conception. For centuries celibacy was *not* practiced by the Christian ministry. St. Patrick of Ireland (died 469) said his *father* and his *grandfather* were both *ministers of the Church*. Celibacy did not become a fixed law of the Church until the Dark Ages—the *eleventh century*. Hildebrand, pope Gregory VII, *compelled* the Church to adopt it, in order to establish his autocratic power over the clergy and religious Orders.

GRAVE ERRORS WERE TAUGHT IN CONNECTION WITH CELIBACY

What other dogmas does the Church of Rome teach in connection with celibacy, which are directly contrary to Holy Scripture?

1. The Church of Rome teaches "that vows may be made *to the saints*." Bellarmine, *De cult, Sanct.*, 3:9.

On the other hand, the Bible teaches that vows like prayer, should be made to *God alone*. There is *not one instance* in Scripture of vows being made *to a saint!*

"Unto *Thee* (God), shall the vow be performed." Ps. 65:1.

"Vow, and pay unto the *Lord your God*." Ps. 76:11.

Bellarmine contradicts himself by confessing that a vow is "a promise made *to God*"; then it should be *paid to God,* and *not* to a saint.

2. The Church of Rome teaches "that children may make vows, and perform them, *without the consent of their parents*." Bellarmine, *De Monach.*, 2:36.

This precept is a direct violation of the Fifth Commandment, as given in Colossians 3:20: "Children obey your parents *in all things;* for this is well pleasing unto the Lord."

It is also a violation of the Fifth Commandment, as explained in Numb. 30:3-5. If Jewish children might *not* perform vows which God approved, *without the consent of their parents, how much more* should children not perform vows which God does *not approve,* without the consent of their parents!

3. "That to enter a cloister, it is permitted to *break the bonds of marriage*." Council of Trent, *sess.* 24:6, 8. Bellarmine, *De Monach.*, 2:37, 38. *De Matrimon.*, 1:14.

This dogma is a *shameful violation of God's command,* "What God hath joined together, let *not man* put *asunder*." Matt. 19:6.

The Roman Church thus dares to sanction what God has *expressly forbidden,*—a mark of *apostasy!*

4. "That mendicant (or begging) friars are in a state of perfection." Bellarmine, *De Monach.*, 2:20, 45.

God's Word declares that *no man* is *in a state of perfection.* Eccles. 7:20, Phil. 3:12.

Also that *no Christian* should be *idle and beg,* but should work and "eat his own bread"; "for if any man will not work, neither should he eat." II Thess. 3:10-12.

The Church of Rome's grave error is that of *the heathen,* of Hindu and Buddhist devotees. Their "holy men" are celibates and beg, instead of working for an honest living. Rome's mistake is based on a wrong interpretation of Christ's words to the rich, young ruler, Matt. 19:21. Here our Lord was *not* teaching that there was holiness or perfection in *poverty;* He was showing the young man his *besetting sin,* viz.: that he loved his wealth more than he loved God, and therefore could not follow Christ and obtain salvation.

5. "That for those who have made the vow of celibacy (continence) it is worse to marry than to *commit immorality"* (literally to "abandon themselves to luxury") . Bellarmine, *De Monach.*, 2:30.

This grossly immoral teaching makes it better to be *guilty of fornication* than to abandon celibacy and *be decently married!,* that is, rather than break rules which the popes have made, it is *better to break the law of Almighty God!* Is not this another mark of apostasy? Matt. 15:9.

THE ATTITUDE OF CHRIST AND HIS APOSTLES TOWARD MARRIAGE

What was the attitude of Christ toward marriage?

He endorsed Marriage, declaring that it was of *divine institution "from the beginning."* Matt. 19:4-6.

He showed His approval by attending the marriage feast at Cana. John 2:1, 2.

He chose *married men as apostles.* St. Peter was married; so also Philip the evangelist. Mark 1:30, 31, Acts 21:9. The holy prophets were married, as Noah, Moses, Isaiah, Ezekiel and Hosea. The high priest of the nation was a married man. Levit. 21:13-15.

In the pastoral epistles, written specially for ministers, St. Paul, under the guidance of the Holy Spirit, wrote: "A bishop (i.e., a presbyter or minister) must be blameless, the *husband of one wife*." I Tim. 3:2-5.

"Let the deacons be the husbands of one wife." I Tim. 3:12. The apostolic church evidently did not believe that celibacy was a holy state.

While St. Paul himself remained unmarried, it was *not* because he regarded celibacy as *holy*, and the marriage of Christian ministers as "*a pollution and a sacrilege!*" Paul declared plainly that it was lawful for him to marry (I Cor. 9:5, 6:12). But it was "not expedient," because he was constantly traveling, visiting churches, and because of the hardships and persecutions to which his family would be exposed. I Cor. 7:25.

Regarding his counsels, which seem to discourage marriage, he says plainly they were *his personal opinions,* and were *not the commandment of God.* I Cor. 7:6, 12, 25.

He sums up the matter thus:

"If thou marry, thou hast *not sinned:* and if a virgin marry, she hath *not sinned.*" I Cor. 7:28. Thus it is clear that the Church of Rome's position regarding the celibacy of the clergy is *wholly wrong:* it is directly opposed to the doctrine of God's Word.

If without sanction in Scripture, why did the Roman Church make this unchristian law forbidding the clergy to marry? Pope Gregory VII made this law in order to have absolute control over the Roman clergy and religious Orders. Having been cut off from family and social ties, priests, monks and nuns, became entirely dependent on his will, so that the *pope's* interests and *not God's service,* became their chief concern. The pope thus obtained an army sworn to carry out his behests, and won the conflict which had been waged for centuries concerning the supreme authority in the Church; and also increased his temporal power over princes and states.

THE NATURAL AND DISASTROUS EFFECT OF ENFORCED CELIBACY

What was the result of enforcing this unnatural law forbidding the clergy and religious Orders to marry?

The result of the law enforcing celibacy was just what might have been expected, viz.: *unspeakable license and immorality,* which one would prefer to pass over in silence. Pope Gregory VII, after making the law, was accused by Cardinal Hugo Candidus of adultery and of procuring the murder of his predecessor, Alexander II, and was superseded by pope Clement III, whom he denounced as Antichrist! Gregory in turn was denounced by Cardinal Peter Damiani as *"Saint Satan"!* Dallmann's *"How Peter Became Pope,"* Section V, pages 53, 54.

In the 9th Century immorality and vicious practices became so widespread and virulent, that the Emperor Charlemagne issued an edict to restrain the clergy and monastic Orders. He said, "We have been informed to our great horror that many monks are addicted to *debauchery* and to *all sorts of vile abominations,* even to unnatural sins. We forbid all such practices and command the monks to cease swarming over the country, and forbid nuns to *practice fornication* and *intoxication.* We shall not allow them any longer to be prostitutes, thieves and murderers, nor to spend their time in debauchery and singing improper songs. Also priests are forbidden to haunt taverns and market places for the purpose of *seducing mothers and daughters."* *Catholicism and Protestantism,* by J. Demetrius, p. 26.

An Italian bishop of the tenth century, describing the morals of his time, declared that if he were to enforce the canons against unchaste persons performing ecclesiastical rites, *no one would be left in the Church* except the boys; and if he were to observe the canon against *bastards, these also* must be excluded!

A tax was systematically levied by princes on clergymen for *license to keep concubines.* Lecky's *History of European Morals.*

During the eleventh century no less than *80 councils* were held in France, *every one of* which *denounced the simony and unchastity of the clergy.*

Bernard of Clairvaux vigorously protested against enforcing celibacy on the priesthood, as contrary to reason and Divine law. He said, *"Deprive the Church of honorable marriage, and you fill her with concubinage, incest, and all manner of nameless vice and uncleanness."*

11

Bernard severely reproved pope Eugenius III for his gross sins. "Who art thou? You, who were ordained to be a shepherd of souls,— are better suited to be a shepherd *of devils*. You call yourselves servants of Christ: you are rather *servants of Antichrist!*"

Cardinal de Vitry declared the older monastic houses were not fit for a decent man or woman to live in! The clergy *owned brothels*. The papal authorities at Rome taxed the earnings *of prostitutes*. McCabe, page 71, 72.

The Dominican, Henry of Hereford, England, wrote in the 14th century that the clergy "traded the holy things of the Church *for women and concubines*, and *diced for them.*" *How Peter Became Pope*, by William Dallmann, page 70. The German abbot, William of Muenchen-Gladbach, made a similar declaration.

St. Catharine of Siena told pope Gregory XI that in Avignon there was "the stench of *infernal vices.*" Of the monks she said, "Their God is *their belly;* during the night, when they ought to be chanting psalms, they have unfortunate women visit them; and the nuns have become *public prostitutes*. They who ought to bring life, *bring death.*" Engert, 2:67. She denounced Pope Clement VII as Antichrist! Dallmann, page 73.

St. Teresa of Spain affirmed that many religious houses and convents were "*a short cut to hell.*" "If young women will be wicked at home, their wickedness cannot long be hidden; but in monasteries such as I speak of, their wickedness can be completely covered up from every human eye. Many of them honestly wish to withdraw from the world, only to find themselves in *ten times worse worlds* of *sensuality and devilry.*"

Do not these papal pronouncements requiring celibacy, with their grossly immoral results, fulfill the warnings of Scripture regarding Apostasy?

These papal pronouncements requiring celibacy *exactly fulfill the predictions* of Holy Scripture regarding *false teachers forbidding marriage*. "The Spirit speaketh expressly that in the latter times some shall depart from the faith (the Greek for 'depart' is 'apostatize') giving heed to seducing spirits and doctrines of devils, speaking lies in hypocrisy, having their conscience seared with a hot iron, *forbidding to marry,*" etc. I Tim. 4:1-3.

Here it is plainly declared that to forbid marriage, as the Church of Rome does to the clergy, is a mark of apostasy, a "doctrine of devils." These are not the words of erring man, but the infallible word of Almighty God, from whose all searching eye nothing is hid, and who will render to every man according to his works. Thus both Holy Scripture and history show the grievous sin of *popes who presume to alter the Law of God;* of attaching to the celibate state the notion of holiness, and of forcing on the clergy and on religious Orders an unnatural law which, sooner or later, was sure to produce disastrous results.

It was inevitable that in the loneliness and morbid condition which celibacy often induces, there should arise grave temptations to immorality which ordinary human beings were unable to resist; and as a result, multitudes of well-meaning, but misguided men and women have not only themselves fallen into a deep pit, but have also *dragged down with them thousands of innocent souls to perdition.* Most of them, perhaps, did not do wrong deliberately; they were *victims of an arbitrary and oppressive system* for which their "infallible" leaders were responsible! But God's law is *eternally true;* men cannot break it with impunity." "Be not deceived: God is not mocked; for whatsoever a man (or Church) soweth, that shall he (or it) *also reap!"* Gal. 6:7.

Chapter XII

PILGRIMAGE, INCENSE, "HOLY WATER," ROSARIES, RELICS, ETC.

The year 1933 was called a "holy year" by Pius XI, who exhorted the "faithful" everywhere to make pilgrimages to Rome. Are pilgrimages enjoined in the Word of God?

Pilgrimages are *not* enjoined in the Word of God, nor can they, according to Scripture, be considered pious, meritorious acts. They are much in vogue in pagan religions, as Buddhism, Hinduism, Mohammedanism, etc., as a means of making merit, and winning the favor of their gods.

THE MISTAKEN BASIS OF PILGRIMAGES

Pilgrimages are founded on the mistaken assumption that they are a mark of *fervent piety*, and help *to win salvation*. It is reported that in the summer of 1933 two zealous pilgrims carried large wooden crosses from northern Italy to Rome; they were much noticed in the public press as *winning merit* and a *reputation for sanctity!*

A second mistaken assumption is that certain localities are *peculiarly holy*, where God is *specially accessible;* as if finding God and obtaining His blessing depended on the place, and *not* on a repentant, believing heart.

The Lord's Word, spoken through Moses nearly 15 centuries before Christ, and repeated in substance by St. Paul, shows the mistaken notion involved in pilgrimage; that *certain places* are specially *favorable* for worship and for *obtaining access to God*, an idea commonly entertained among heathen nations. Referring to salvation he said, "It is not beyond the sea that thou shouldst say, 'who shall go over the sea and bring it unto us? But the Word is very nigh thee, in thy mouth and in thine heart, that is, 'the *Word of faith*' *which we preach*." The Apostle used this passage and enforced its meaning, to show that holiness and acceptance with God do *not depend on locality, nor on long pilgrimages,* but on a *believing heart,* for God can be *found everywhere* and is ready to bless, if we *seek Him with the whole heart in the way that He commands.* Deut. 30: 11-14, Rom. 10: 6-10, Jer. 29: 13.

Our Saviour in conversation with the woman of Samaria also stressed this momentous truth, that there is no need of pilgrimage, for true worship does *not depend on place or outward circumstance,* but on the *state of the worshipper's heart.* "Woman, believe me, the hour cometh, when you shall neither in this mountain, nor yet at Jerusalem, worship the Father. God is a spirit, and they that worship Him must worship Him *in Spirit and in truth.*" John 4: 21-24, Isa. 57: 15, 66: 2.

If Pilgrimages are not sanctioned by the Word of God, why do popes presume to urge them?

Because they accord with the natural notions and desires of the *sinful human heart* which wishes to be doing something to procure salvation; they make a fair show before the world, *widely advertise the papal religion;* and bring *large revenue to the Vatican.* Boniface VIII (died 1303) proclaimed a jubilee with *plenary indulgence,* to be repeated *every hundredth year,* and crowds of pilgrims flocked to Rome, bringing the pope enormous sums of money. The historian, Gibbon, mentioned that at the jubilee "two priests stood day and night with rakes in their hands to gather, without counting, the heaps of gold and silver that were poured on the altars." Later popes considered a hundred years too long a time to wait for such a lucrative harvest, so Clement VI (died 1352) reduced the interval to *fifty years;* Urban VI (died 1389) still further reduced it to *thirty-three years,* and Paul II (died 1471) finally reduced it to *twenty-five years.*

INCENSE, CANDLES, ETC.

Is it proper to use incense, candles, etc., in the worship of God?

No; for the Word of God does not prescribe them for the Christian Church, and whatever is *not prescribed by God* should *not be used.* "Ye shall *not add* unto the Word which I command you." Heb. 8: 5,

Deut. 4:2, 12:28, 32. All of these texts teach,—*"Follow exactly the directions that God gave for His worship."* Note that the Apostolic Church *did not use them;* for the aim of that Church was *simplicity,* the *avoidance of all outward show,* and *concentration of thought* on what was *spiritual.* The Church of Rome borrowed incense and candles from *heathen worship,* as acknowledged by Gregory I, and later by Cardinal Newman. See final note of Chapter IV, *The Church's object of worship.* Christian converts of the *first four centuries* considered incense, etc., *as an abomination,* because they knew the heathen origin of these things, and their *debasing association with idolatry.*

But were not incense and lamps used in Old Testament times in the service of the Tabernacle and Temple?

Yes, for God specially commanded their use then; but He *nowhere commands their use in the New Testament.* Moreover Scripture shows that incense, candles, etc., like circumcision, animal sacrifices, and the whole Old Testament ritual were *"types and shadows,"* which were *done away in Christ.* Heb. 8:5, 8:23, 10:1.

The only references in the New Dispensation to incense, etc., are found in Revelation, where it is used in *a figurative sense,* referring to the *prayers of God's people.* "Golden vials full of odors (incense), which are the *prayers of saints."* Rev. 5:8, 8:3, 4.

HOLY WATER

"Holy Water," so called, is an empty superstition of the Dark Ages, also *borrowed from paganism,* and introduced about A.D. 1000. Pagan temples had holy water stoups long before the Church of Rome had them. Justin Martyr, who died about A.D. 163, wrote: "The pagans (Gentiles) on entering their temples, *sprinkle themselves with water."* One looks in vain in Scripture for any word that allows its use. Holy Water, and other inventions, like making the *sign of the Cross,* etc., do *not help true worship,* but *really hinder it,* for they distract attention from what is inward and spiritual to outward things, which too often *are a "vain" show, only to be seen of men."* The Holy Spirit warns of this in Matthew 6:1-5.

ROSARIES

What is the harm of using rosary beads in prayer?

The practice of "telling beads" in prayer was borrowed *from Buddhism,* and antedates Romanism many centuries. Mohammedans also use rosaries. They were introduced into the Church about the year 1090. The practice not only has *no sanction in Scripture,* but is *opposed to the whole spirit of the Gospel,* which *forbids mechanical forms in the worship of God.* Using beads destroys the true spirit of prayer; it is like the *praying by rote of the Tibetans,* using prayer wheels and hand rattles. Our Lord uttered a solemn warning against such methods when He spoke of "vain repetitions" and "much speaking" like the heathen. Matt. 6:5-8.

The Roman rosary seems to exalt a human being more than God. It is said to consist of 166 beads; one bead representing the Creed; 15 beads representing *Paternosters,* addressed to *God the Father;* and 150 beads are *Ave Marias,* addressed to *the Virgin Mary.* The prayers to Mary are thus *ten times* more numerous than those addressed to God—"worshipping and serving the creature more than the Creator!" and no prayers seem to be addressed to our Saviour or to the Holy Spirit.

During the pilgrimage of 1933, it is reported that the pope prescribed a set form of prayers for pilgrims, who in order to receive Indulgences must visit four leading Churches in Rome, each one three times and each time prayers must be repeated in three places; before the altar, six *paternosters,* six *Ave Marias,* and six *glorias;* before the crucifix, repeat the Creed three times, and before Mary's image, seven *Ave Marias.* As one reads the Scriptures, one cannot but note how different is the praying of saints recorded there! Note how solemn was King Solomon's prayer in I Kings 8:22-53; see Ezra's humble confession of sins in Ezra 9:6-15, and Daniel's heartfelt confession in Daniel 9:4-19, as well as the beautiful outpouring of his heart's longing by St. Paul, in Ephesians 1:17-23 and 3:14-21. These are the *genuine expression of hearts that long for God,* as contrasted with the cold, mechanical repetitions of souls *doing penance!*

How should true believers pray?

The Word of God teaches that true believers, avoiding repetitions and praying by rote, should *"pray in the Holy Spirit,"* reverently, humbly, with a believing thankful heart, thinking of what they are doing, and of the great King to whose throne they are coming.

"Ye beloved,—*praying in the Holy Ghost,* Keep yourselves in the love of God." Jude 20.

"I will pray with the spirit and with the understanding." I Cor. 14:15, Eph. 6:18.

"Always laboring-fervently (Greek, ἀγωνίζομαι *agonize*) in prayers that ye may stand perfect and complete in all the will of God." Col. 4:12.

What other acts of penance do pilgrims often perform?

Pilgrims often ascend the "sacred stairway" (*scala santa*) at St. John Lateran, on their knees, repeating prayers on each step. It was here that Martin Luther, burdened with a deep sense of sin, *vainly sought peace*, until *the light of the Holy Spirit shone into his heart*, showing him the *folly of penances, pilgrimages and other "dead works,"* and leading him to *trust in the all-sufficient Redeemer alone for salvation.* The glorious truth revealed to the prophet Habakkuk and expounded by St. Paul, brought peace and joy to his heart, and *made a new man of him,—*"THE JUST SHALL LIVE BY FAITH!" Hab. 2:4, Rom. 1:17.

RELICS

What is meant by Relics?

Relics are supposed to be parts of the body, or of the clothing, or of some object associated with *the person of a saint or the Virgin Mary,* or even of our *Lord Himself.* It is a most regrettable and harmful superstition that members of the Roman Communion venerate these, and often attribute miraculous power to them. Some of these relics exhibited as genuine at the Vatican and in other Churches are: pieces of the Saviour's Cross, two thorns from the crown of thorns our Lord wore; part of His cradle at Bethlehem, and His swaddling clothes; part of the penitent thief's cross; one of the thirty pieces of silver paid to Judas to betray Christ; the *tail of*

Balaam's ass; a *feather from the angel Gabriel's wing;* and many heads, five arms, and several dozen fingers, said to be those of John the Baptist; Veronica's handkerchief, etc., etc.

Are these relics genuine?

Probably very few, if any. Most of them *cannot be genuine,* for the many pieces of wood exhibited as parts of Christ's cross, are *enough to make many crosses.* And how could John the Baptist have as many heads, arms and fingers as those attributed to him? Many cases of *fraud* in relics are proved by the conflicting testimony of "infallible" popes. Take for instance the case of *St. Bartholomew's Body.*

The Roman *Breviary* and *Martyrology* allege that this apostle's body was removed *from Benevento to Rome* by the Emperor Otto, who reigned A.D. 983 to 1000. The *Bulls of pope Alexander III and Sixtus V declare this was a fact.* But *the Church of Benevento* asserts that Bartholomew's body is *still there* in the Church, and produces as proof the *Bulls of Leo IX, Stephen IX, Benedict XII, Clement VI, Boniface IX* and *Urban V!* Thus two "infallible" popes with the Breviary and Martyrology declare one thing, and six "infallible" popes declare just the opposite! Whom must one believe? Note also that *17 other Churches claim parts of Bartholomew's body!*

The Handkerchief of St. Veronica

The Handkerchief of St. Veronica, with which she is alleged to have wiped the Lord's face in His agony, and on which his likeness was said to be imprinted, is claimed *by 7 different places,* viz.: *Rome, Turin, Milan, Cadouin, Besançon, Compiegne* and *Aix-la-chapelle!* Four papal briefs *guarantee the genuineness* of the handkerchief shown at *Turin,* and *14 briefs* the one at *Cadouin!* Which are "the faithful" to believe? How can intelligent, honest men avoid *disbelieving all such relics and the papal guarantees of them?*

Amulets and Charms

Similar to relics is the superstitious use of the mechanical appliances called amulets or charms among members of the papal church, which in no respect differ from those worn by *members of African savage tribes to ward off danger or disease.* Take for example,

THE CARMELITE SCAPULAR

which is alleged to have been miraculously bestowed by the Virgin Mary on St. Simon Stock. This scapular is said to confer on the wearer a *share in the merit of all good works done throughout the whole Church and by all fraternities existing up to the time of pope Sixtus IV* (1471-1484). It also confers on the wearer, unless rebellious, *absolute immunity from hell!* It is alleged also that Mary promised pope John XXII (1316-1334) that she would *go every Saturday to Purgatory and release any Scapularists who might be there and take them to heaven!* This amulet is *vouched for* by John XXII in the Bulla Sabatina, A.D. 1322, and was *confirmed by five other popes,* Alexander V, Clement VII, Pius V, Gregory XIII and Paul V! (Clement VII was the pope whom St. Catharine of Siena called *Antichrist!*). Dallmann, page 73.

THE CORD OF ST. FRANCIS

This charm, in addition to other benefits, is supposed to confer *6 times a year,* a general absolution, *"restoring completely baptismal innocence!"*

Is it not incredible that people who profess to be Christian and to believe the teachings of Holy Scripture, should tolerate such childish and palpably false superstitions?

The incident mentioned in II Kings 13:21 of a corpse which was cast into Elisha's sepulchre and revived, is sometimes cited as ground for belief in relics. Is this at all applicable?

No, it has *no application whatever* to relics. No hint of the use or veneration of relics is found in God's Word. It is deplorable to see the Church of Rome substituting empty superstitions for Gospel doctrine, and thus *leading unbelievers to belittle and ridicule the Christian faith.* The use of relics is one of the many additions to the Gospel which popes have presumed to make in *direct violation of God's command,* "Thou shalt not add thereto." Deut. 12:32.

Is there anything in Holy Scripture to justify the use of relics?

No, there is nothing in Holy Scripture to justify the use of relics or veneration of them, or belief in any miraculous power in them.

They are a survival of the ignorance and superstition of the Dark Ages, which ought to be *discarded by intelligent, sincere people;* and they lead ignorant people to *commit idolatry,* by bowing down to them, kissing them, and paying worship to them. John Huss, "the man of truth," fearlessly denounced the priests who organized false miracles, and sold relics, dispensations, and indulgences; and *the charlatans who proclaimed pilgrimages to revere apocryphal relics."* Huss said, "Religion should *return to the Gospel;* the priests to *humility and verity.* He who humbles himself profits more in his soul than he who should go upon a pilgrimage from one end of the world to the other, shedding his blood along the way. He who is humble, pleases God. Pilgrimages are *not a divine institution,* but rather a *foolish invention of men!"* Mussolini's *John Huss, the Man of Truth.*

How does the Roman Church try to justify the use of relics?

The Church of Rome asserts that relics are intended to "excite good thoughts and increase devotion." But instead of doing this, they generally *excite irreverent curiosity* in careless sightseers, and discredit true religion by *exhibiting as genuine* what *men know to be counterfeit.* Why not rather use *the means God has given* "to excite good thought and increase devotion," viz.: by reverent *study of God's Word* and *by prayer?* The right way to honor a good man who has passed away, is *not* to *venerate a piece of bone,* but to *emulate his virtues* and *serve God in sincerity and truth.*

THE WORSHIP OF RELICS

Members of the Roman Communion often deny that they worship relics; they say they only "venerate" them. But leading Roman Church theologians, like the Jesuit Dens, declare that the *supreme worship of latreia* should be paid to the relics of our Lord's Passion, as nails of the Cross, the crown of thorns, the seamless coat, etc., and the *second grade of worship,* δουλεία, should be paid to relics of saints. Dens' *Theology,* V, page 45.

What folly thus to deceive the people by imaginary verbal hair-splitting! Christ said plainly, excluding all worship of human beings and material things: "Thou shalt worship the Lord thy God, and *Him only* shalt thou serve!" Matt. 3:10.

The Church of Rome has many things to get rid of, as the "Proposed Reformations of the Benedictine Abbey," near Cologne, testify: Benediction of the Blessed Sacrament, repetitious rosaries, miraculous shrines and medals, imaginative meditations, morbid self-analyses, regimenting of consciences, devotional confessions,—all these were unknown in the early Christian Church, and are useless not to say highly harmful today! The chaff should not be husbanded and the wheat cast aside! *The Converted Catholic*, page 67.

What attitude should sincere believers take concerning relics?

Sincere Christians should *wholly reject them* as *without warrant* in Scripture and as *unworthy of true religion*. Relics like other unjustifiable additions to the Gospel, *turn men's thoughts away from God and saving truth*, and fix them on external things, which are "unprofitable and vain." Titus 3:9. They are a *form of will-worship* which St. Paul says, "make a fair show in the flesh." They are among *the "dead works"* from the practice of which "the blood of Christ *should purge our consciences*." Heb. 9:14.

It is easy to perceive that as true religion of the heart declines, men vainly try to fill the aching void by additions which, while having the *appearance of piety, and pleasing the thoughtless masses of the people*, are wholly *displeasing to God* because *contrary to His revealed will*.

All churches should heed the warning of a thoughtful writer, concerning the *deadening effect of ritualism*, of which the Church of Rome furnishes a melancholy example. Forms and ceremonies may impress the eye and ear, but they *deaden the soul to spiritual truth*. The habitual use of elaborate rites is like an *opiate;* they soothe the senses, but *harden the conscience*, leading the worshipers to *forget the truth*, which the rite was originally meant to convey, and be satisfied with mere *outward mechanical performance*. "When men come to think that rites possess in themselves material and magical virtues, the purpose they were intended to serve is *gone*. Instead of impressing truth and aiding devotion, they *hide God from us*, and make men *practical atheists*." Again, "when ceremonies become an end instead of a means, they *prevent direct communion of the soul with God. It is faith which saves the soul, not the mechanical practice of religious ceremonies. The world has been besotted with ceremonies!*" T. de Stitny, quoted by B. Mussolini.

Chapter XIII

THE RELATION OF CHURCH AND STATE

What does the Word of God teach concerning the relation of Church and State?

The Word of God teaches clearly that Christian ministers and people, being citizens, should render all due respect and obedience to rulers and to the laws of the land. Since the spheres of Church and State are wholly different, they should be kept separate and distinct, neither infringing on the sphere of the other. The Church should faithfully discharge its spiritual duties, and not attempt to control the State; and the State should faithfully discharge its civil and political duties, and not attempt to control the Church.

What Scriptures prove that this is the correct relation?

Our Lord Jesus Christ's own words: "My Kingdom is *not* of this world!" Again, "Render unto Caesar the things that are Caesar's, and unto God the things that are God's." John 18:36, Mark 12:17, Luke 20:25.

Also Matthew 17:24-27, which records that our Lord, although He was King of heaven and earth, yet obeyed the laws and paid tribute to the Roman Emperor.

The apostles also, following Christ's precepts and example, enjoined obedience to the civil government and respect to all rulers.

"Let every soul be subject to the higher powers (i.e., civil rulers). For there is no power but of God; the powers that be are *ordained of God*." Rom. 13:1-7, I Tim. 2:1, 2.

"Put them in mind to be subject to principalities and powers, *to obey magistrates*, to be ready to carry good work." Titus 3:1.

"*Submit yourselves to every ordinance of man for the Lord's sake;* whether it be to the King as supreme, or unto governors as unto them that are sent by him for the punishment of evil doers, and for the praise of them that do well."

"Honor all men. Love the brotherhood. Fear God. Honor the King." I Peter 2:13-17.

THE POPE'S CLAIMS CONFLICT WITH SCRIPTURE, AND DENY DUTY TO CIVIL LAWS AND RULERS

What is the teaching of the Church of Rome concerning the relation of Church and State?

The Church of Rome's teaching is exactly opposite to that of Holy Scripture, and to the practice of the Christian Church for several centuries. Rome holds that the State should be subject to the Church, and that the pope should be supreme over all civil rulers. The Roman Church asserts that "the pope can change kingdoms, take them from one and give them to another, as the sovereign spiritual prince." "The authority of Kings is of human right, and the clergy are *exempt from their jurisdiction.*" Bellarmine, *De Pontif.*, Rom. 5:2, 6. Boniface VIII, *Bull. Unam. Sanctam.*, Leo XIII, *Encyclical Letter Immortale Dei.*

"The clergy cannot be judged by any secular judge, although they do *not observe the civil laws,* i.e., although they violate the laws of their country! Bellarmine, *De Cleric.*, 1:28: "The goods of the clergy as well ecclesiastical as secular, are *free, and ought of good right to be so, from the tribute of secular princes.*" *De Cleric.*, 1:28.

Note how the papal dogmas *directly contradict Christ and the Scriptures. The Church of Rome says:*

"The authority of Kings is of *human* right." God's Word declares, "They are *ordained of God.*" Rom. 13:1, 2.

Christ and His apostles paid tribute to the Roman government. The Church of Rome says, that pope and priests ought *not to pay tribute.*

The popes contradict St. Peter. They say the clergy are "exempt from the jurisdiction of Kings and rulers." St. Peter enjoins clergy as well as laity, *"Submit yourselves to every ordinance of man* for the Lord's sake"; both to Kings and to governors.

St. Paul enjoins: "Wherefore we must needs be subject, not only for wrath, but also for conscience sake. For this cause *pay ye tribute also:* for they (civil rulers) are *God's ministers, attending continually upon this very thing.*" Rom. 13: 5, 6.

The Apostles thus declare that it is a solemn obligation of all Christians, ministers and people, to obey the laws and to pay taxes;

and that because rulers and magistrates are God's ministers in civil government. It is plain, therefore, that concerning the relation of Church and State, the Church of Rome's dogmas quoted above put the papal Church into *direct conflict with the teachings of Christ and Holy Scripture,* thus creating a condition which is hostile to the civil government that protects the Church and to which all Christians owe allegiance.

Does the pope still maintain this attitude of disobedience toward the teachings of Holy Scripture and toward the civil government of the land?

He does. In a letter[1] addressed to the bishops of France dated February 11, 1906, pope Pius X declared: "That it is necessary to separate Church and State is a thesis *absolutely false, a most pernicious error.*" He is thus, by implication, repeating the claim that the State should be subject to his control.

POPE GREGORY VII

WHEN DID THIS FALSE TEACHING CONCERNING THE RELATION OF CHURCH AND STATE FULLY DEVELOP?

In the Dark Ages under Hildebrand, who as Gregory VII, was pope from 1073 to 1085,—a time of utter ignorance and disorder.[2] We have already seen that his claims to absolute authority in Church and State were *based on fraudulent documents,* the so-called "Donation of Constantine," and the "Decretals of Isidore," which *later popes and reputable Catholic leaders acknowledge were forgeries.*

What has been the result of this false teaching of the Roman Church, claiming absolute power for the pope over civil rulers and governments, as well as over the Church?

---

[1] *Readings in Modern European History,* page 229, by T. H. Anderson and C. A. Beard.

[2] The Papacy probably attained its highest power under Innocent III at the time of the Fourth Lateran Council in 1215. This Council was attended not only by the Church leaders of every country, but also by representatives of the civil governments of Europe. It condemned all heretics to death, and forced the civil governments to swear to destroy all whom the pope condemned! *The Century Cyclopedia,* Vol. IX, page 529. Dallmann's *How Peter Became Pope,* page 61.

History shows that the arrogant claims of popes,[1] and their unholy ambition to rule without regard to the rights of others, have been like firebrands cast into Europe, often destroying the peace and prosperity of Kingdoms, causing endless intrigues, rebellions, war and bloodshed; in England, France, Germany, Italy, Holland, etc. There was constant meddling in the internal affairs of almost every country by the pope and his emissaries to the great injury and distress of both rulers and people. See the struggle between Henry II of England and Thomas Becket, who opposed needed reforms; the wars of the Guelphs and Ghibellines in Germany and Italy, which lasted 300 years, till the end of the 15th century; the Thirty Years War from 1618 to 1648, etc., etc. Note also the anathemas and bitter denunciations by the Pope, of the Treaty of Westphalia, which sought to promote religious peace and peace among nations.

THE THIRTY YEARS WAR, AND THE TREATY OF WESTPHALIA

The Thirty Years War was a fierce religious and political struggle, which involved not only Germany, but the whole of Central Europe. The immediate cause of the war was the oppression of the Bohemian people by Austria, which forced Bohemia to revolt in May, 1618. On one side were the Catholic League and Wallenstein, the Austrian General, chief leaders; on the other side King Christian of Denmark and Gustavus Adolphus II, King of Sweden. Victory and defeat alternated with both parties, until in 1648 the Treaty of Westphalia finally brought peace to war-torn Europe. By this Treaty, Switzerland and Holland became independent of the German Empire. France received Alsace and other possessions, and the territory of Sweden was enlarged. The peace of Ausburg, 1555, was ratified, including Calvinists as well as Lutherans and the sovereignty of the Papacy, and the oppressive power of Innocent X were brought to an end.

Have later popes continued to hold the unjustifiable position of Gregory VII regarding the relation of Church and State?

They have. Such is the inordinate lust for power of the human heart when uncontrolled by the Spirit of God, that later popes,

---

[1] The Emperor Charles V's Spanish minister wrote from Genoa in 1527: "I have lived 25 years in Italy, and have observed that *the pope has been the sole cause of all the wars and miseries during that time.*" (Ang. Brief, 310.) This is the testimony of *one Romanist to another.* (Italics ours.)

regardless of the plain teachings of Holy Scripture and the fundamental rights of rulers and people, have continued to hold these absurd and false claims. A brief glance at the record of subsequent popes will show this.

INNOCENT III

Innocent III, on becoming pope in 1198, with childish extravagance proclaimed: "I sit on high above Kings and all princes. This steward is the Viceroy of God, the Successor of Peter; he stands in the midst between God and men. He is *the Judge of all*, but is judged by no one. Christ has committed the whole world to the government of the popes! I alone enjoy the plenitude of power. The pope *holds the place of the true God!" Ang. Brief*, 93.

A gloss in the Canon Law of the Church called the pope *"Our Lord God!"*

BONIFACE VIII

Pursuing the policy of his predecessors in 1302, Pope Boniface VIII declared: "In her (the Church) are two swords, the spiritual and the temporal. Both are in the power of the Church. The former by the hand of the priest, the latter by the hand of princes and Kings, but *at the nod and sufferance of the priest*. The one sword must be subject to the other, the *temporal authority* to the *spiritual*."

Again, "We declare and pronounce that it is *absolutely necessary to salvation* that *every human being be subject to the Roman Pontiff*."

(What is really necessary for salvation and the maintenance of true religion is for our Romanist friends to discard their *mistaken subjection to the Papacy*, and *return to the Lord Jesus Christ* as the *true and only Head of the Christian Church*.)

But Boniface's absurd claims soon got him into trouble. Becoming involved in a quarrel with King Philip IV of France, Boniface was accused of many crimes, was imprisoned in his own palace, and died soon after (A.D. 1303).

PAUL IV

Declaring the cruel Inquisition to be the chief support of the papacy in Italy, Paul IV in 1558 issued the Bull, *"Cum ex apostolatus officio*, asserting that "the pope as God's representative, has full power over nations and Kingdoms; he judges all, and can be judged

12

in this world by none. All princes and monarchs, as soon as they fall into heresy, are deposed, and incur sentence of death. If repentant, they are to be imprisoned the rest of their lives, and do penance on bread and water. No one may give aid to a heretical prince, and any monarch who dares to do so, forfeits his dominions and property, which lapse to princes who are obedient to the pope!"

PAUL V

Pope Paul V allowed himself to be called "Vice-God!" Dallmann's *How Peter Became Pope*, page 98.

INNOCENT X

Opposing the spirit of religious tolerance ushered in by the Peace of Westphalia,[1] October 24, 1648, Pope Innocent X (1644-1655), *"speaking as the very mouthpiece of God,"* said in a papal bull, "We therefore, decree and declare by these peace pacts (that is, the pact of Osnabruck of August, 1648, and that of Westphalia, October, 1648), that everything herein contained are, and forever will be, null, void, *invalid, iniquitous, unjust, damnable, reprobate, inane,* and altogether lacking in force; that no one is, or ever will be, obliged to observe them, *even if bound thereto by oath.* (Note that the pope, *sanctions the breakings of a solemn oath to God!*)—they must therefore be forever held as if they had never been issued, as never existing, and as never made."

It should be carefully observed that the pope here, as always, "runs true to form." Though professing to be the representative of the "Prince of Peace" on earth, and to have a sincere interest in the welfare of the European nations, Innocent X refused to sanction a sorely needed treaty of peace, and deliberately encouraged the continuance of war. He was more anxious to press his selfish claims to power than he was to heal the wounds of bloodshed and violence from which Europe had suffered for more than three decades.

PIUS IX

Holding the same pernicious opinion of the relation of Church and State, Pius IX in 1864 wrote—"In case of conflicting laws, enacted by the two powers, temporal and spiritual, to hold that the civil law should prevail is *an error*." That is, the pope's opinion must *override the laws of the land!*

LEO XIII

Leo XIII officially declared—"Over the mighty multitude God has set rulers with power to govern, and He has willed that one of them should be head of all," i.e., the pope. Going out of his way to criticize the American Government he said, "It would be very erroneous to draw the conclusion that the most desirable status for the Church is to be *sought in America*. It is an error to hold that it would be universally lawful or expedient for State and Church to be *dissevered and divorced as in America*." Again Leo said in substance, "There must be complete obedience to the Roman Pontiff as *to God Himself*, for we hold upon earth *the place of God Almighty!*" Remember that this awful blasphemy was uttered in the 20th century, for Leo XIII died July, 1903.

Does not conflict with civil governments inevitably grow out of the false claims of supremacy which the Papacy has constantly made for itself?

It does. See the false claim of Leo XIII that "we hold on earth the place of God Almighty"; or the claim made for the priest in the Confessional, that what he hears, "he *knows as God*." Or the false assertion that "the Pope here on earth *is Christ*." (*Il Papa qui in terra è Christo*.) L. Lucantonio, *La Supernazionalità del Papato*, page 71. This book was recently published and dedicated to Cardinal Gasparri, Papal Secretary of State under Pius XI.

How do these papal claims accord with the basic principles of the Constitution of the United States, and with the practice of the U. S. Government from its beginning?

They do *not accord at all*, but *directly conflict with the basic principles of the United States Constitution*, which *clearly affirms the entire separation of Church and State*, which declares the equality before the law of all religious systems, that all may enjoy the inalienable right to worship God according to the dictates of conscience; and especially forbids that partiality or special privilege be shown toward any religious system whatever.

Moreover, had not the papal See distinctly expressed its disapproval of the American Constitution, when Leo XIII went out of his way to criticize the U. S. Government, saying, "It would be very erroneous to draw the conclusion that in America is to be sought the most desirable status for the Church. It is *an error* to hold that it would be *universally lawful or expedient for the State and Church* to be, as *in America, dissevered and divorced?*"

Remember, too, that the pope claims to be a spiritual ruler, who has absolute control over every Church member's conscience, and who holds over him the power of eternal life or death!

It is apparent in what an impossible situation an honest citizen of a free Republic finds himself who, while pledging his unswerving loyalty to his own government, *also solemnly pledges loyalty to an autocratic and unscriptural* alien government, whose fundamental principals are *totally different!*

The chief matters over which the Church of Rome claimed control, and so came into collision with the State, in addition to the right to interfere in political affairs whenever it saw fit to do so, were Education, and Marriage (Matrimony). The Church also bitterly opposed distribution of the Bible among the people.

EDUCATION

The Roman Church has always been keen to criticize severely what it considers defects in education by the State. But can any defect in State education remotely compare to the colossal falsehood and fraud on which the Popes' claim to supreme power are based?

The Church of Rome continually denounces the Public School system of the United States, and Pius IX declared in substance that education outside of the Roman Church was a damnable heresy. But who can approve the intolerance and selfishness which led the Roman hierarchy to oppose a school system that gives the children of the poor an opportunity to gain an education, and which promotes sympathy and friendliness among all classes of society? Remember, too, that many men who have become leaders in commerce, industry and political life owe the beginnings of that life to the public school system. It may reasonably be asked, if the Roman Church is so bitterly opposed to the school system of the nation, why do so many Romanists seek and obtain positions as teachers in the public schools? Surely if loyal to the teachings of their Church superiors, such teachers cannot contribute much to the efficiency of the schools in which they are employed. In 1933 Romanists secured the passage of a law in the New York State legislature, purporting to be against "intolerance" (!) which makes it a grave offense, punishable with fine and imprisonment, even to inquire about the religious affiliations of applicants for teachers' positions. Thus, contrary to the spirit of the U. S. Constitution, American citizens in New York State are *deprived of one of the safeguards of civil and religious liberty,* viz.: the right of free speech and inquiry, and by this law teachers, who are unfriendly to the public school system, may be *forced upon* the public schools, *contrary to the wishes of the majority of the citizens of the community.* Such a law should never be allowed to remain on the statute book!

Notice should be taken of the Encyclical Letter of Pius XI on the Christian Education of Youth, Dec. 31, 1929, in which the claim is made that education should belong exclusively to the Roman Church; and the rash charge is made that the State in the matter of education "violates rights conferred by God on the family"; and makes the boast that the Roman Church has "ever protected and defended these rights." One may well ask, What did education IN the Church of Rome do for the ignorant masses of Spain and of Italy, prior to the coming of Victor Emmanuel in 1870, or for Latin America and the Philippines? In countries where education has been controlled by the Roman Church a far greater degree of illiteracy is found than in other countries, as statistics published by these countries show. For instance, Brazil reported 75.5% of its people illiterate, and Portugal 68%. Whereas in countries where education is not controlled by the Roman Church, the rate of illiteracy is low: as in Finland and Norway only 1%; and in Great Britain less than 1%! In reply to the boast as to what the Roman Church has accomplished in education, let the report of Governor-general W. H. Taft to the U. S. Government be read, showing the shocking conditions in the Philippines, for which the Roman friars were largely responsible.[1]

---

[1] Cardinal Manning attributed the Revolution in Italy, by which the pope lost control of "the States of the Church," largely to the *immorality of the priesthood* and to *the neglect of educating the people.* The papal States were considered the worst governed regions in Europe. Poverty and ignorance prevailed among the people who hailed Napoleon, and later Victor Emmanuel, as welcome deliverers. The expression "Prisoner of the Vatican" was not true to the facts; it was a pretext

A well-known writer on social and economic questions in Brazil declares: "It is true that if our country had been peopled by a Protestant nation, there would be no illiteracy in Brazil. Because it was colonized by a Catholic nation, illiteracy in Brazil *reaches the highest percentage, known among nations called civilized.* In Europe there is practically no illiteracy in Protestant lands: in Catholic countries of the Old World *illiteracy is intense.* Since the rural population of Brazil is ninety percent illiterate, how can the Catholics of Brazil consider themselves *'benefactors of national education?'*" Mario Pinto Serva, *Revisto do Brazil,* No. 77, 1922.

MARRIAGE

THE CHURCH OF ROME OPPOSES THE LAWS OF THE STATE CONTROLLING MARRIAGE

It took the Church of Rome many centuries to discover that there were *seven* sacraments instead of *the two taught by the Word of God,* and at the Council of Florence in 1439 "Matrimony" was placed among them. The Protestant or Reformed Church refused to recognize Marriage as a sacrament, because Christ, the only Head of the Church, did not so recognize it. The laws of the United States, originally made by Protestant leaders, carefully guarded the marriage bond. The deplorable laxness of marriage laws in recent years was in no sense due to Protestant influence, as has been wrongly charged, but was due to *irreligious legislators* who, in spite of earnest protests, lowered the Christian standard of Marriage and Divorce. No marriage performed according to the law of the land by a Protestant minister or a civil magistrate is regarded as valid by the Church of Rome; only those performed by a Roman priest are recognized. The *Syllabus* of Errors, published by Pius IX in 1864, declared: "Whoever says that marriages should be contracted according to the civil law, and *not* according to the directions of the Council of Trent,

---

used by the pope to win sympathy, as if he were a martyr. As a matter of fact, he had liberty to go where he pleased. Pius IX, a weak pope, was *dominated by Cardinal Antonelli,* whose lack of religion and morals was notorious. It is reported on good authority that the Cardinal on his death-bed refused the sacraments, saying that he *had never believed in them.* After his death his illegitimate children sued his estate for their share of the property to which, according to Italian law, they were entitled, and which they received.

let him be *anathema*" (accursed). Roman bishops have called the married life of parties married by a Protestant minister, or a civil magistrate, *concubinage;* in saying this they were merely echoing the harsh and unjustifiable statement of Pius IX, who declared that such marriages were a *"shameful and abominable concubinage."* *Allocution* of September, 1852. Bishop Colohan of Cork, wrote in the *Catholic Bulletin,* January, 1917, page 25, to the same effect. Such discourteous and untrue denunciations only injure the Church whose representatives are guilty of them!

THE CHURCH OF ROME "ANNULS" MARRIAGE, BUT DOES NOT GRANT DIVORCE

The Roman Church while maintaining a legalistic regularity, discarded in the administration of its marriage law the moral principles and legal rules which the State established *for the control of fraud.* Thus, those salutary principles concerning the validity of contracts and the suppression of fraud, which the experience of mankind has found absolutely necessary, have been disregarded by the Papacy to the great injury of society and of the good name of the Christian faith. Roman dignitaries grow eloquent concerning the sanctity of marriage and the evils of divorce; but under the name of "annulment" the Church finds reason sufficient for granting permanent separation. A pre-nuptial agreement between the contracting parties to separate permanently should the marriage prove undesirable, has been considered sufficient cause for annulment. Witness the Case of the Duke of Marlborough, and that of Marconi in 1927.

The boasted doctrine of the Roman Church, which is supposed to teach marital sanctity and high moral conduct received stunning blows through papal misconduct in the 16th century.

In both Church and State morality was at a low ebb, for Alexander VI and his illegitimate son, Caesar Borgia, were guilty of gross crimes. Ceasar caused his own brother to be murdered, and his body to be thrown into the Tiber. He caused his brother-in-law to be stabbed on the palace steps, and, as his victim was recovering, broke into his bedroom and had him strangled. He killed his father's favorite, Peroto, while taking refuge under the pope's mantle, and the pope's face was sprinkled with his blood. Finally the pope lost his life by drinking a poisoned cup which he caused his steward to prepare for one of his cardinals, who succeeded in bribing the steward to give the cup to the pope.[1]

Pope Julius II's immorality was flagrant. Though a priest and monk, he was the father of 3 daughters illegitimately, the marriage of one of whom, Lucretia, he twice dissolved.

Pope Clement VII was also guilty of breaking the laws of God and of the Church. When Henry VIII of England appealed to him to divorce Catherine of Aragon, because she bore him no son, he refused, as contrary to the law of the Church and because Catherine's nephew, Charles V, as Emperor, was considered all-powerful.[2] Clement himself was born out of wedlock, but was made legitimate by a dispensation of his cousin, Pope Leo X. Clement married his young relative, Catherine de Medici,[4] then 14 years of age, to Prince Henry of France, and Margaret of Parma, the illegitimate daughter of Charles V, to Alessandro the Moor; and after the latter's death, Charles V and Pope Paul IV married her to Ottavio Farnese,[3] the illegitimate grandson of Pope Paul III! In view of these facts, the Roman Church had no cause for boasting. The unchaste lives of its dignitaries not only struck a blow at the sanctity of marriage and demoralized society, but led an unbelieving world to scoff at the Christian religion.

The Roman Church has shown a ruthless disregard of the rights and feelings of non-Catholics whenever its members happened to be in a majority in the community, or the judge a Catholic lacking in Christian feeling. No matter how much suffering it caused to an innocent contracting party, the Church law was enforced, if it was to the Church's advantage to do so.

In Quebec, Canada, in 1934, a Roman Catholic judge annulled a marriage between a Protestant and a Romanist, the ceremony of which had been performed *25 years before* by a Protestant minister! This was directly *contrary to the laws of Canada* and of the British Empire. How could a judge, who had *solemnly sworn* to *uphold the law of the land,* do such an unchristian act, which tended to break up a

---

[1] Ranke, *History of the Popes,* Vol. I, pages 49, 50.
[2] Ranke, *History of the Popes,* Vol. I, page 89.
[3] Ranke, *History of the Popes,* Vol. III, pages 170, 172, 173.
[4] Guizot, *History of France,* Vol. IV, pages 118, 119.

family, was contrary to the laws of the British Empire, and contrary to the dictates of humanity? Why? *Because of bondage to a foreign pope, who ignored the Word of God, which he professed to obey!*

Regarding the duty of obedience of members of the Roman Communion to the laws of the country, the advice of the Rev. Mr. Ryan, already quoted, seems strangely at variance with Christian precepts. He said in substance: "In deciding whether an obnoxious law ought to be obeyed (St. Peter made *no exception of obnoxious laws*), the non-Catholic citizen may consult his Bible, or his minister, or merely his own conscience; in a similar situation the Catholic may consult *his priest, his bishop,* or *the pope!*" That is, Mr. Ryan declares that an erring human being should be the Catholic's guide, rather than *the Holy Spirit speaking through the Scriptures and the God-given conscience!* Here appears one of the "impassable gulfs" which separate Romanism from the true Christian faith!

THE POPES CURSE BIBLE SOCIETIES

The popes of Rome have bitterly cursed the Bible Societies for obeying God's command, "Holding forth the Word of Life," and thus enabling the people of all lands to "Search the Scriptures."

Who can estimate the vast blessing which these noble institutions and their faithful colporteurs have brought to the nations of the earth by the distribution of God's Holy Word! Think of the splendid work of the British and Foreign Bible Society, the American Bible Society, the Bible Society of Scotland, and others, in translating the Holy Scriptures into over 1000 languages and dialects and in circulating millions of Bibles and Gospels year by year! This unselfish, life-giving service is truly one that angels may rejoice over, yet Pius VII in 1816, denounced these societies as a "horrible invention, which undermined the foundation of religion!" Leo XII cursed the Bible Societies in 1824. Pius VIII repeated the anathema, "for preaching *the gospel of the devil* in the language of the people!" In 1844 Gregory XVI again condemned these societies and the Evangelical Alliance; and Pius IX denounced "those *cunning and infamous societies,* which call themselves Bible Societies, and give the Scriptures to inexperienced youth"; as if there were no Holy Spirit who gave the Word, "to guide them into all truth!" John 16:13.

And in this 20th century wherever Romanism dominates, the same opposition to the distribution of the Holy Scriptures is seen.[1] Colporteurs often report that Roman priests desecrate and burn Bibles, and denounce and persecute God's faithful servants for obeying His command, just as was done in the Dark Ages. But still the glorious work goes on; the good seed of the Kingdom is sown far and wide; the living Christ, the Incarnate Word, and the Bible, God's written Word, go forth, *"conquering and to conquer,"* for His promise to the Church is *sure, "My Word shall not return unto Me void";* "The earth shall *be filled with the knowledge of the Lord* as the *waters cover the sea!"* Isa. 55:11, 11:9, Hab. 2:14.

In April, 1941, propagandists advertised widely in the secular Press that the Roman Church was now issuing a new translation of the Holy Scriptures—this fact is published especially for Protestant consumption, and to deceive ignorant people who do not know the Church's record of bitter hostility to the Word of God for centuries.

Showing this hostility to the Bible, the British Minister to Chile relates that on one occasion the misplaced zeal of the hierarchy *burnt even its own version of the Scriptures!* The Minister wrote that when Rev. Kenelm Vaughan visited Chile to collect funds for Westminster Cathedral, he brought to that land a large stock of *Spanish (Douay) New Testaments for distribution.* But alas! he was met on the frontier by an emissary of the Archbishop of Santiago with instructions that the testaments *must all be burnt before Rev. Vaughan could enter the Province*—which *was promptly done! The Church Times,* Sept. 22, 1922, p. 291.

The Rev. Dr. Cahill is reported by a Roman Catholic paper to have declared with more heat than wisdom, that "he would rather have a Catholic to *read the worst books of immorality* than *the Protestant Bible—that forgery of God's Word!"* He thus *"runs true to form!"* Roman Catholic *Tablet,* Dec. 17, 1853, p. 804.

---

[1] The excuse which Roman Catholic clergy often allege for their hostility to the work of Bible distribution, viz.: that what they curse and denounce is the Protestant Bible, is altogether *without foundation.* For the Protestant translations of the Scriptures have been made with *the utmost care* by *learned and devout men,* and are *thoroughly trustworthy versions.* The real ground of objection is, the *Church of Rome fears the Bible, because it exposes Rome's many errors!* Cardinal Bellarmine expressed the hostility of the Church of Rome toward the Bible when he falsely said: "that Holy Scripture does NOT CONTAIN ALL THAT IS NECESSARY TO SALVATION; that it is NOT SUFFICIENT"; and "that it is NOT FOR THE PEOPLE TO READ!"

Reasonable men should base their beliefs concerning the relation of Church and State, and all other matters, on the Word of God and on the facts of history. For God clearly says in His Word, "Should not a people seek to their God? To the Law and to the Testimony? If they speak not according to this Word, it is because there is no light in them!" Isa. 8:19, 20. Again the Bible enjoins: "Prove all things, hold fast that which is good!" I Thess. 5:21. Test every dogma of men by the Word of God, and NOT by man's word or human tradition. Sad to say, the Church of Rome is deceived and led captive by tradition! Hear the testimony of an honest, able Roman Catholic, who says, "the Dogmatic Commission of the Vatican Council proclaims that 'the existence of Tradition *has nothing to do with evidence!* That objections taken from history are *not valid* when *contradicted by ecclesiastical decrees!* '" That is, men's mere unproven statements must prevail over historic fact! Did not pope Pius IX, deceived by such sophistries, say, "I am *Tradition! La Tradizione* son' io." Thus also Fénelon declared, "The Church is supreme *over fact* as *over doctrine!*" Cardinal Newman fell into the same error when he spoke of "doctrines which lie beyond the evidence of history," and which Roman Catholics receive, *not* because they are "proved by reason or history, but because Revelation has declared them by the pope." But the pope's words are *not* Revelation! True Revelation is the *Word of God, the Bible, given by the Holy Spirit,* and *nothing else!* Acton, *History,* pp. 515, 549.

We respectfully urge our Catholic friends to take God's Holy Word *alone* as their rule of faith, and the Holy Spirit as their guide. Trusting Tradition and relying on pope and priest, men forsake God, and sink deeper and deeper into the quicksands of error. But trusting in Christ and His Holy Spirit, and guided by the Word of God, the light and joy of heaven shall fill their souls! Thank God, there are many Roman priests and laymen who are finding out this blessed truth, and are rejoicing in the liberty wherewith Christ makes His people free; Christ "delivers them from the bondage of corruption," and brings them *into the glorious liberty of the sons of God!*

Chapter XIV

RELIGIOUS LIBERTY AND PERSECUTION

What precious truth and right does the Bible give to Christian believers, a right which all enlightened Governments now guarantee to their citizens?

The Bible proclaims religious liberty to all men, the sacred right to worship God according to the dictates of one's own conscience; which right no man and no Church may interfere with, or take away.

"Proclaim liberty throughout all the land, unto all the inhabitants thereof." Levit. 25:10.

"Brethren, ye have been called unto liberty." Gal. 5:13.

"Be not ye the servants of men." I Cor. 7:23.

"And ye shall know the truth, and the truth shall make you *free*." "If *the* son therefore shall make you free, ye shall be *free indeed*." John 8:32, 36.

"Stand fast, therefore, in the liberty wherewith *Christ* hath made you free, and be not entangled again with the yoke of bondage." Gal. 5:1.

Persecution Contrary to the Christian Faith

Does the Christian faith teach, or allow, persecution of those who do not accept it?

The Christian faith not only does not teach, but does not allow, persecution under any circumstances; for persecution is wholly contrary to the Spirit of Christ, and is of Satan. The Christian method of propagation is by persuasion, by appeal to conscience, by presenting the Gospel. It seeks to win by love, and by the power of the Truth. II Tim. 2:24-26, I Peter 3:15.

How was the Gospel propagated in the early days of the Church?

In the early and purer days of the Church, Christians abhorred the use of force and shedding of blood on account of religious beliefs.

(174)

This was true not only of apostolic days, as we read in the book of Acts, but also in post-apostolic times.

TERTULLIAN warmly defended freedom of conscience. He declared it was unchristian to use force in spreading the truth: that real worship must come from the heart.

The same view was expressed by CYPRIAN; and

LACTANTIUS earnestly argued that Christian doctrines should not be propagated by force.

Is not persecution on account of religious belief both foolish and wicked?

Persecution is both foolish and wicked, because it tramples on the sacred rights of others, and because the use of force and violence *never make an honest man change his beliefs*. His convictions are really deepened by suffering for conscience sake. Only weak men yield to persecution, and are *made hypocrites by it;* they profess to change their faith merely to escape punishment. Moreover, evil men, by inflicting persecution, usurp the right to control men's consciences, a right which belongs to God alone, as Creator and Judge.

THE PROTESTANT CHURCH THE CHAMPION OF LIBERTY

Has the Reformed Church uniformly championed religious liberty and opposed persecution?

The Reformed or Protestant Church has *always been the champion of civil and religious liberty*. Where can a nobler record be found than that of Admiral Coligny and the Huguenots of France? Of William of Orange in the Netherlands? Of Cromwell and the Puritans in England? Of John Knox and our forefathers in Scotland, and the Pilgrim Fathers, who founded the Colonies in America?

Roger Williams[1] who planted the Colony of Rhode Island was rightly called "the apostle of religious toleration" in America! See Guizot's *History of France*, Motley's *Dutch Republic*, Green's *History of the English People*, and Bancroft and Woodrow Wilson's *Histories of the United States*.

---

[1] The Encyclopedia Britannica contains this record: "Roger Williams (1604-1684) founder of the Colony of Rhode Island, and *pioneer of religious liberty*. . . . In June 1636 Williams and his companions founded their new settlement upon the basis of

A distinguished historian pays this tribute to Calvinism, as the basis of the Reformed faith: "Calvinism was *not* an opinion, but an attempt to *make the will of God as revealed in the Bible* an *authoritative guide for social as well as personal direction.*"

Of Geneva, Calvin's home, John Knox said: "Elsewhere the Word of God is taught as purely, but never anywhere have I seen God obeyed as faithfully." The Calvinists abhorred all conscious mendacity, all impurity, all moral wrong-doing of every kind so far as they could recognize it.

"Calvinism purged England and Scotland, for a time at least, of lies and charlatanry. Whatever exists at this moment in England and Scotland of conscientious fear of doing evil is the remnant of the convictions which were branded by the Calvinists into the hearts of the people; for all that we call modern civilization, in a sense which deserves the name, is the visible expression of the transforming power of the Gospel; though they failed to destroy Romanism, they drew its fangs; they forced it to abandon that detestable principle that it was entitled to murder those who dissented from it." Froude's *Calvinism,* pp. 49, 50.

HAS NOT THE CIVIL AND RELIGIOUS LIBERTY, BESTOWED BY GOD THROUGH THE PROTESTANT CHURCH, PROVED TO BE AN UNSPEAKABLE BLESSING, BRINGING PROSPERITY WHEREVER IT IS FOUND?

Civil and religious liberty has brought *unspeakable blessings,* and it has *always gone hand in hand with the Reformed or Protestant faith.* To see this truth one need only compare Protestant England with Romanist Spain; Italy prior to 1870 with Denmark and Sweden; Germany under Emperor William I with Austria; and the new world of the Pilgrim Fathers with Mexico and South America.

---

complete religious toleration, with a view to its becoming a shelter for persons distressed for conscience. . . . He was the first and foremost exponent in America of the theory of the *absolute freedom of the individual* in *matters of religion.*"

It is sometimes claimed that the principle of religious liberty in America was first established in the Province of Maryland under Cecil Calvert, Lord Baltimore. But this is clearly proved to be erroneous by the Maryland Statute entitled "An Act concerning Religion" enacted April 21, 1649 and *approved by Lord Baltimore himself,* which provided that *"all persons within the province who deny Jesus Christ to be the Son of God, or who deny the Holy Trinity, or speak reproachfully thereof shall be punished with death and confiscation of all lands and goods."* Archives of Maryland, vol. I, p. 244. Woodrow Wilson's *History of the American People,* vol. I, pp. 130, 131. The statement of the Encyclopedia Britannica is undoubtedly correct.

THE LOW MORAL CONDITION OF EUROPE PRIOR TO THE REFORMA-
TION WAS MAINLY DUE TO THE DEMORALIZING INFLUENCE OF THE
CHURCH OF ROME AND THE LOVE OF POWER AND GREED FOR GAIN OF
THE ROMAN CURIA.

The cause of the low moral condition of Europe in the time of
John Huss is thus described by Signor Mussolini: "The Church of
Rome had become a slave of profane commercialism, had been bound
over to the God Mammon, to the money that undermines all faith."
Quoting the eminent authority F. von Bezhold, he says: "The
Roman Curia had become a gigantic money-making organization.
The saying that in 'Rome everything was for sale' was by no means
an exaggeration, for with money one could buy anything, from the
smallest prebend to a cardinal's cap, from permission to use butter
on fast days even to absolution for murder and incest. . . . From the
sensuality and cupidity of the monks no one was safe." Mussolini's
John Huss, the Man of Truth.

In contrast to this deplorable condition of Europe caused by papal
control, the historian Froude describes the well-being of the Scotch
people as a result of the Protestant Reformation. Instead of being
gloomy, as some represent, "I should say that the Scots have been
an unusually happy people. Intelligent industry, the necessaries of
life moderately provided for; a sensible contentment with the situation of life;—this through the week, and at the end of it the 'Cottar's
Saturday Night'—the homely family, reverently and peacefully
gathered together and irradiated with a Sacred Presence,—Happiness! such happiness as we human creatures are likely to know in
this world will be found *there*, if anywhere!" *The Influence of the
Reformation on Scottish Character*, Froude.

A CARDINAL CONFESSES THE BARRENNESS OF HIS CHURCH

That the Protestant Church has almost without exception orig-
inated and supported the great enterprises of public charity for
relieving human suffering and promoting the public welfare, is un-
deniable. Cardinal Manning, of London, acknowledged this, and
confesses the sterility of the Church of Rome in the matter *of dis-
interested public charity*.

The Cardinal wrote: "All the great works of public charity in England had their beginning *outside the Church* (i.e., outside of *the Roman Catholic Church*). For instance, the abolition of slavery and the slave trade. Not a Catholic name, so far as I know, shared in this. Then the whole Temperance movement,—it was *a Quaker that made Father Mathew a total abstainer!* Catholic Ireland, and the Catholics of England until now, have *done little for Temperance.* The Anti-vivisection Act, also the Act of Parliament for the protection of animals from cruelty, were the *work of Dissenters.* So the Acts against the horrible depravity which destroys young girls, multitudes of *ours,*—I was literally denounced by Catholics,— *not one* came forward! There are endless works for the protection of shop-assistants, overworked railway- and tram-men, women and children ground down by sweaters, and driven by starvation wage upon the streets. *Not one of these works in their behalf was started by us (Romanists);* hardly a Catholic name is to be found on their reports!" E. S. Purcell's *Life of Cardinal Manning,* vol. II, page 781.

EMANCIPATION FROM THE PAPACY NECESSARY FOR NATIONAL PROSPERITY

The prosperity of Protestant nations due to their faith in Christ and the Bible, and the cramping, repressive effect of Romanism on the intellectual and moral life of peoples, are often referred to *by non-Protestant writers.*

Pere Hyacinthe of Paris wrote in the London Times, August 15, 1904: "France and Italy can only advance in proportion to their *emancipation from this fatal servitude to a foreign power (the papacy),* which was *never instituted by Christ,* and which was *unknown during the early centuries of the Church's history."*

Another thoughtful Roman Catholic observer asks: "What were the present Reformist (Protestant) nations while they were still Romanist, with respect to others? Who will gainsay that we were greatly superior to them in everything,—in literature, philosophy, theology, social culture, and so forth? And what has happened since then? The *Romanist* nations have *declined more and more,* so that now many of them are spoken of as *dead nations,* while the *Reformist nations are steadily advancing,* in knowledge, in morality, and in general progress." Fradryssa, pages 248, 252, 295.

HAS THE CHURCH OF ROME EVER FAVORED CIVIL AND RELIGIOUS LIBERTY AND SOCIAL REFORMS?

The history of the countries controlled by the Church of Rome, like Spain, Austria, Mexico, and the South American States, shows clearly that the Church has constantly *opposed social and political reforms.* It has *always been reactionary.* "There was a time in all Latin America when there was no religious liberty, no freedom of speech, no public education, no civil marriage, no burial rites for Protestants in public cemeteries, no valid baptism for Protestant children, and in some Catholic countries, no right of inheritance: These intolerable conditions have passed away. Did they pass away *without opposition from the Roman Catholic Church? It fought every one of these reforms. It is fighting some of them still. Not one advance has been made toward free institutions and free education in Latin America without encountering relentless opposition from the Roman Organization." Open Door in Brazil,* by Dr. J. P. Smith.

Another missionary, who for years saw the ill-effects of Roman Catholic teachings, testifies thus: "South America is cursed with a *baptized paganism,* which has hung like a millstone around its neck for centuries. Romanism, with its *open hostility* to the *circulation of the Scriptures,* with Mariolatry of the *most debased character,* with its *traffic in indulgences,* its *exorbitant charges* for baptisms and confession, for the marriage of the living and the burial of the dead, has reached a depth of superstition and immorality, which can find no parallel in any other continent."

Concerning the effect of Romanist teachings on the moral and religious character of the Brazilian people, a "four-square" Roman Catholic jurist wrote: "Romanism has produced an apparent unity of belief, but *no true religious spirit.* There is no more Catholic people than the Brazilian, *nor one less really religious."*

An intelligent physician thus testifies: "When I was director of the Penitentiary in Bahia, a study of the religious psychology of the criminals showed that almost all were religious. They did not miss going to Mass; but almost all of them wore *charms and prayers around their necks;* and one day the old chaplain complained that his flock were *breaking the 'ara' (altar stone),* in order to *make*

13

fetishes to render them invisible to the sentries, and thus escape from prison!" Dr. J. P. Smith's *Open Door in Brazil*, 1925, page 43.

The Rev. Edward C. Pereira, a native Brazilian, testifies: "The great sore of Romanism is its *failure to create moral character.*" Concerning chastity, he points to "a celibate clergy filling society with *illegitimacy* under the complacent eyes of ecclesiastical authority." Pointing to the confessional, he says, *"There* the stains of adultery and licentiousness are *easily washed away."* *O Problema Religiosa da America Latina*, 1920, page 434.

These reliable testimonies are confirmed by the Roman Church's *own Reports.* According to the statistics presented at the first Plenary Council of Latin America in 1889, "Among 18,000 priests, 3,000 were living *illegally in wedlock;* 4,000 were living *in concubinage with their housekeepers;* and 1,500 in relations more or less open *with women of doubtful reputation."* *History of Sacerdotal Celibacy,* vol. II, page 243. *South American Problems*, page 159.

Is it just to hold the Church of Rome responsible for the low moral and religious state of the South American people?

Yes, the Church of Rome is justly held responsible for the moral and religious state of the people, for, for centuries, it *has had exclusive control of their education, and has guided their thinking on morals and religion.*

Persecution the Natural Outgrowth of Papal Dogma

Is not Persecution the inevitable result of belief in the absolute power and infallibility of the pope?

Persecution is the natural outgrowth of the papal dogmas of absolute power and infallibility. History shows that weak human nature, once clothed with absolute power, whether civil or religious, has *never failed to abuse it.* It is so easy, even for a well-meaning person, to deceive himself. He reasons: "This proposed measure I consider beneficial: I am infallible, and have power to enforce it. Therefore even if severity and cruelty are used, it is *right to use them."* Thus men have justified the *most hideous wrongs,* the most *brutal cruelties.* They have deliberately trampled on the sacred rights of others, and have brought untold grief and agony to thousands, all because they *considered themselves infallible*. They became *monsters without knowing it*, shielding themselves with the delusion of infallibility, and clothed with unlimited power, which they *should never have been allowed to possess.*

History furnishes abundant proof of these statements all down the centuries. Reference has already been made to the crusade of Innocent III against the Albigenses, "a war of extermination, lasting for about 15 years, one of the bloodiest in history."

Note the presecution of *John Wycliffe*, "the morning star of the Reformation," and the marytrdom of *William Tyndale*, who gave the English people the Word of God in their native tongue. So bitterly was Wycliffe pursued by his papal foes that his very bones were exhumed, burnt, and their ashes scattered on the river Swift!

See also noble John Huss, burnt at the stake by Council of Constance in 1415. In spite of the Emperor's guarantee of safe conduct, the Council declared that *"faith need not be kept with heretics!"*

Huss' death was followed the next year by the marytrdom of Jerome of Prague,[1] also by fire.

Savonarola was put to death at Florence in 1498, because he fearlessly denounced the wickedness of pope Alexander VI, and earnestly sought the reformation of the Church.

In England nearly 300 Protestants fell victims to the fanaticism of the Romanist queen, "Bloody Mary."

In Paris on St. Bartholomew's Day, 1572, 30,000 Huguenots, "the flower of France," were massacred at *the instance of pope Pius V,* who *so rejoiced at the news* that he had a special *Te Deum* sung, and a medal struck, inscribed with his name and the words, *"Strages Ungonotorum," "the slaughter of the Huguenots,"* to commemorate his infamous crime.[2]

---

[1] Jerome of Prague, so-called to distinguish him from Jerome *the translator of the Vulgate*, was born at Prague, the capital of Bohemia about 1365. Educated at the University of Prague, he was shocked by the *prevailing godlessness of the Roman Church*, and co-operated with John Huss in promoting reform. Having incurred the hatred of the hierarchy, he was imprisoned, condemned by the Council of Constance, and was *burnt at the stake in 1416*. Faithful unto death, Jerome's intrepid witness for Evangelical truth will never be forgotten by a grateful nation.

[2] Pius V, as we have seen, not only persecuted the Huguenots in France, but *sent troops* to help King Charles IX destroy them. The pope gave orders to Count Santafiore the leader, "to take no Huguenot prisoners, but *instantly kill everyone that fell into his hands!"* Catena, *Vita di Pio V*, page 85.

The Duke of Alva's "Council of Blood" cruelly destroyed thousands of faithful Christians in the Netherlands; for the success of this crusade the *pope "earnestly prayed,"* and sent Alva a " 'consecrated' *hat and sword!"*

During no less than 30 persecutions the blood of the noble Waldenses was shed in the valleys of Piedmont, and yet they *heroically kept the faith!*

In 1562 the Roman Inquisitors under Pius IV brutally massacred 2,000 Waldenses in Calabria. The pope then urged the Duke of Savoy to do the same to the Waldenses in Piedmont, and complained loudly when the Duke refused to commit the crime.

What was the fault of the Waldensians, that they should be so bitterly and constantly persecuted?

A thoughtful historian answers: "Their crowning offence was their *love and reverence for Scripture,* and their burning zeal in making converts. They had translations of the Bible in the vulgar tongue, and many of them *knew the whole New Testament by heart.* After a hard day's labor, they would devote the night to instruction; they sought the lazar houses to carry salvation to the lepers. Surely if there ever was a God-fearing people, it was these unfortunates who were under the ban of the Roman Church.

The Noble Leyczon declares the sign of a Vaudois deemed worthy of death was that "he *followed Christ,* and *sought to obey the commandments of God." Lea's History of the Inquisition,* vol. I, page 89.

Theodore Beza, the eminent Reformer, paid a just tribute to these noble servants of Christ, saying: "Permit me to call them (the Waldenses) the true primitive Christian Church who, through God's Providence, stood firmly against the storms that blew, opposing the usurpation and idolatry of Rome."

Again, the Government of Lucca, having enacted a law offering a reward of 300 crowns and reversal of any sentence of outlawry to all persons who should succeed in murdering any of the Protestant refugees who had fled from that city, Pope Pius IV (1499-1565) described it as a *"praiseworthy act, piously and wisely enacted,* and that nothing could *redound more to the glory of God, provided it were thoroughly carried into execution!" Letters of Lord Acton,* in *The Times,* London, of November 9 and 27, 1874.

LORD ACTON DEPLORES THE MURDEROUS SPIRIT OF THE POPES

Lord Acton, an intelligent and honest member of the Roman Catholic Church, was professor of history in the University of Cambridge. Testifying plainly about the cruelties of the Inquisition, and *the responsibility of the popes for them,* he wrote: "The principal obstacle on the way to Rome is the *moral* obstacle. The moral obstacle, to put it compendiously, is *the Inquisition.* The Inquisition is peculiarly the weapon and work of the popes. It stands out from all those things in which they co-operated, as the *distinctive feature of papal Rome.* No other institution, no doctrine, no ceremony is so distinctly the creation of the papacy, except the Dispensing power. It is the principal thing with which the papacy is identified, and by which it must be judged. The principle of the Inquisition is the *pope's sovereign power over life and death.* Whosoever disobeys him, should be tried, *tortured and burnt.* That is to say, the principle of the Inquisition is *murderous,* and a man's *opinion of the papacy* is *regulated and determined* by his *opinion about religious assassination!" "Letters of Lord Acton,* edited by Herbert Paul, June 19, 1884, page 185.

THE TESTIMONY OF HON. WM. E. GLADSTONE AND LORD MACAULAY

Regarding the hostility of the Church of Rome toward civil and religious liberty, and the disastrous effect of this hostility on the welfare of nations, the Honorable William E. Gladstone, former Prime Minister of Great Britain, said concerning the papacy: "Its influence is *adverse to freedom* in *the State,* the *family,* and the *individual.* When weak, it is too often crafty; when strong, tyrannical. The pope's policy is, that in the Church of Rome, nothing shall remain except an Asian monarchy, nothing but one giddy height of *despotism,* and one *dead level of religious subserviency.*" Again Mr. Gladstone said: "Romanism is a *perpetual war against the progress of the human mind.*" Bishop of St. David's *Charge to the Clergy,* 1872, page 17.

The Honorable J. B. Macaulay's testimony is to the same effect: "Among the contrivances which have been devised for *deceiving* and *controlling mankind,* it (the papacy) occupies the *highest place.*" *Lady Trevelyan,* 1868, vol. VI, page 476.

About what time did persecution begin in the Church?

It was about the 5th Century, when Leo I was bishop of Rome, that persecution began to be practiced, and heresy was punished by death.

Pope Urban II, who died in 1099, declared with a dishonesty unworthy of a Christian, "We do not consider those as murderers, who, burning with zeal for their Catholic faith against excommunicated persons have *happened to slay* some of them." Epistle, xxii, *ed. Migne.*

Note that the pope by the words "Happened to slay" deliberately misrepresents a *premeditated murder* as if it were a *sudden, accidental act!* Was the massacre of the Huguenots on St. Bartholomew's Day, over which the pope *rejoiced,* and the terrible Inquisition, accidental occurrences, or were they *deliberately planned crimes,* with the full approval of the popes?

INNOCENT III's CRUSADE AGAINST THE ALBIGENSES

One of the most brutal crimes which ever blackened the pages of human history was the wholesale slaughter of the Albigenses at the instigation of Innocent III, and led by Arnold of Citeaux and Simon de Monfort, who butchered the peaceable people of Languedoc in Southern France without mercy. De Monfort's report of the campaign was, "Neither age, sex nor rank have been spared. We have put all to the sword." Ranke's *"History of the Popes,"* Book I, Ch. I, page 40.

Like King Ahab in Naboth's vineyard, the pope seized the lands of the slaughtered victims. Dallmann's *How Peter Became Pope,* VI, page 60.

THE ALBIGENSES WERE MEN OF NOBLE CHARACTER, WHO DIED TRUE MARTYRS TO THE CHRISTIAN FAITH.

That the Albigenses were true Christians, and that the charges brought against them were false, is proved (1) by the reputation they enjoyed among their neighbors, (2) by the testimony of the King of France and by their local rulers, and (3) by the admissions of the *Roman Church authorities themselves*. The Albigenses were commonly known as *"les bons hommes,"* "the good people," and also as the *Cathari* or "Pure Sect," showing that their neighbors considered them upright, law-abiding citizens, similar to the Puritans of later times. They were hated because they protested against the false claims of the papacy, holding firmly that *Christ* was the *only Head of the Church;* protesting also against the corruption of the priesthood, they *exalted the one atoning sacrifice of Christ* as opposed to the false, sacerdotal pretensions of the hierarchy and to the dogmas of Transubstantiation and the Mass, as set forth by the 4th Lateran Council of 1215.

Their rulers also bore witness to their blameless character. When Count Raymond of Toulouse was urged to persecute them, he refused. "Why should I persecute them? They are guilty of no wrong-doing." The King of France, Philip Augustus, was shocked by the brutal cruelty of their enemies, especially of Simon de Monfort. When told of the wanton destruction caused by Simon and his brother, the King said, *"God was just,* and that *they would surely suffer for their nefarious deeds."* And so it was, for Simon was crushed by a mass of stones which fell on him at the siege of Toulouse in June, 1218.

The Roman Church authorities openly acknowledged that the *Church had brought on itself* the danger which threatened it, viz.: the alarming *progress of heresy, caused by priestly corruption and neglect of duty.* In his opening address at the Lateran Council, Innocent III had declared to the assembled fathers, "the corruption of the people has its chief source *in the clergy.* From *them arise the evils of Christendom."* And pope Honorius III repeated the assertion.

Egged on by the pope and the Inquisiton, nothing could exceed the ferocity of the persecutors. Religious fanaticism was inflamed by *lust for loot,* for the pope had promised the leaders of the crusade not only the lands of the victims, but also the domain of any noble who dared to protect the heretics. Wholesale massacres of innocent people continued *for 15 years.* When the Abbot of Citeaux was asked "How distinguish between heretics and the faithful?" He replied, "Slay them all! God will know His own!" The Inquisition worked ceaselessly, and towns and castles were given over to pillage, massacre, and the flames.

The Albigenses deserve to be remembered as a noble people who were "faithful unto death," laying down their lives as witnesses for Christ and His Gospel.[1]

Regarding the attitude of the Vatican toward persecution in recent years, two comparatively recent demands of pope Pius XI deserve to be noticed. They show the severity with which he would treat heresy, or those censured by ecclesiastical authority, by *inflicting upon them civic outlawry*. In Malta the Vatican demanded that an offending priest (Father Micallef) should be *deported against his will*, in *violation of the civil rights* which *he enjoyed under State laws*.

In the Concordat, Art. 5, of Italo-Vatican Agreements, the pope demanded, and secured, that those under censure of the Church should be *cut off from all employment by the Italian Government*, thus practically making the supposed offender *an outlaw in the State*, depriving him of *his right to earn his daily bread* as school teacher, or postmaster in an Italian village; so the pope demanded in his letter to Cardinal Gasparri. Such demands are unchristian and most reprehensible.

---

[1] It is most regrettable that the late pope, Pius XI, ignoring the plain facts recorded by careful historians, defames the character of the Albigensean martyrs, calling them *"a terrible sect," "guilty of craftiness and violence," "worse than the Saracens,"* and tries to justify the cold-blooded massacres inflicted upon them. In 1937 Pius XI recommended prayer to the Virgin Mary against Communists in Spain, saying, "As the *terrible sect of the Albigenses was overcome by the invocation of Mary,* so we hope that those shall be overcome who as Communists of today remind us of them by their craftiness and violence." The childish accusation of "craftiness and violence" recalls Aesop's fable of the wolf and the lamb, suggesting the *fierceness* of the *lamb* and the *gentleness* of the *wolf!*

The pope did no honor to the memory of the Virgin Mary by imagining that the foul massacre of God's faithful servants was due to her influence. There is no proof that Mary knew of this hideous crime, or that she prayed about it. If Mary had prayed, it would *not* have been for the destruction of the innocent Albigenses, but rather that *their brutal murderers* should *repent of their sin,* which was one of *the foulest blots* that *ever stained the pages of history.*

THE UNWARRANTED PAPAL CLAIMS OF SUPREMACY OVER THE CIVIL POWER HAVE INEVITABLY CAUSED CONFLICT WITH STATES.

What has been the practical result of Rome's false theory of supremacy over civil governments; has it led popes to assume authority which does not belong to them, and frequently meddle in the political affairs of nations?

It has. The whole history of the papacy in relation to civil government, both in medieval and modern times, shows repeated instances of unwarranted and disastrous interference, directly ignoring the plain declaration of Christ, "My Kingdom is not of this world," and disobeying the injunctions of Saint Peter and the other Apostles, "Submit yourselves to every ordinance of man (i.e., civil government) for the Lord's sake." I Peter 2:13.

For instance, in medieval times the subjection of Ireland to England, which Irishmen have bitterly denounced, was the *work of a pope.* Adrian IV, pope from 1154-1159, sold Ireland to Henry II, King of England, for selfish considerations. These were the acknowledgment by the King of the *pope's overlordship;* and the promise that he would *compel the Irish people to pay tribute to Rome* ("Peter's pence"), which was then in arrears.

In Germany the same pope began the struggle between the papacy and the House of Hohenstauffen.

He also incited the leaders of the Italian party to oppose the Emperor Frederick I, (Barbarossa). Thus by his political intrigues, this pope well deserved the name of "trouble-maker."

The Vatican also has frequently interfered with the affairs of the British Government, threatening serious complications, as in Parnell's time in Ireland, and recently in Malta. The attitude of the Roman Curia and the priests of Malta toward the civil government of that island was strangely contrary to the teachings of Scripture, which they professed to obey, for it *tended to incite the populace to open defiance of the civil power.* So strained became the relations between the Government and people that on May 23, 1937, an attempt was made *to assassinate the premier,* Lord Strickland, simply

---

Green's *History of the English People,* vol. 2, page 176.

because he *obeyed his Government's instructions* rather than submit to the dictation of ecclesiastics! Rom. 13:1-7, I Peter 2:13-15.

The conflict between the Government of Mexico and the Roman hierarchy a decade or more ago is well known. Was the accusation that the Mexican Government was persecuting the Roman Church true?

The charge of persecution against the Government of Mexico was *not* sustained by the facts of the case. The Government properly desired to maintain its sovereignty in civil affairs, and its requirement that Roman priests, like all other Mexican citizens, should obey the laws of the land seems reasonable. The testimony of competent witnesses shows this.

In 1925, a mining engineer who had lived 20 years in Mexico, was asked concerning the conflict between the Government of Mexico and the Roman Church. He replied, "It is nothing new: it is merely the age-long controversy between Church and State." The accusation that the Government was anti-religious, he said, "was *not* true. It was *not* anti-religious, but *anti-clerical,*" i.e., opposing the defiant attitude of the priests.

A former President of Mexico, Emilio Portes Gil, also stated the case clearly and dispassionately,—"Definitely, the Government is *not opposed to religion.* The trouble is due to the Catholic clergy who continue to aspire to a worldly or *temporal mission* which *the Constitution denies to all religions.* Considering itself superior to the Civil Power, the Church has continued to interfere in the internal policy of Mexico." He cited as proof the past history of Mexico saying, "It is well known that the clergy and influential laity of the Roman Church brought to Mexico the monarchy of Augustin de Iturbide in 1822, and later the Second Empire in 1864. Maximilian and his Empress left documentary proof of their difficulties in dealing with a clergy *which was determined to dominate a government* that was favorably disposed toward the Catholic religion. Their letters attest the *unpatriotic attitude of the Catholic clergy in Mexico.*"

"Alas! the Church has not mended its ways. Whatever wealth and power it acquires, it continues to use to *further its selfish aims,* and to increase its *influence in temporal affairs.*" The President added, "In Mexico all religions are welcome to worship, and their ministers are allowed ample freedom in pursuing their spiritual tasks. There is no interference with religion *so long as its leaders do not preach disobedience to the political institutions of Mexico.* No other religion among the many practiced in Mexico, has presented any complaint to the Government, alleging that its ministry has been handicapped, or its worship interfered with."

Again, the Roman hierarchy tried to force the United States Government to interfere in Mexico's internal affairs, on account of a purely Church quarrel, in which the U. S. Government had no right to interfere.

Nine years later the Vatican repeated the same offense. In 1935 a cablegram from Rome was widely published in American newspapers entitled, *"The Pope urges Catholic Action in Politics";* and for months Roman Church authorities and Societies carried on a propaganda which was highly prejudicial to the public welfare. The U. S. Ambassador to Mexico, Hon. Josephus Daniel, was publicly denounced by name, and repeated demands were made for his recall, simply because he declined to interfere in matters which were outside of his sphere. Happily the U. S. Government refused to yield to the pressure of the hierarchy, and *firmly maintained the American principal of the separation of Church and State.*

Also in the Philippine Islands in 1938 the Church of Rome presumed to interfere in Government business. President Quezon, having vetoed a bill in the National Assembly, which would have placed national education *under the control of the Roman clergy,* the Roman bishops criticized him for exercising his constitutional right, whereupon the President administered a deserved rebuke, saying, "It seems that the Archbishop and bishops are blind to the situation invariably created whenever Church authorities have attempted to *interfere in affairs of State.* They seem to have closed their eyes to the situation in Mexico and in Spain. They have forgotten the lesson everyone should have learned from our own Revolution against Spain in 1896. The country is now facing one of the most menacing evils which can confront the Government and people of the Philippines, viz.: *interference by the Church in the affairs of State.*"

President Quezon had abundant reason for vetoing the bill, for he remembered Governor-General W. H. Taft's report to the U. S. Senate. In this was revealed the maladministration of education in the Philippine Islands under the *control of the Roman Friars,* whose immoralities and gross neglect of duty were plainly exposed.

CAN OBEDIENCE TO THE POPE'S COMMAND "URGING CATHOLIC ACTION IN POLITICS" BE HARMONIZED WITH WHOLEHEARTED LOYALTY TO THE CIVIL GOVERNMENT?

No, it cannot be. "No man can serve two Masters"—a foreign pope and a civil ruler. Sooner or later conflict with the Civil Power must arise. It has always been so in the past, and will always be so in the future.

In view of the Pope's message urging "Catholic Action," and the public statements of an American Archbishop's[1] attempting to *justify ecclesiastical interference in politics,* it is apparent how valueless have been the public assertions of Roman Church leaders in the past that their Church does *not* interfere in politics. In 1928 when a member of the Roman Communion was candidate for the Chief Office of the U. S. Government,[2] frequent assertions were made that, if elected, his official acts would be entirely free from Vatican influence; and Protestants were called "intolerant" and "bigoted" for receiving these assertions with reserve. At that time it was pointed out that the *Vatican's insistence on the supremacy of the Church over State* and *its frequent interference in politics,* directly *conflicted with the principles of civil and religious liberty,* and therefore, it was *not* "intolerance and bigotry" but simple recognition of the facts of history which led American citizens to challenge an allegiance which professed entire loyalty to one's own national government, and at the same time loyalty to a *foreign government,* whose principles were *totally different.*

Space does not permit mention of the persecutions by the Papal Inquisition during 300 years, spreading death and terror over Europe.

---

[1] Archbishop Curley, who without just cause criticized the President of the United States for pursuing the proper American policy of declining to interfere in the internal affairs of a neighboring, friendly power.

[2] Former Governor of New York, Alfred E. Smith.

It is estimated by competent authorities that in the 16th century hundreds of thousands of Protestant martyrs laid down their lives for Christ. Even in this so-called "enlightened" 20th century, the Roman Church still persecutes, whenever it has the power to do so.

A few years before the Revolution in Spain which put an end to the monarchy, a Spanish woman who had been converted to the true faith was *put in prison for two years* for declaring that the *Bible states that the Virgin Mary had other children* beside our Saviour! Matt. 12:47, 48, John 7:5.

During the summer of 1933 two young men in Quebec, Canada, who had been converted by reading the Bible, were arrested and imprisoned on complaint of a Roman priest because they *distributed Christian tracts.*

In 1935 the Rev. Victor Rahard, formerly head of a religious Order of the Church of Rome, was converted to the true faith, and became minister of the English Church of the Redeemer in Montreal, Canada. He was bitterly denounced by the Roman Church, was arrested, tried in the Civil Court and fined $100.00 because he exhibited at the door of his church a statement of Christian truth *taken verbatim from the "39 Articles of the Church of England."* Fortunately, as in the case of St. Paul, God made the persecution of this faithful servant turn out "to the furtherance of the Gospel," for many fair-minded Catholics were drawn to his Church and were *won to the original Christian faith.*

The Church of Rome's boast, *Semper eadem,* "Always the same," is certainly true of her unchristian persecution of those who differ from her in faith; wherever she has the power, she still persecutes, just as in the days of the cruel Inquisition.

A missionary in Brazil writes: "Ten years ago a mob of Romanists raided one of my chapels and burnt all the furniture, *including the Bible,* which was approved by Roman Church authorities."

"As we were leaving Brazil on furlough in 1937, a mob, incited by the local priest, *burnt the Presbyterian Church at Ventanis.* Again, since our arrival in the United States, news has come of the *destruction by explosives* of the Presbyterian *chapel* at *Rio Parana-hyba.*"

The same year two Indian converts at Tayabamba on the upper Amazon, were imprisoned in a cell, the floor of which was covered with water. For 34 days they were kept *without trial,* on charges which were *proved to be false.* They wrote to the missionary in charge, "pray that we may be kept faithful to the Lord, and that our wives and children may be comforted in their sorrow." *Letter of Dr. E. E. Lane,* February, 1938.

The Reverend Augusto Bersani, pastor of the Italian Protestant Church in *Montreal,* knows by experience the unjust attempts of the Roman clergy to deprive of their religious liberty those who desire to follow the dictates of conscience. When it becomes known that an Italian has become a Protestant, he is denounced to the civil authorities as a *Communist,* and his deportation to Italy is demanded. Rev. Bersani wrote: "During the past year (1937) I have had to appeal to the Department of Immigration on behalf of *27 Italians* who have committed no other offence than *changing their religious beliefs!* In one case, a young man was arrested and held for deportation *within 24 hours* after declaring *his faith in the Protestant Church!*"

It is well known that this flimsy pretext of charging persons with *Communism* was used by the Insurgents in Spain to excite odium against the Spanish Republican Government. Loyalists were called Communists, although the rebels knew perfectly well that they were good Republicans. They knew that there were thousands of loyal Catholics, like the Basques, who heartily supported the Republican Government, though it suited the purpose of the Vatican to declare otherwise.

More attempts at persecution were revealed by the passage of the *"Padlock Law"* of Quebec, which was clearly a menace to religious liberty. Newspapers of Toronto of February 6, 1938, published front page dispatches headed, "Sale of Bibles banned by Quebec City Police," and "Circulation of Bibles halted by Padlock Law." The Padlock Law was rightly called "an astounding piece of legislation." The law made *no provision* in the case of an accused person, for *trial by jury,* or for a *hearing before a judge.* In the Attorney-General *alone* was vested the power of deciding what under this law were illegal activities or utterances! "This law enabled the Government of Quebec to padlock any newspaper, building or private home, which might be suspected of disseminating *any views on faith, morals* or *economics,* of which the *Government disapproved!* Here is an enactment so constructed that it might be turned to any purpose, good or bad, depending solely on the will of the man, or group of men, behind it."

The *Globe and Mail,* and Toronto *Star, The Evangelical Christian,* March, 1938, pages 64 and 117.

Roman Church authorities strenuously try to deny the widespread and virulent persecution which for centuries were inflicted on those who rejected their teachings, and which they still inflict as far as they have the power. But their denials are useless in view of the plain facts of history. It would be well to remember the words of an impartial historian, who wrote regarding the cruel persecutions which the Roman Church inflicted:

"The so-called horrors of the French Revolution were a mere bagatelle, a summer shower, by the side of the atrocities committed in the name of religion and with *the sanction of the Catholic Church.*" Estimating the number of unfortunates who perished in the French Revolution at 5,000 at most, Professor Froude says, "Multiply the 5,000 by ten, and you do not reach the number of those who were murdered in France alone in August and September, 1572. 50,000 Flemings and Germans are said to have been hanged, burnt or buried alive under Charles V."

"Add to this the long agony of the Netherlands under Philip II, the 30 years war in Germany, the ever recurring massacres of the Huguenots, and remember that the *Roman Catholic religion alone* was at *the bottom of all these horrors;* that the crusades against the Huguenots especially were *solemnly sanctioned by successive popes,* and that no word of censure ever issued from the Vatican, except in the brief intervals when statesmen and soldiers grew weary of bloodshed and looked for some means to admit the heretics to grace." Froude's *Condition and Prospects of Protestantism,* pp. 143, 144.

Why should such facts as these be recounted?

Because *they are true,* and the publication of truth is *always salutary,* while the *ignoring or suppressing of the truth* is *always harmful.* There is no better way of appraising an institution or religious system than by ascertaining its effect on human conduct. "By their fruits ye shall know them." The warnings of history should be heeded. They show the *baleful effect of false principles* on the life of a nation, which result in dishonor to God and immense suffering to multitudes of innocent people. Moreover, like causes produce like effects. What has taken place in the past, may recur in the future. Those mistaken principles which formerly wrought great injury to individuals and governments, will cause the same injury in the future, if *unchecked.* The *greatest safeguard of the public welfare,* against the repetition of wrongdoing, is to *make it known,* and *point out its causes.*

Have the popes of Rome ever expressed sorrow for the dreadful persecutions for which they were responsible, *or have they* ever renounced the false dogmas which led to them?

Sad to say, so far as is known, no pope has ever publicly expressed sorrow for the bitter persecutions they have caused; nor have they renounced the grave errors which have led to such gross violation of human rights. Some apologists for the Papacy have *vainly tried to deny the plain facts of history;* while others have attempted to *deny the responsibility of the Roman Church for persecutions* by alleging that the Church only condemned heretics, and the civil government put them to death!

A Church history under the imprimatur of Archbishop Glennon, 1904, even attempts to "whitewash" the Roman Inquisition, asserting that the Inquisition *"has never shed a drop of blood!"* But this is a childish subterfuge, an unworthy attempt to dodge the verdict of history and escape the odium which justly attaches to papal persecutions; for it is a universally recognized principle of law that the party who instigates, or procures the commission of a crime is as truly responsible for that crime as the actual perpetrator. The *Church of Rome was the power behind the act,* which urged and procured the bitter persecution and death of heretics, and impartial public opinion will always hold her responsible for these acts.

As long as the popes of Rome *continue falsely to claim supreme spiritual and temporal power over the world,* the Roman Church will *rightly be held responsible* for *the hideous persecutions which have disgraced the Christian name.*

THE PAPAL CHURCH STILL UPHOLDS PERSECUTION TO DEATH FOR RELIGIOUS BELIEF

Not only has the Roman Church not repudiated the unchristian dogma of the persecution to death of heretics, but it has *continued to justify and teach it,* certainly up to the year *1910.*

PIUS IX

Pius IX upheld persecution and all its attendant cruelties, when he pronounced it an error to hold that "in the present day it is no longer expedient for the Roman Catholic religion to be considered the only religion of the State to the exclusion of all other modes of worship"; and "also *an error to hold* that the Church should *not avail itself of force,* directly or indirectly, *through the temporal power."* The pope thus teaches that no Church other than that of Rome has a right to exist, and that it is right and proper to use force to crush those who do not accept the papal system. Remember that Pius IX did not live in the Dark Ages, but in the 19th Century. The Church of Rome therefore had no excuse for *maintaining a barbarous dogma,* which was repugnant not only to the Christian faith, but also to the best teachings *of pagan sages.*

LEO XIII

Pope Leo XIII (died in the 20th century, 1903) maintained the same odious dogma of persecution, that "heretics" ought to be put to death. In 1901 a book entitled *Institutiones Juris Ecclesiastici,* by Marianus di Luca, professor in the papal college at Rome, was issued from the Vatican Press. This book declared that the Church "has a *coercive power, even to the extent of the death sentence."* "It must put these wicked men (heretics) to death."

Mr. A. B. Sharpe, in *Questions and Answers,* page 46, defines as "heretics" all Christians "who reject the teaching of the Roman Catholic Church" among whom he generously includes such excellent company as Milton, Bunyan, Whitefield, the Wesleys, Wm. Penn, George Fox, Chalmers and Moody, mentioning them by name, and

14

by implication including them among the *"wicked men, who ought to be put to death!"*

Again in a duly authorized book entitled *Aquinas Ethicus,* by Joseph Rickaby, S.J., vol. I, pp. 332, 333, the execution of death sentence for heretics is urged. In reply to the question, "Are heretics to be tolerated?" it is said, they should "not only be excommunicated, but also *banished from the world by death.* If coiners or other malefactors are at once handed over by secular princes to a just death, *much more may heretics,* immediately they are convicted of heresy, be not only excommunicated, but *done to death."*

Cardinal Lépicier, twice legate of the pope, in a volume published by him in 1910 entitled, *"The Stability and Progress of Dogma,"* wrote, "If heretics profess publicly their heresy, and incite others to embrace the same errors, none may doubt that they deserve not only to be separated from the Church by excommunication, but even *to be cut off by death from the number of the living!"*

PROSCRIPTION OF PROTESTANTS SUGGESTED

Rev. J. A. Ryan, of the Catholic University, Washington, D. C., in his book, "The State and the Church," 1922, upholds persecution for religious belief and even the proscription of non-Catholics. He says: "A Catholic State could tolerate only such religious activities as were confined to the members of the dissenting group. It could not permit them (Protestants, etc.) to carry on a general propaganda, nor accord their organizations certain privileges that had formerly been extended to all religious corporations, for example, exemption from taxation."

Knowing that the Supremacy of Church over State, which popes advocate, is not possible under the Constitution of the United States, Mr. Ryan adds: *"But constitutions can be changed,* and non-Catholic sects may decline to such a point that the *proscription of them may become feasible and expedient!"* The Century Dictionary and Cyclopedia defines proscribe as, "to outlaw," "to publish one's name as condemned to death, and liable, to confiscation of property." In other words, Rev. Ryan suggests that if a Roman Catholic party ever got firm control of the U. S. Government, they could *change the constitution,* and *"proscribe,"* or outlaw all Chris-

tians who *prefer to follow the Bible and conscience rather than the pope!* Who would imagine that such intolerant dogmas could be held in this 20th Century? Does this not indicate a *relapse to the superstition* and *despotism of the Dark Ages?* Surely "eternal vigilance is the price of liberty!"

The present position of the Church of Rome regarding the punishment of heretics is that, in principle, it follows the teachings of St. Thomas Aquinas, who declared that "the Church, no longer hoping for the heretic's conversion, delivers him to the secular tribunal to *be exterminated thereby from the world by death.*" It is greatly to the discredit of the Roman Church that it has not repudiated its barbarous cruelty in the treatment of heretics, but continues to try to justify itself, and now merely holds the infliction of the death penalty *"in abeyance."* The *Catholic Encyclopedia* states: "the present day legislation (of the Roman Church) against heresy has *lost nothing of its ancient severity;* but the penalties on heretics are now only of a spiritual order; all the punishments which require the intervention of the secular arm have fallen into abeyance." Reading between the lines this means: "Humane and enlightened civil governments have deprived us of the power to murder heretics that we once had; we are now obliged by civil law to refrain, so we hold the barbarous practice *'in abeyance.'* " Think how deplorably far Papal teachings and practice are from the love and mercy of Him whose example the Church professes to follow! Rom. 12:19-21, II Tim. 2:24-26.

WHAT WAS THE ATTITUDE OF POPE PIUS XI TOWARD THE ETHIOPIAN WAR AND THE WAR IN SPAIN? DID HE BRAVELY STAND FOR PEACE, REGARDLESS OF CONSEQUENCES?

It is most deplorable that Pius XI, while uttering vague platitudes favoring peace, in reality yielded to political pressure and *approved the war.* Did not the pope *bless the Italian armies* as they embarked *on their unrighteous crusade of conquest,* a crusade of brute force and violence against a weak nation, which had given no provocation for the attack made upon it? And did he not try to gloss over his unjustifiable attitude before a disapproving world by miscalling the crusade a *"mission for civilization?"* The pontiff had a rare opportunity to prove his sincerity by standing firmly for the law of God, upholding right against might, and law against brute force; but alas for the weakness and inconsistency of human nature which in the hour of crisis chooses expediency not principle, and, disregarding the Divine voice, *"follows the multitude to do evil!"*

Concerning the tragic onslaught on Ethiopia, Mr. William Teeling, a Roman Catholic, remarks in a recent book, "The fact must be faced that practically without exception the whole world *condemned* Mussolini, *except the pope!"*[1]

As for Spain, pitiful were the frantic appeals made to the pope by loyal Catholics beseeching him to use his influence to stop the war, but *all in vain!* M. Aquirre, President of the Basque Government, who signed himself "a practicing Catholic," wrote urging the Papal See to break its silence in view of the massacre of Catholic women and children, but *no reply came!*

M. Francois Mauriac also addressed the pope, pleading that the terrible destruction of life and property might cease, but *to no purpose.* M. Mauriac wrote—"General Franco is one of 'the faithful'; *one power alone* can lower his arm" (that is, *your* power, as a supposed minister of Christ), but the pope turned a deaf ear to the cry of distress of Catholics, who were maligned as *Communists!*

M. Maurice Dargaud, commenting in the Lyon *Républican* on the ominous silence of the Papal See, which meant ruin to Spain, declared: "Whether they wish it or not, their silence expresses this— 'Back, ye who implore and weep! *The Vatican diplomacy requires these things!*' It blessed the massacres of Ethiopia: it is indifferent when 'the most Catholic country of Europe' is ravaged with fire and sword! It is no longer deniable that the high dignitaries of the Church are visibly allied with the powers who control *the forces of money and violence!*" *S. S. Times,* October, 1937, page 747.

Bear in mind that these statements were made, not by men who were unfriendly to the papacy, but largely *by Catholics,* who indignantly protested against the wars in Ethiopia and Spain as *blots on the Christian name, perpetrating hideous wrongs which caused the cruel death of thousands of innocent people!*

No thoughtful observer can help asking—"Would it not be well if the Papal See, instead of using plausible generalities to exhort the

---

[1] *The Pope in Politics; The Life and Work of Pope Pius XI* by William Teeling, September, 1937.

nations of the world to peace, would try to realize how weak and unchristian its attitude toward the wars in Ethiopia, Spain, and China appear, not only to impartial observers of the outside world, but also *to many earnest souls in its own flock?* When the Great Day of Reckoning comes and all nations stand before the Bar of Almighty God, will the specious plea, *"the Vatican diplomacy required these things"* then avail?

Concerning China and the brutal war inflicted on her by Japan, the *Daily Telegraph* of London in 1938 referred to a circular which the pope addressed to Chinese Roman Catholic bishops, in which he wished to correct the impression that his sympathies were with the Japanese in their invasion of China.

The pope said in substance that he had expressed no opinion about the war, but his circular ended with *a pro-Japanese hint,* that "it would be well to remember that the Japanese armies were fighting against Bolshevism." A commentator in the British Weekly remarked, "We had always supposed that it was General Chiang Kai-shek who was fighting Bolshevism in China till the Japanese invasion! The papal policy seems dominated by an anti-Bolshevism which is little short of obsession. It is an international disaster that, as Mr. William Teeling says, "The Political policy of Rome seems to become more and more identified with *organizations on totalitarian lines."* While the pope complained of persecution of the Church in Germany, "in the rest of the world he seems everywhere to give his blessing to *the forces of reaction.* He has condoned, or seems to be condoning, the two most ghastly international crimes of recent years. He has shown himself in all these matters to be little more than a small Italian politician. This is more dangerous to the Roman Church than all the machinations of the enemy!"

Even Turkey was shocked by the painful contrast between the Vatican's *profession* and *practice.* Concerning the war in China the journal *Tan* of Ankara expressed surprise at the Vatican's announcement condoning Japan's unjustifiable assault on a peaceable nation, saying, "When Jesus wrote the Gospels, He took the side of the slaves who were being killed by torture, and announced that Christianity was against the cruel aggressors. In our day when we write about those who are savagely treated, we point to the victims of Ethiopia and the Chinese, who are being murdered by the million.

Has the task of defending all the Judases who are crushing the oppressed to earth fallen to the 'holy' spiritual Head of the Vatican?" Revelation, June, 1938, page 246.

In 1938, the Mexican journal *Naçional* rebuked Mexican bishops for "using a message of sympathy sent to the Spanish clergy to *play a political rôle in Mexico,"* and indignantly commented as follows: "The Mexican bishops express sympathy *only* with those who died in the Spanish *rebel ranks!* They forget that the Basque people, Catholic by tradition, do not regard their religious creed as an obstacle to aiding the cause of the Spanish Republic. They also forget the Church buildings destroyed by the 'holy' machine guns of General Franco's foreign legions! Today Mexican bishops cannot assert that they are being attacked, or call attention to one single act of intolerance by Mexican Government authorities. The aim of the Mexican Episcopate is *political domination,* and it does not mind what alliances it uses to obtain its end—agitation abroad, or foreign alliances *not sanctioned by law or justice."*

A Canadian journal[1] comments—"This last paragraph presents the case in a nutshell. Mexico has found out what every other country has had to find out by painful experience, viz.: that *spiritual and political freedom are impossible, where the Church of Rome holds sway!"*

Thus it is clear that the attitude of the Mexican Government toward the Church of Rome was reasonable and fair. It rightly wished to manage its own affairs without interference from a hierarchy which sought power that did not belong to it, and which held a theory of the Church, that *has no foundation in Holy Scriptures,* and is *impossible,* if true civil and religious liberty are to be preserved.

IN AUSTRIA DID NOT THE VATICAN PRACTICALLY SURRENDER TO THE DEMANDS OF THE GERMAN GOVERNMENT, AND HEARTLESSLY SACRIFICE THE RIGHTS OF ITS PEOPLE?

It did. Cablegrams from Vienna of April, 1938, reported that Cardinal Innitzer, primate of Austria, and five Roman bishops had issued an official order which was read in the Austrian Churches, urging all Catholics to support the "union" of Austria with Germany

---

[1] *The Evangelical Christian,* Toronto, *February, 1938, page 65.*

—"union" being an euphemism for the *enforced surrender of Austria to the German Reich,* and its complete extinction *as an independent State!*

In this official order "four duties were enumerated which should bind every Catholic,—Obedience to the new worldly authority; unbounded loyal co-operation in the development of the Fatherland; manifestation of Catholicism in the new situation; and a *daily prayer for the great German nation and its Fuehrer!"* In other words, surrender without protest your national life, and "Kiss the rod" by praying for the prosperity of the *Church's ruthless enemy!* No little perturbation and vacillation seemed to have followed the Cardinal's announcement. A sharp rebuke was flashed from the Vatican radio station, denouncing as disloyal Catholics those who favored surrender to the German Government! This was at once followed by a second message from the Vatican *disclaiming responsibility for the previous one!* Amid the babel of conflicting voices, a perplexed laity could not discern the Vatican's real meaning. Meanwhile the pope had hastily summoned the Austrian Cardinal who, to smooth over a humiliating situation and "save face," published a vague statement like the Delphic Oracle of old, that the order to submit to the Nazi demands "obviously did not mean approval of that which was not, and is not, compatible with the laws of God and the liberty of the Catholic Church!"

Later dispatches revealed that the German Government, throwing aside its cloak of "union," and intent on pressing its advantage to the utmost, was proceeding sweepingly to Naziize the whole fabric of Austrian public life,—military, judicial, political and financial,— even the Austrian *schilling* being at once replaced by the German *mark;* and the famous Library of Vienna was "purged" of all books deemed "objectionable." Before long the promised "union" became a *conquest,* and the former Head of the Austrian Government, Count von Schuschnigg, who, as in duty bound, had striven to protect his country's interest against armed aggression, was arrested and imprisoned as a conquered enemy!

Thus a proud Empire, which for 400 years under the Hapsburg dynasty had played a leading part in the affairs of Europe, and whose capital had been famous throughout the world as a center of learning, science, music and art,—forever disappeared from the pages of history!

It is reported on good authority that concentration camps were filled with patriotic Austrians, who bitterly protested against such summary and treacherous treatment, and not a few, overwhelmed with grief, committed suicide! Alas, one looked in vain for any courageous, determined effort on the part of the Papal See to stand in the face of danger for justice and right! What a pitiful surrender apparently without even a dignified, earnest protest, for the Fuehrer had distinctly promised that the union of Austria should *not* be *forced!* Did the pope and the Austrian Cardinal lack the martyr-spirit of John Huss and Martin Niemöller?—*New York Times* and *Philadelphia Journals* of April 20-25, 1938.

One must be blind indeed who cannot read, at least in part, the lessons of these grave events; the sin and folly of a fallible human being attempting to be the Head of a Church of which *Christ alone is the true Head:* and at the same time claiming in direct violation of Christ's words, "MY KINGDOM IS NOT OF THIS WORLD," to be an earthly ruler, who, by dabbling in the muddy stream of politics, *degrades and brings reproach upon the Christian faith!* What floundering in the bogs of inconsistency and moral compromise could be avoided by humbly obeying the plain teaching of Holy Scripture, —*Render to Caesar the things that are Caesar's, and unto God the things that are God's!*

THE PERNICIOUS EFFECT OF THE TEACHINGS OF ULTRAMONTANISM IN THE ROMAN CHURCH

Lord Acton, though a Romanist, spoke plainly of the great injury resulting from the dogma of Ultramontanism, that is, the *Italian theory which centers in the absolute infallibility and power of the pope* and lays *claim to civil as well as religious jurisdiction;* this in contrast to the theory of the Gallican or French Church. Acton wrote: "In requiring submission to papal decrees on matters not articles of faith, they (the ultramontane clergy) were investing with new authority the existing bulls and giving *unqualified sanction to the Inquisition* and *the Index,* to *the murder of heretics* and the deposing of Kings. They approved what they were called upon to reform, and blessed with their lips *what their hearts knew to be accursed." Introductory Memoir* to Lord Acton's *Letters,* pp. xliii, xliv.

Again, holding the papacy *justly responsible for the Inquisition* which was murderous, he wrote: "Therefore, the most awful imputation in the catalogue of crimes rests upon those whom we call Ultramontanes. The controversy is not primarily about problems of theology: it is about the spiritual state of a man's soul who is *the defender, the promoter, the accomplice of murder."* "I will show you what Ultramontanism makes of a good man by an example very near home. St. Charles Borromeo, the pope's nephew and minister, wrote a letter requiring Protestants to be murdered, and *complaining that no heretical heads were forwarded to Rome,* in spite of the *reward that was offered for them!* His editor (Cardinal Manning) published the letter with a *note of approval.* The Cardinal thus not only holds up to the general veneration of mankind the authority that *canonized the murderer,* but makes him (Borromeo) in a special manner his own patron." In other words, Borromeo's *demand for the heads of Protestant victims to be sent to Rome,* Cardinal Manning's *approval* of *this murder,* and *the pope's making a saint of him,* may all be accounted for by the *virus of Ultramontanism! Letters of Lord Acton,* page 186.

Perhaps, one may ask, surely intelligent Romanists do not now hold these medieval fictions regarding papal power, which are impossible from the viewpoint of Holy Scripture, and also from that of free, enlightened governments? Alas! many still hold them. For though they see how inconsistent they are with the Word of God, and how prejudicial to the welfare of free governments, yet they have been taught from youth to believe that popes are infallible, and therefore *dare not, under penalty of anathemas and excommunication, reject these false dogmas.* Being in bondage to these beliefs from childhood, they are blind to the fact that loyalty to a pope means *disloyalty to their Creator,* whose high place he usurps, and that loyalty to a pope may also mean *disloyalty to the free government* to which every citizen owes the rights he enjoys, and to which his wholehearted allegiance is due.

If intelligent laymen in the Roman Catholic body will carefully examine the Scriptures and trustworthy history, they will be convinced that *the claims of the papacy* are *entirely unfounded,* and *that it is their duty to acknowledge the Lord Jesus Christ* as the *true and only Head of God's Church,* whom they will henceforth obey and serve. *Christ is now calling honest laymen in the papal body,*—"COME YE OUT OF HER, MY PEOPLE, THAT YE BE NOT PARTAKER OF HER SINS!" Rev. 18:4, II Cor. 6:14-18.

May all governments and peoples come to see that *the Holy Scriptures are the root of civil and religious liberty;* that *the papacy has no foundation in Holy Scripture,* but is merely the *false principle of totalitarianism grafted on religion;* and *acknowledging Christ alone as Head of the Christian Church and Lord of the conscience* may all men thus be brought "*into the glorious liberty of the children of God!*" Rom. 8:21.

CHAPTER XV

SUMMARY

In the preceding chapters we have endeavored to set forth something of our priceless heritage as the children of God; "the riches of grace" that there are for every believer in His glorious Gospel; the all-sufficiency of our Lord Jesus Christ as Redeemer, in whom every need of the individual soul and of the human race is abundantly supplied; His perfect atoning work and the full provision He has made through the Holy Spirit and the Word for the salvation of men and for the establishment of His Church.

It has been the aim to show constructively from Holy Scripture that the Protestant faith is the original Christian faith taught by our Lord and His apostles; and that the Protestant or Reformed Church, since it holds the original Christian faith, is therefore the true Church of God. Though we acknowledge with deep sorrow our many sins and how far short we come of the divine standard, yet we rejoice that at last Christ will present our beloved Church "faultless before the Father's presence with exceeding joy," "a glorious Church not having spot or wrinkle or any such thing." Eph. 5:27, Jude 24.

We have seen from Scripture that Christ is the only Head and Foundation of the Church; and that for any man to claim to be the head and foundation of God's Church is to usurp the place of the Creator, and is a mark of apostasy.

We have seen that there is no Scriptural warrant whatever for a pope; that Peter was not the rock on which Christ built the Church, but that Christ Himself was the Rock; that the papacy was not invented till centuries after Christ; that the whole papal power was founded upon fraud, as leading Romanists acknowledge; that while the papacy has continued to exist in spite of its total lack of Scriptural warrant and the great harm it has caused, its continued existence can be explained on perfectly natural grounds, because it offers immense prizes of wealth, power and prominence, which am-

bitious, worldly men have always coveted and will continue to covet
to the end of time.

We have seen also that the Holy Scriptures of the Old and New
Testaments, being the very Word of God, are through the guidance
of the Holy Spirit an all-sufficient rule of faith and life, making men
"wise unto salvation," and "thoroughly furnished unto all good
works." To teach, as the Church of Rome does, that the traditions
of men are also the rule of faith, and that the Holy Scriptures are
"not all-sufficient," are "not the judge of controversy," and are "not
for the people to read," is a deadly error, which grossly dishonors
the Author of the Scriptures, and robs men of that divine light which
alone can guide them to the haven of eternal rest.

We have seen the Word of God teaches that the Holy Trinity
alone is the Object of Worship in the true Church; that no mere
human being, however good, may share in any degree in that worship, nor may any image or visible representation be used in worship.
Also that the Church of Rome, by worshipping human beings and
images, has directly disobeyed two of God's commandments and has
apostatised far from the true faith.

The Scriptures also plainly declare that only God can forgive
sins. Any human being who claims to forgive sins or grant absolution is guilty of falsehood, and usurps the honor which belongs to
God alone. The papal church by asserting that its priests have power
to forgive sins, "not only as ambassadors of Christ, but as judges
and by way of jurisdiction," is guilty of this great impiety.

The Scriptures also declare that there is only one Mediator between God and men, the incarnate Son of God, through whom alone
sinners may approach the holy God, and through whom alone they
may receive blessings from Him. The Roman Church falsely asserts
that there are other mediators, thus contradicting Scripture, and
making sinful human beings usurp the place of the divine Saviour.

We have seen the Word of God declares that Christ offered Himself
on the cross as the one perfect sacrifice for the sins of the world,
which forever avails for all who put their trust in Him. This saving
truth the Church of Rome denies, by asserting that her priests in

the so-called Mass offer a real atoning sacrifice for sin. She is thus guilty of an unspeakable sin, for she deceives men by the gross error of a counterfeit atonement and makes sinful priests usurp the place of the only divine Redeemer.

The Lord's Supper, which our Saviour appointed as a simple memorial of His atoning death and everlasting love, the Church of Rome has grievously perverted, as if her priests had magical power to change bread and wine into human flesh and blood. The laity are made the victims of a fatal delusion; for under threat of eternal condemnation they are forced to worship a wafer as God. When the priest "elevates the host," as is said, they are required to believe that they are adoring God, whereas they know they are only adoring a piece of bread!

Again, the Scriptures show that God alone is Lord of the conscience, and no human being may claim that high position or dare to come between the soul and its Maker. This grievous sin the pope commits, usurping the place of Almighty God, and keeping souls in bondage by claiming the right to dictate to men's consciences.

So also, papal Indulgences and Masses for the dead; according to Holy Scripture, these are a travesty of God's salvation, a traffic in men's souls, a bartering of the precious blood of Christ.

In all of these things, which concern the very heart of the Gospel, the Church of Rome has apostatised far from the faith, and has forfeited all right to be considered a part of the true Church of God.

In contrast to these soul-destroying errors, the Protestant or Reformed Church proclaims, as the Word of God proclaims:

No Head of the Church, but the one divine Lord,
No Foundation of the Church, but Christ the Rock,
No rule of faith, but the Word of God,
No object of worship, but the Holy Trinity;
No Mediator but the Lord Jesus Christ,
No priest but the one divine Saviour,
No sacrifice but Christ's one atoning death,
No Confessional but the Throne of God;
Absolution, not by man, but by God alone,

Not penances, but Repentance unto life,
Not Indulgences, but separation from all sin,
Not Purgatory, but eternal life in heaven;
Christian liberty and freedom of conscience,

Unity in diversity, the "unity of the Spirit,"—this is our priceless heritage as the children of God; here is "the Word of Truth, the Gospel of your salvation!"

True to Holy Scripture, the one aim of the Protestant and apostolic faith is to exalt God, not man; to ascribe all glory to the Holy Trinity alone, to whom it rightly belongs; as John Calvin's favorite text declares:

"For of Him, and through Him, and to Him are all things; to whom be glory for ever, Amen."

"That God in all things may be glorified through Jesus Christ: to whom be praise and dominion for ever and ever, Amen."

These things being true, what is our duty as Protestants?

We should believe the Truth with all our heart, and live the Gospel by a consistent life. Let it be said of Protestants now, as was said in France at the Reformation, "as honest and true as a Huguenot!"

We should teach the children in the home to love the Word of God; have family worship with them; teach them the catechism, to honor the Sabbath Day, to love the Church of God and be loyal to it.

We should shun Modernist infidelity on the one hand, and Romanism on the other,—whose "word will eat as doth a canker." Shun false teachers who mutilate the holy Scriptures; and shun Romanisers in the Church, who, regardless of common honesty, betray the sacred truth entrusted to them, and undermine the foundation of the Church to which they owe allegiance and whose benefits they enjoy.

Christian parents under no circumstances should send their children to Roman Catholic schools. Mixed marriage of Protestants and Catholics should also be avoided, for on account of the pope's *Ne Temere* decree such unions too often result in bitter sorrow and broken homes.

Protestants should pray and work more earnestly to win Romanists to the true faith. We should distribute broadcast sound Protestant literature, and strive with all patience and kindness to show our Romanist friends from God's Word the deadly errors of the papal system, and lead them into the light and liberty of the children of God. 2 Tim. 2:24-26, James 5:20.

Oh, for the mighty power of the Spirit of God to arouse the Church from indifference and compromise, from prayerlessness and paralyzing doubt of His Holy Word, to realize its danger, and EARNESTLY CONTEND FOR THE FAITH ONCE FOR ALL DELIVERED TO THE SAINTS!

INDEX